Ideas, Products, Services...
'Social Innovation' for Elderly Persons

Edited by

Elena Urdaneta

and

Brian Worsfold

Edicions i Publicacions de la Universitat de Lleida

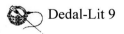 Dedal-Lit 9

June 2018

First published in 2018 by
©Edicions i Publicacions de la Universitat de Lleida
Campus Cappont
Jaume I I
Lleida 25001
Catalonia (Spain)

Opinions expressed or implied by contributors to this publication are not necessarily shared by all copyright holders or members of the research group Grup Dedal-Lit.

Cover design: Andrea-Mersey de Castro · www.mrsmersey.com
Layout: Francesc Català i Alòs

ISBN 978-84-9144-106-9
Authorized Registration Number: L 786-2018

Contents

Part One: Ideas

Intergenerationality and Social Participation

A Space to Grow Old In

A Language to Age With

Part Two: Products

Part Three: Services

The Need for 'Social Innovation'

Socially-Dynamic Environments for 'Active Ageing'

Acknowledgements

The editors gratefully acknowledge the knowledge input of the Consortium Partners of The SIforAGE Project (2012-2016), and European Commission funds (FP7-SFS-2012-1-321482) that have made the compilation of contributions to this book possible.

The editors also gratefully acknowledge the support of the research group Grup Dedal-Lit of the Department of English and Linguistics at the University of Lleida.

Introduction

'Social Innovation' is a nebulous and malleable concept. Our understanding of what exactly 'social innovation' is and what it signifies has transmuted over the years.

In 2007, in *Social Innovation. What it is, why it matters, and how it can be accelerated*, Geoff Mulgan, Simon Tucker, Rushanara Ali, and Ben Sanders defined 'social innovation' as "new ideas that work," responding to a wide range of social requirements "from gay partnerships to new ways of using mobile phone texting, and from new lifestyles to new products and services." Moreover, Mulgan, Tucker, Ali, and Sanders saw such innovations as being "predominantly developed and diffused through organisations whose primary purposes are social."[1]

Then, in 2008, in their article "Rediscovering Social Innovation," James Phills Jr., Kriss Deiglmeier, and Dale Miller refined the concept, holding that "innovation is both a process and a product," and that, on the one hand, the concept demands academic study of "*social* processes that produce innovation, such as individual creativity, organizational structure, environmental context, and social and economic factors" while, on the other hand, *innovation* manifests itself in the form of "new products, product features, and production methods,"[2] or, as they went on to point out later, "a principle, an idea, a piece of legislation, a social movement, an intervention, or some combination of them."[3]

In the same year, in the same journal, Sarah Soule, Neil Malhotra, and Bernadette Clavier saw 'social innovation' as generating administrative responses to issues confronting governmental and social institutions that would, by definition, contribute to social progress. In this, Soule, Malhotra

---

[1] Geoff Mulgan, Simon Tucker, Rushanara Ali, and Ben Sanders. *Social Innovation. What it is, why it matters, and how it can be accelerated*. (London: The Young Foundation, 2007). 8.
[2] James A. Phills Jr., Kriss Deiglmeier, and Dale T. Miller. *Stanford Social Innovation Review*. 6. 4, 2008.
<www.gsb.stanford.edu/faculty-research/centers-initiatives/csi/defining-social-innovation>
[3] James A. Phills Jr., Kriss Deiglmeier, and Dale T. Miller. *Stanford Social Innovation Review*. 6. 4, 2008.
<www.gsb.stanford.edu/faculty-research/centers-initiatives/csi/defining-social-innovation>

and Clavier rule in collaboration between "government, business, and the non-profit world.[4]

In their "Introduction" to *The Open Book of Social Innovation* (2010), Robin Murray, Julie Caulier-Grice, and Geoff Mulgan asserted that social innovations must be "social both in their ends and in their means," understanding social innovation to be…

> new ideas (products, services and models) that simultaneously meet social needs and create new social relationships or collaborations. In other words, they are innovations that are both good for society and enhance society's capacity to act. (Murray, *et al.* 2010)[5]

This understanding was taken up and expanded by the European Commission in 2013. The European Commission's *Guide to Social Innovation* (2013) reiterated the perception that 'social innovation' is about "the development and implementation of new ideas (products, services and models) to meet social needs and create new social relationships or collaborations," but the *Guide* went on to say that the overall goal of social innovations is "to improve human well-being," and that, since "they rely on the inventiveness of citizens, civil society organisations, local communities, businesses and public servants and services," such innovations are social in both their ends and their means, enhancing "individuals' capacity to act."[6]

In 2015, in their article entitled "Complexity Theory and the Development of the Social Innovation," Ani Matei and Catalina Antonie noted that the National Endowment for Science, Technology and the Arts (NESTA) pointed out that 'social innovation' is a means for responding to "social needs which can be neglected by traditional forms of private market provision and which have often been poorly served or unresolved by services organized by the state."[7] Matei and Antonie went on to amplify the NESTA

---

[4] <www.gsb.stanford.edu/faculty-research/centers-initiatives/csi/defining-social-innovation>
[5] Robin Murray, Julie Caulier-Grice, and Geoff Mulgan. *The Open Book of Social Innovation.* (NESTA / The Young Foundation, 2010). 3.
<youngfoundation.org/wp-content/uploads/2012/10/The-Open-Book-of-Social-Innovationg.pdf>
[6] European Commission. *Guide to Social Innovation.* (Sup. Mikel Landabaso) DG Regional and Urban Policy (European Commission), February 2013.
<s3platform.jrc.ec.europa.eu/documents/20182/84453/Guide_to_Social_Innovation.pdf>
[7] Ani Matei and Catalina Antonie. "Complexity Theory and the Development of the Social Innovation." *Procedia – Social and Behavioral Sciences.* 185, 2015: 62. [3rd World Conference on Psychology and Sociology, WCPS- 2014]

definition saying that 'social innovation' must generate "new ideas (products, service and models)" that can be used "to fulfil unmet social needs."[8] In a similar vein, Alan Walker has acknowledged that 'social innovation' is a "highly-contested" concept and that, when applied to the concept to Active and Healthy Ageing (AHA),

> (s)ocial innovations are ideas, products, services or models that are new or applied in new contexts and which are designed to improve the well-being and quality-of-life of people as they age.[9]

Again, similar objectives were at the core of the research carried out within the remit of The SIforAGE Project. The SIforAGE Project – "Social Innovation in active and healthy ageing for sustainable economic growth" (2012-2016) aimed at promoting Active and Healthy Ageing (AHA) in society by strengthening cooperation between researchers, policy-makers, product- and service-developers, civil-society organisations, and society in general.[10]

More recently, in 2018, the LEED Forum on Social Innovations placed the emphasis on the organisational and financing implications of 'social innovation,' contending that such innovations would bring about "new relationships with stakeholders and territories." The Forum perceived 'social innovation' as a motor force, an administrative strategy that identifies and fosters new services aimed at improving the quality-of-life of individuals and communities, while at the same time introducing new processes and standards into the labour market, thereby enhancing the welfare of both consumers and workers.[11]

<ac.els-cdn.com/S1877042815021643/1-s2.0-S1877042815021643-main.pdf?_tid=fa6c9dc4-0533-11e8-8bac-00000aab0f6b&acdnat=1517258324_3a6d7881381d0e94f1aed3ff34bd4856>

[8] Ani Matei, and Catalina Antonie "Complexity Theory and the Development of the Social Innovation." *Procedia – Social and Behavioral Sciences*. 185, 2015: 62-63. [3rd World Conference on Psychology and Sociology (WCPS), 2014] <ac.els-cdn.com/S1877042815021643/1-s2.0-S1877042815021643-main.pdf?_tid=fa6c9dc4-0533-11e8-8bac-00000aab0f6b&acdnat=1517258324_3a6d7881381d0e94f1aed3ff34bd4856>

[9] The Final Conference of The INNOVAGE Project was held in Brussels on 14th October 2015. <www.youtube.com/watch?v=piA3aumLWvE>

[10] The SIforAGE Project (2012-2016) was a European Union research project funded by the European Commission (FP7-SFS-2012-1-321482). <www.siforage.eu>

[11] See the Organisation for Economic Co-operation and Development (OECD). LEED (Local Economic and Employment Development) Programme. Forum on Social Innovations.

* * *

As an academic discipline, 'social innovation' lies on the cusp of scientific enquiry and the humanities. In his afore-mentioned address, Alan Walker posited that the aim of 'social innovation' projects should be…

> simply to combine the highest quality science with stakeholder perspectives to find new ways of improving healthy life-expectancy and to enable people to age better over the life-course.[12]

In this sense, social innovation is a crossover discipline, and any activity within the field of 'social innovation' is, by definition, interdisciplinary, cross-cultural, and multi-tasking.

Ideas, products, services … these are the stuff of social innovation. Yet, while the emphasis of many of these definitions of 'social innovation' is on the 'newness' of the ideas and products, 'social innovation' is also about the application and adaptation of ideas and products that already exist, and that have existed for a long time, to the 'new' phenomenon of the large and exponentially-growing ageing population of the modern world. With this in mind, 'social innovation' may also be perceived as a construct whereby 'innovation brings about social change.' This contention is in line with the approach undertaken in the internationally-recognised Oslo Manual in which the goal of 'social innovation' is to bring about social change:

> Just like not all enterprises are social enterprises, not all innovations are social innovations. Compared to mainstream innovations, 'social innovations' are critically driven by an extra motive: a social mission, and the value they create is necessarily shared value, at once economic and social.[13]

Ultimately, in a social sense, 'social innovation' is required to create ideas and products that transform and update modes of behaviour and change attitudes, perceptions, prejudices, and stigmas that relate to ageing and to

---

<www.oecd.org/cfe/leed/Forum-Social-Innovations.htm>
[12] <www.youtube.com/watch?v=piA3aumLWvE>
[13] The European Association for Social Innovation (EaSI)
<www.easi-socialinnovation.org/index.php/2014-11-17-15-30-48/social-innovation-what-and-why>

elderly persons in general, such that stereotypes are deconstructed and equality fomented at all levels amongst all generations.

* * *

This book is a compilation of research studies carried out in several European countries – England, Ireland, Italy, Germany, Latvia, Poland, Spain, Turkey – and in Canada, by persons working in diverse disciplines – sociology, gerontology, anthropology, economics, legal studies, psychology, literary studies, computer technologies, interior design – a diversity that provides an insight into the major areas of interest and focus of researchers of 'social innovation' as applied to ageing persons and populations.[14] The contributions are allocated to sections labelled *ideas*, *products*, and *services* according to the type of 'social innovation' they present. The sections are sub-divided into areas that reflect major fields of interest in ageing studies. These areas are: *Intergenerationality and Social Participation*; *A Space to Grow Old In*; *A Language to Age With*; *New Technologies and Cultural Difference*; *New Technology Systems as 'Social Innovation'*; *Industrial Design as 'Social Innovation'*; *Care Services and Caring*; *Social Exclusion (Female Elderly)*; *Concerning Dementia (Alzheimer's)*; *The Need for 'Social Innovation'*; and *Socially-Dynamic Environments for 'Active Ageing.'*

Ideas

Intergenerationality and Social Participation

A need for government-backed policy on intergenerationality is at the core of Eleonora Barone's chapter "Rethinking ageing societies: working on a shared value for a new leadership," in which she advocates re-formulation of the whole concept of ageing in Spanish society. She argues that, interacting together, elderly and young Spanish men and women are best-situated to bring about such re-thinking. The association "memory in motion between Young and Old" (mYmO) has carried out three projects designed to achieve interaction between the elderly and the young on public, private, and personal levels. Furthermore, Eleonora Barone recommends the creation of

---

[14] These contributions represent some of the research studies presented at the The SIforAGE International Conference "Envisioning a New World" – Social Innovation for Active and Healthy Ageing that took place in Barcelona on 19th, 20th, and 21st October 2016.

intergenerational environments and platforms as examples of "good practice" for companies and administrations.

Eleonora Barone sees business environments and the marketplace as potential driving forces for the intergenerational re-formulation of elderliness and as major players in the push for a less-ageist society. She points out that it is long-term dedication to work in 'life-less' work-place environments which bring on stress, fatigue, ill-health, and exhaustion amongst the ageing workforce. This leads her to conclude that organisations and companies should encourage the continued employment and application of elderly workers in the work-place. Using "Service Design Methodology" and "problem-solving approaches," Eleonora Barone foresees intergenerationality as a driving force in the generation of new ideas and projects, but she warns that if the potential of elderly persons in the workplace is not recognised urgently by administrations and companies in the Mediterranean Area, then the economies and product-development of countries such as Spain will miss out on a golden opportunity. One way of achieving the recognition of this potential is through intergenerationality.

* * *

Intergenerationality, that is, the interaction between individuals of different generations, is a major strategy in the management and administration of ageing persons and communities, and the concept is focusing the attention of many researchers in the field of 'social innovation.' However, in "'Intergenerational Solidarity' in Community Practice," Baiba Bela, Liga Rasnaca, and Anna Stepcenko note that, to date, comparatively little attention has been given to 'intergenerational solidarity.' Research focused, at the community level, on intergenerational communication, emotions and attitudes, mutual help and mutual respect, and, at the level of society at large, on policies contributing to a user-friendly society-for-all-ages, revealed that 'intergenerational solidarity' reduces stereotypes, helps elderly people share their feelings, and facilitates bonding between young and elderly individuals, sharing of resources, and reducing loneliness.

Three 'intergenerational solidarity' projects were carried out in Latvia: 1. "Connect, Latvia," which enhances interconnectivity amongst Latvia's old-age pensioners, providing free computer training services and creating a space for interactivity; 2. "Grandmother Exchange," by which elderly women are trained to act as proxy 'grandmothers' to young families; and 3. a Latvian Parliament project (2013) to promote improved coordination, at national, regional and local levels, of services for Active and Healthy Ageing (AHA). The policy-making discussions that derived from this government-brokered project have led Baiba Bela, Liga Rasnaca, and Anna Stepcenko to conclude that 'intergenerational solidarity' is a basic building block in the construction of any social model of Active and Healthy Ageing (AHA).

* * *

A concern with the paucity of environments for the practice of intergenerationality in Spain is also the focus of attention in Pedro Moreno-Abellán, Silvia Martínez de Miguel-López, and Andrés Escarbajal-de Haro's chapter. The authors recognise the fact that, in the Spanish Welfare State, elderly people today are more demanding of social participation than previous generations. In "Social Participation of the Elderly Through Intergenerational Programmes in the Region of Murcia (Spain)," the authors posit that there is a need for 'spaces of participation,' that is, custom-conceived 'interactive spaces' designed to motivate elderly persons. To test this out, Intergenerational Programmes (IPs) were established to see just how elderly persons might be helped to develop new, appropriate interactivity with young people. It is contended that the nature of such heightened intergenerational activity should then give rise to the development of 'discreet personal spaces' that will maximise the innate productivity of elders, representing "a new culture of ageing" that is characterised by intergenerational participation.

Following the creation of several Intergenerational Programmes (IPs) in social centres in Murcia (Spain), it was shown that the younger participants empathised readily with the elderly participants, and that Intergenerational Programme (IP) participation kept the elderly persons satisfied and active, believing that, thanks to the depth of their personal experience, they were helping the younger participants acquire positive social values and grow into "better" citizens. As for the effect of the Intergenerational Programmes (IPs) on the elderly persons themselves, the participants saw their image as 'elderly adult' transformed and improved in the eyes of the community. In general, the research revealed that the spread of organised, intergenerational activities can bring about greater social cohesion between all generations in a society, reducing generational difference and narrowing social divisions.

* * *

Along similar lines, in their chapter "Social Gatherings and Healthy Breakfasts. New Strategies for Participation: an 'Intergenerational Education' Project at the University of Murcia," Juan Antonio Salmerón-

Aroca, Antonia María Sanchez-Lazaro, and Gema Belchi-Romero report on research carried out into intergenerational education between students and elderly people at the University of Murcia (Spain).[15] During 2015-2016, meetings based on equality and mutual respect were organised between persons of similar social and cultural backgrounds, with the aim of sharing knowledge and values.

At the meetings,[16] attended by sixty-two students (age 20–27) and thirty-three elderly persons (age 65–88), 'Social Conversation' sessions discussed the topic of 'immigration,' allowing for an exchange of opinions on cross-cultural matters that underscore diversity and anti-discrimination. The sessions, which included a series of 'breakfasts' during which the topic of 'healthy living' was discussed, revealed that the more active the elderly person is, the more significant the contribution he/she can make to society. Positive findings to emerge from the 'Social Conversations' were the breakdown of stereotypes and the facilitating of intergenerational communication, resulting in the conclusion that intergenerational education should become standard practice for the administration of communities of the elderly.

A Space to Grow Old In

In their respective chapters, Emine Özmete, Katarzyna Ziomek-Michalak, and Pei-Wen Chu find a significant linkage between and elderly person's quality-of-ageing and the social and cultural environment in which the ageing takes place. In "Place Identity in Doris Lessing's *The Diary of a Good Neighbour* (1983)," María del Rocío González-Torres narrows this down to 'the home' – the place in which the elderly person lives – which she sees as being a singular feature of a person's ageing identity. It is the place, the domestic space, that is 'home' that constitutes the focal point for social interaction, experience, and memory, the repository of an individual's 'self.' In her study of Doris Lessing's *The Diary of a Good Neighbour* (1983), Rocío González-Torres points to the example of 90-year-old Maudie Fowler whose rented home is cold all-year-round, is a reservoir of past experience, of scarcities, and of tribulations. Yet, in terms of her 'self,' for the elderly

---

[15] The authors took their cue from the report of the Third National Congress for Elderly People, *Relaciones Intergeneracionales*, published in 2009 by the Spanish Ministry of Health, Social Policy, and Equality – IMERSO.

[16] The meetings took place at centres of the Institute in Murcia for Social Action (IMAS) and of the University of Murcia.

woman it is a retreat, a refuge, a personalised, minimalist space which affords some user-friendly comforts, among them an old chair, an empty fireplace, and an unplugged electric heater. Despite its seemingly infrahuman state, it is this space that forms part of Maudie Fowler's identity, and she cannot leave it because it is part of her identity. And when Janna, a younger woman-friend, advises her to get her own place, Maudie declines: the two – the space and its occupant – have aged together. Her identity is inextricably linked to the space that is her 'home,' and for Maudie Fowler to abandon her 'home' would be to deny part of her 'self.' In this sense, a person's home is a construct, a physical rendition of the individual's past and present.

For Rocío González-Torres, what is significant in Doris Lessing's novel is that, following the intergenerational encounter between Maudie and Janna, the former's subsequent rebuttal of any change in her physical surroundings causes Janna's own attitude towards 'the space to grow old in' to be transformed. She comes to realise that, for an elderly person, the space he or she has constructed over the years, however untidy and grim, is the most desirable and subjectively-appropriate space for that person to grow old in.

A Language to Age With

Just as 'the space one grows old in' is of fundamental importance to a person's quality-of-ageing, so too is language and language-usage – lexicon, articulation, expression, and style – at all levels of personal communication to the management of elderly persons. It is a truism to say that we age in a language, that is, usually our first- or early-language, our mother-tongue. Because ageing is a social and cultural construct, the language we age in is significant in that, to a certain extent, it conditions the quality of our ageing, 'quality' being used in its strict sense.

The individual constructs his/her own ageing in his/her own language. Likewise, in most cases, the individual's social and cultural environment constructs ageing in his/her own language. For example, there is an adage in English which goes: "You're only as old as you feel!", an adage used in a culture which, with its wide range of anti-ageing cosmetics and 'active ageing' gyms, among countless other products and services, makes the elderly person more conscious of his/her relatively-advanced age, that is, makes him/her feel 'older.' Furthermore, cultural concepts such as 'birthdays,' 'Saints' Days,' anniversaries, commemorations, and so on, will acquire a more or less meaningful status, depending on the culture and the language group in which they are articulated and expressed.

Aphorisms, adages, clichés, mottoes, epithets, and platitudes abound in an individual's language and, as one grows older, such formulaic sayings come to the surface and find expression, unexpectedly, spontaneously, without warning, rising, as it were, from deep within the elderly person's sub-conscious and language-usage memory. For these reasons, David Rampton's "Browning's Rabbi, the Gerontologists, and the Aphorism," presented in the section *A Language to Age With*, is an important and significant contribution to this volume. In his chapter, David Rampton cautions that, on spontaneous recall, sayings that have lain deep within our memory since early adulthood, are recalled only in part, often replete with ambiguity and half-digested meaning.

Centring his argument basically on the Victorian poet Robert Browning's[17] popular verse from "Rabbi Ben Ezra": "Grow old along with me! / The best is yet to be, / The last of life, for which the first was made,"[18] David Rampton claims that such aphorisms have been used and abused, in particular by doctors, medical researchers, and gerontologist to cheer elderly persons up. He cites a review by Avram Mark Clarfield of the book *Contesting Aging & Loss* (2010)[19] that reveals different perceptions of ageing of poets and pathologists, some of the former seeing positive aspects in ageing, some of the latter seeing ageing as an entirely negative process. Ultimately, however, as references to William Shakespeare's *As You Like It* (1599) show, it is the way old people are treated by society that will determine whether ageing is perceived as being positive or negative.

Yet David Rampton sees a third, middle way, as posited by such medical researchers as Atul Gawande (1965-) and Tom Kirkwood (1951-), a way that is further endorsed in writings by Helen Small (*The Long Life* 2007),[20] Karen Chase, (*The Victorians and Old Age* 2009),[21] and Kay Heath (*Aging by the Book. The Emergence of Midlife in Victorian Britain* 2010). Returning to Browning's aphorism, David Rampton contends that when the Poet writes "Grow old along with me," it underlines the ager's indefinite commitment to the "pain of deterioration." But "the best is yet to be" is a clarion call for this commitment to be active and unwavering. Others of

---

[17] Robert Browning (1812–1889).

[18] From "Rabbi Ben Ezra" *Dramatis Personae* (1864).

[19] Janice E. Graham, and Peter H. Stephenson. Eds. *Contesting Age and Loss*. (Toronto: University of Toronto Press, 2010).

[20] Helen Small. *The Long Life*. (London: Oxford University Press, 2007).

[21] Karen Chase. *The Victorians and Old Age*. (London: Oxford University Press, 2009).

Browning's verses, for example, "Ah, but a man's reach should exceed his grasp / Or what's a heaven for?"[22] and "God's in his heaven – All's right with the world,"[23] read in their respective contexts, bring David Rampton to conclude that context is everything. However, it is also true that, while the meaning of the aphorism is conditioned by context, the aphorisms themselves take on their real power, as aphorisms, if recalled taking "the long view," that is, in late old age.

The inference is clear: it is crucial that administrators, social and cultural service workers, and carers in general, recognize the importance of language and language-usage in the management of elderly communities and elderly persons.

Products

New Technologies as 'Social Innovation'

Usage by the elderly of products deriving from new technologies is an important area of study, both for gerontologists and administrators. In her chapter "Exploring older adults and the use of digital technologies in the context of everyday life in Taiwan," Pei-Wen Chu reports on a study undertaken in 2013 which looked at the use by elderly persons, aged 50 years old and over, of products such as computers, social media platforms, email accounts, and others. The pilot study undertaken by Pei-Wen Chu focuses on how people in Taiwan, aged between 52 and 62 years old, react to new technologies. Observations showed that the uptake of new products by elderly people is conditioned by the students' cultural context.[24] Results show that elderly persons pick up new skills more efficiently when they learn competence and usage of the products in the company of their teachers and other elderly learners.

In Taiwan, taking into account surroundings, activities, and feelings, the 'hands-on' part of the study was carried out in a primary school classroom, in which the chairs and tables are designed for children. Any fear that this seemingly-deficient logistics might prove an obstacle to learning activities, skills-acquisition, and personal-development proved baseless. Pei-Wen Chu reports that, as the elderly persons were Taiwanese, that is,

---

[22] From "Andrea del Sarto." *Men and Women* (1855).

[23] From "Song from Pippa Passes" *Pippa Passes, A Drama* (1841).

[24] This is in line with what Emine Özmete and Katarzyna Ziomek-Michalak say about quality-of-ageing and cultural context.

members of a culture not given to complaining, none of the elderly participants registered a complaint.

Of the various Internet platforms and online interfaces used, work with Facebook proved to be the most motivating, the new users seeing Facebook as a tool for avoiding social exclusion. However, because the keyboard input is designed for Taiwanese users, typing speed is slowed down and access to platforms made arduous and slow, to the extent that elderly users became impatient and frustrated. Pei-Wen Chu considers that, while this factor, together with the dysfunction between corporeal comfort and mental activity may prove to be a serious constraint for elderly persons in Western cultures, it is not a significant factor for Asian elderly. In short, the experience of active ageing will depend on the culture within which that active ageing takes place.

New Technology Systems as 'Social Innovation'

A team of researchers at the German Research Center for Artificial Intelligence (DFKI – Saarbrücken) are working on ways to improve mobility-potential for elderly persons, specifically on public transport in Saarbrücken and in Saarland as a whole. In the chapter "'mobisaar' – a technology-based service providing mobility for everybody in public transport," Maurice Rekrut, Jan Alexandersson, Jochen Britz, Johannes Tröger, Daniel Bieber, and Kathleen Schwarz present research aimed at developing an integrated-technology-based system designed, essentially, to help elderly persons use the bus service in Saarbrücken. The "from door to door" service, which operates custom-designed buses equipped with fold-out wheelchair ramps and safety door-step mechanisms, is controlled by digital-communication platforms and smartphone apps. Trained mobility-guides assist elderly and mobility-impaired travellers to use the system, thereby facilitating access to health and social services, and to socialising environments in general.

It is foreseen that the Call Centre, the passenger app, and the guide app of the 'mobisaar' system can be developed for enhanced integration between railway and alternative transport networks, in both urban and rural areas. As it stands at present, the system can provide transport information to be used for improving routing on a minute-by-minute basis. Recently, the city of Homburg has been linked up with the 'mobisaar' system.

Industrial Design as 'Social Innovation'

As in Rocío González-Torres' study of Doris Lessing's *The Diary of a Good Neighbour* (1983), the space an elderly person grows old in is the focus of attention, too, for P.J. White, but this time from the perspective of an interior-furniture designer. In "Designing a Domestic Heating Product for Older People Within the Concept of 'Contained Living Spaces,'" P.J. White presents a research protocol for the design and manufacture of products that are purpose-built for use by elderly persons who live in their own homes.

Recognising the importance of independence and of ageing 'at home,' P.J. White argues that interior designers can play a part in striving for a degree of comfort and convenience in that space by creating products that enhance quality-of-life and reduce dependency. Moreover, the author posits that such design innovation will help sustain an active and healthy ageing population.

Research has shown that room-temperature has a direct bearing on the elderly person's health and wellbeing, and that adverse temperatures can even be a cause of death. With this in mind and taking into account the domestic heating requirements of elderly people in the Republic of Ireland, P.J. White describes the stages in design and production of a portable, mobile 'contained living space,' with integrated heating-source to control the temperature of the space at all times. Following sketch-based brainstorming sessions, a sketch-book is used to design a prototype 'hot-desk.' The 'hot-desk' is a small desk on wheels with a built-in, rechargeable-battery heater "to warm user's hands, arms, and legs as they sit at the desk." P.J. White concludes by saying that the prototype 'hot-desk' will undergo further 'in situ' testing.

Services

Care Services and Caring

Caring, the carer, and the administration of care together form a key component in the institutionalised management of elderly persons. Through 'social innovation,' the type, manner, and logistics of care and care services can be tailored to the specific requirements of the individual and to the social environment in which he or she lives. In "New Services for New Elders. Welfare vs Free Market: Technology, Cost Governance, and Human Caring," Dario Bracco and Ugo Marchisio focus attention on a region of Italy and point to an urgent need for more-personalised, institutional care of the new elderly – those of the 'Baby-Boomer' generation – in line with characteristically Mediterranean humanity. To make matters worse, the cost of the new elderly is becoming untenable for modern societies, especially for the younger generations who are becoming increasingly dependent on the new-elderly, wealthier family members.

Dario Bracco and Ugo Marchisio note, first, that, in Italy, increasing longevity is having an impact on the health services nationwide, with elderly men spending on average four of their final years in a severely disabled condition, and women on average just over six years. In the city of Turin, in 2014, over 25% of the population was more than 65 years old. Because of inadequate state-funding, residential and hospital requirements have increased proportionally and are now overcrowded. Moreover, statistics show that, in Turin, 75% of persons aged 65 years old and over live in their own homes, including frail and disabled persons, and that 35% of these individuals live alone.

Dario Bracco and Ugo Marchisio conclude from their research and from their observations that, in the short term, the solutions are three-fold: 1) to care for the new elderly in such a way that they remain active and healthy for as long as possible; 2) to resort to the 'free market' to cover optional requirements,[25] and 3) to revamp the concept of the 'nursing home' by making residential homes meet the needs of active and healthy elderly persons and of those elderly people who become increasingly dependent. In short, the authors recommend that a mixed model – State-financed services and 'free market' initiatives, that is, Public Private Partnerships (PPPs) – are the most rational way to tackle the care of the elderly in Italy.

Social Exclusion (Female Elderly)

As far as any form of 'social innovation' is applicable, that feature of the ageing process known as 'social exclusion' falls within the scope of responsibility of care-services. In "Older Women and Social Exclusion. A Descriptive, Exploratory, Qualitative Study," Andrés Escarbajal-de Haro, Silvia Martínez de Miguel-López, and Juan Antonio Salmerón-Aroca inform that, as 'female aging'[26] is fast becoming a distinctive feature of longevity in

---

[25] State-funded welfare and health services must continue to satisfy basic needs, that is, a roof, appropriate care services, appropriate and adequate food, and free health cover.

[26] Women in Spain live longer on average than men – 85–86 years for women and 79–80 years for men.

Spain,[27] elderly women are at greater risk of social-exclusion than are elderly men[28] and, for this reason, they are becoming increasingly dependent.

With this in mind, a project was launched to study gender and environment of the elderly population in the Autonomous Region of Murcia, with specific attention to the social-exclusion of elderly women that this may result in.

The authors' research findings, gathered from interviews and discussion groups involving eighty women over sixty-five from the Valle de Ricote in the Autonomous Region of Murcia (Spain), were structured in seven categories, including 'Life trajectory,' 'Interpersonal relationships,' and 'Socio-community participation.' In respect of 'social-exclusion,' the collated information revealed that elderly women, married or widowed, between 65 and 75 years old, usually live in their own homes, and that the formation they received as girls and young women conditions their late-aging, a period seen as liberation from the traditional division of labour as housewives. While showing a strong disposition to take all precautions recommended to keep themselves healthy, all the women showed some anxiety about future care options. The authors present evidence to show that close family support and affectivity reduces the elderly person's sense of social-exclusion, but they end with a warning; active association in socio-cultural environments can help promote social-inclusion, but it can also create dangerous stereotypes.

Concerning Dementia (Alzheimer's)

Alzheimer's and, more specifically, the management and care of elderly persons suffering from Alzheimer's, is concentrating the minds and the efforts of managers, administrators, and carers in institutions and agencies entrusted with the care of elderly persons across the world. It is Alzheimer's and its effect on the elderly sufferer and family members that is the discursive subject of Matthew Thomas's novel *We Are Not Ourselves* (2014).

Aware of the urgency and gravity of the current situation regarding Alzheimer's and other forms of cognitive-impairment,[29] in *"We Are Not*

---

[27] Elderly women currently make up 10% of the total population in Spain.

[28] This is due partly to reasons of income, partly to their expected roles of 'carer' or 'nursemaid,' and partly to a lower level of formal education than men.

[29] Statistics warn that, currently, 50% of those persons aged 85 years old and over will suffer from some form of memory-loss, 25 million in the world at present, Alzheimer's being the

Ourselves: Matthew Thomas's Portrayal of Alzheimer's," Cristina Garrigós observes that Alzheimer's has been presented in novels and films for over a decade now. She notes, too, that textual and audio-visual fictionalisations of Alzheimer's are frequently conceived and created by persons for whom the effects of Alzheimer's has been part of their personal experience, as a son or daughter of a person suffering from Alzheimer's,[30] and she points out that such fictionalisations are helpful because they articulate inscrutable factors such as a sufferer's gradual loss of 'self,' modulations in his/her identity, our understanding of a person's humanity, and the impact of Alzheimer's on the sufferer's close family. Through a skilfully-devised narrational strategy, Matthew Thomas is able to present the Alzheimer sufferer Edmund Leary through the behavioural responses and emotive reactions of his wife Eileen and son Connell. Following her analysis, Cristina Garrigós concludes that it is memory, not just memory-loss, that is key – "it is what configures a person" – and that it is how an Alzheimer's sufferer wishes to be remembered by his/her family members and friends, and how these same family members and friends will remember the Alzheimer's sufferer.

By way of a two-fold word of warning, noting that Alzheimer's disease is among the costliest of all diseases in the United States of America, Cristina Garrigós points out that, on the one hand, it is the economic circumstances of the Alzheimer's sufferer and his/her family that will condition the amount and quality of the care the sufferer receives, the type of relationship the sufferer will have with individual family members, and relations between those same family members. On the other hand, reading Matthew Thomas's *We Are Not Ourselves* as a denouncement of the lack of administrative support and institutionalised preparedness for the exponential spread of Alzheimer's disease and its consequences in the United States of America, Cristina Garrigós contends that, if the modern, Westernised communities and their governments do not wake up to the implications inherent in the proliferation of mental-impairment diseases, Alzheimer's disease and its effects have the potential to break down North American society and destroy the hopes of all United States citizens in the fulfilment of their 'American Dream.'

* * *

---

prevalent form. For society at large, the cognitive-impairment brought on by Alzheimer's leads to a state of almost total dependency for the sufferer.

[30] Matthew Thomas's father suffered from Alzheimer's and his novel *We Are Not Ourselves* (2014) is about his experience as the son of an Alzheimer's sufferer.

As a clinical psychologist, in "Preventing Dementia as a Defence Against Ageing: A Pilot Study at the Primary Care Service," Glòria Mateu-Vives looks at the anxieties of persons aged 60 years old and over who are showing the first signs of dementia, one type of which affects one-fifth of all persons aged 80 years old and over. Her research has shown that there is one worry in particular that presents itself as a person grows older, namely, when "to stop *being* oneself" – that is, when to allow one's 'self' to fade away, or when to start denying one's 'self.' Glòria Mateu-Vives argues that a person's experiences in his/her youth and early adulthood can give rise to his or her resorting to one form of dementia that minimizes emotional pain. In these instances, when such minimization strategies are brought into play and develop to a certain intensity, then psychotherapy is required.

Glòria Mateu-Vives' Pilot Study put into practice thirty-five group-psychotherapy sessions that took place between October 2010 and July 2016. The psychoanalytic, psychotherapy groups were made up of twelve elderly primary-care outpatients, who, during the sessions, revealed their anxieties, and the defences they employ to suppress these anxieties. By expressing openly in the group their early-lifetime anxieties, their experience of parenting, and their currently diminishing independence, the elderly participants found relief and emotional containment. The group-sessions were shown to foment social-interaction and to help fight social-exclusion. Significantly, it also became evident that an elderly person's participation in psychoanalytic, psychotherapy group-sessions can obviate perceived self-induced memory-loss, or delay and even prevent the onset of certain types of dementia and cognitive-impairment, thereby greatly enhancing quality-of-life.

The need for 'social innovation' for services

In her chapter "The Need for Social Innovation for Active and Healthy Ageing (AHA): Lessons from Turkey Active and Healthy Ageing Research," Emine Özmete presents statistical data drawn from cohorts of men and women aged 40 years old and over[31] in twelve cities in twelve regions of Turkey. The statistics lead her to conclude that quality-of-life amongst ageing communities is culture-dependent, that is, conditioned by the culture the elderly individual ages in, the values and traditions of that culture, and

---

[31] The "Turkey Active and Healthy Ageing Study" involved face-to-face interviews with 3,082 individuals, 1,546 individuals in the 40–64 age group, and 1,536 individuals in the 65+ age group, with close gender parity. The interviews took place from June to October 2015.

the stability and security offered by that cultural environment. In the case for Turkey, a country in which the elderly population is growing rapidly, proportionally, along with longevity, Özmete finds that the elderly individual's level of education is a major factor in his or her awareness of personal health issues, degree of dependency, willingness to exercise regularly, physical functionality, and ability to access health-care systems and dental care.

On these grounds, Özmete calls for more 'social innovation,' at both societal and individual levels, to be directed at facilitating and improving all strategies and actions that relate to Active and Healthy Ageing (AHA). Such innovation, she contends, should be aimed, especially, at fomenting and facilitating more exercise amongst elderly people, providing improved self-help services and help with Internet platforms and applications (apps), and encouraging attitudes and behaviour patterns that relate to personal health habits and social interaction. She advises that, for service administrators, 'social innovation' means developing policies and formal regulations designed to meet those needs of elderly persons that have not yet been met.

Socially-Dynamic Environments for 'Active Ageing'

Like Emine Özmete in her chapter, Katarzyna Ziomek-Michalak links the dynamics of ageing to the social and cultural environment in which the ageing takes place. In "Social innovative projects for seniors in Poland – the way to a constructive attitude towards ageing," Katarzyna Ziomek-Michalak uses data from innovative projects carried out in Poland that take into account certain lifestyles of Polish elderly citizens. Her research leads her to posit that environments conducive to increased ager activity induce a more positive attitude towards ageing, increase social skills, reduce loneliness, and enhance quality-of-life, such that, when supported by local community organisations, elderly citizens develop a strong sense of self-help, enabling them to take control of their lives and their personal health.

Katarzyna Ziomek-Michalak cites the University of the Third Age (UTA) in Poland as an appropriate state-sponsored initiative that enhances social interactivity, self-esteem, and presentation of 'self' among the elderly students. Moreover, it has added value in that it can also change social perceptions of the elderly. Together with the entrepreneurial "Active Pensioner" programme which enables elderly persons to start up and manage their own businesses in order to earn a supplement to their state pensions, recreational and sporting competitions, carnivalesque depictions of elderliness, skill-development and educational courses, team-work, intergenerational projects, and activities involving the use of the Senior's Card, all of which foment solidarity and a sense of belonging, are all similarly appropriate.

Concluding remarks

'A language to grow old with,' 'a space to grow old in,' 'care and caring services,' 'memory loss,' 'social exclusion' …. these are all features of the ageing process in which all and any form of 'social innovation' can have an impact and play a part. In fact, because of the 'longevity revolution' – the confluence of increasing longevity with the large, ageing, baby-boomer generation in Europe – the role of 'social innovation' is becoming increasingly urgent and critical. 'Social innovation' must serve society in this way or, as Cristina Garrigós warns in her chapter, the whole of Western civilisation as we know it is placed at severe risk of collapse. Economic-, legal-, social-, and political-institutions, and democracy itself are teetering on the brink. Today's pensioners, many former students of the '68 revolution, are demonstrating in the city streets of Europe again, while young persons are trying hard, democratically, to take control of national governments. It may well be that the only 'social innovations' at hand to save the day, at least as a stop-gap until more profound and refined social attitudes and administrative practices emerge, are astute, imaginative, and creative applications of the Internet, social platforms, and those products deriving from the new technologies.

Strange as it may seem, 'growing old' does not appear necessarily to come naturally. There is, no doubt, an art to growing old, especially to 'growing old well,' or 'growing old gracefully,' as the expression goes. Unlike 'ageing' *per se*, 'growing older' is more a creative process than just a natural one. Moreover, just as potential social innovators – age critics and researchers – must be ever-ready to learn more about what it means to 'grow old' in order to achieve a deeper understanding of the ageing process, so too should elderly people remain open to learning more about their own 'getting older' in order to help themselves age better.

At this point, we take our cue from the 1986 winner of the Nobel Prize in Literature, Wole Soyinka, who said in an interview:

I even made the mistake of announcing publicly, once, that I was retiring, and then I had to swallow my words and say, "Oh no, what

I should have said is that I am now a *student* of retirement, and that I'm a *graduate* this year, and then I'll do my *post-graduate* next year, and eventually I'll do my *PhD* on retirement, by which time I'm probably gone!" That's it … and I cope with it![32]

This sentiment is echoed in Núria Casado-Gual's play *Prime Time*[33] in which an elderly female actor, seeing herself as a victim of professional ageism, resolves to live out the rest of her years, not following the exigencies of a play-text written by a playwright, but according to the script she plans to write for herself:

My name is Gloria Aran. I have a dream... to start my own project. It's a 'work-in-progress' which has still to be defined, like me... I am just learning how to grow old. (…) This is the beginning of a time of splendour... a true prime time, for me and for all of you. And, what's really stimulating about it is that the script which is awaiting us, in fact, is as yet unwritten.

With this in mind, it may be that provision should be made by society and its institutions for elderly persons to be taught or instructed on how to improve their 'growing old' experience. For both innovators and elderly persons, 'getting older' should be viewed, perhaps, as a 'learning process': for researchers, administrators, and carers, a better understanding of ageing and the ageing process would enable them to encourage and assist elderly persons to understand their own ageing better and to help them adapt to their new perceptions of their personalised 'growing old'; for the elderly person, 'growing older' might be treated as a task, with the pay-off being a longer life with greater independence, autonomy, and personal freedom.

If, indeed, 'growing older' does imply a 'a learning curve,' then perhaps the aim of every elderly individual should be to increase their personal longevity and enhance their personal quality-of-life. The elderly individual should learn how to 'get older' better, both physically and mentally. As Rabbi Ben Ezra foresees in Robert Browning's dramatic

---

[32] Wole Soyinka, on retirement: <www.emresanli.com/video/?id=qzvVxJa8peU>

[33] The play *Prime Time* by Núria Casado-Gual was commissioned by the organisers of The SIforAGE International Conference "Envisioning a New World: Social Innovation for Active and Healthy Ageing," and was first performed in CaixaForum Barcelona in October 2016. See Núria Casado-Gual. *Prime Time* [Play – version in English] (Edicions i Publicacions de la Universitat de Lleida, 2018).

monologue "Rabbi Ben Ezra," "Grow old along with me / The best is yet to be."[34] In order for this to happen, with the support and input of all the ideas, products, and services deriving from ongoing 'social innovation,' elderly persons should be helped to develop their own potential for 'self-help,' and learn, functionally and practically, how to sustain a low level of social, economic, and health-care dependency for as long as their personal circumstances permit. This is probably the best way forward. The alternative does not bear thinking about.

The editors

---

[34] David Rampton cites these well-known lines in his chapter "Browning's Rabbi, the Gerontologists, and the Aphorism."

Part One

Ideas

Intergenerationality

and

Social Paticipation

Rethinking ageing societies: working on a shared value for a new leadership

Eleonora Barone

Founder and Director of the "memory in motion between Young and Old" Association (mYmO)[1]

Europe is getting older, and the 'Silver Economy' is one of the most relevant markets, sharing the podium with the digital transformation. In Spain, the percentage of older people in the demographic pyramid increases continuously, from 18% in 2016 to a predicted 33% in 2050. Unemployment data shows that 57% of unemployed persons is concentrated in two big age-bands: younger people under 25 years old without expertise (15%), and older people over 45 years old, due to ageism (42%).[2] In the Mediterranean area in particular, our public systems are experiencing problems sustaining the payment of pensions and social subsidies, while social services and care needs increase. We need to create new opportunities and new models to facilitate participation, rethinking ageing societies.

Within this framework, this chapter analyses "the grey revolution" as a way to understand better what matters. How can we work together, seniors and juniors, to build a new, shared leadership? What are the roles of each actor, from citizens to enterprises through to public administrations and NGOs?

* * *

Starting from the assumption that, better than mentors and entrepreneurs, senior citizens could be the drivers of the change and that, together with the younger generation, they could work to reshape the society of the future, this chapter will focus on three main projects that are being worked on at "memory in motion between Young and Old" (mYmO): a) from the elderly centre to the talent centre in the City Hall; b) diversity programmes in companies; and c) the intergenerational innovation laboratory. These

---

[1] "memory in motion between Young and Old" (mYmO)

[2] Ageism – the personalised and institutionalised discrimination against elderly persons.

projects relate to three ways of crossing generations from three different perspectives: public, private, and personal. Put a senior in your life, cross generations in your company, promote intergenerational communities in your neighbourhood, and everything will be different!

Today there is a clear discrepancy between the new and increasing interest in the 'old style,' as a new fashion market, and the ageism that is evident and powerful in every sector of our lives. The good news is that grey hair has started to become fashionable, not only amongst adult people but also among the young. The first senior agency has been created in Russia – Oldushka[3] – and Dolce e Gabbana have started to use older models to dress their photos and their firm. In fact, marketing and advertising are the first markets to have seen senior citizens as a niche to explore.

So now we should look to convert those first interests in something more than love for vintage, fashion, and super heroes.

* * *

If we look at the market, knowing that we live every year longer and in better conditions, we really have the chance to re-design a lot of products and services. In fact, we have great opportunities ahead because, clearly, we still have a lot to invent. This is the premise. The challenge is to understand what we can do to take advantage of these opportunities.

First of all, to have a global vision, we should stop thinking in separated boxes, isolating concepts and problems. In fact, after years of policies that segregate by age – youth policies, policies for children, policies for the elderly – we have been creating tools and resources for specific generational groups only. We are not used to working in an inclusive way, nor in an intergenerational way, if by intergenerational – intergenerational equates to interaction + cooperation + influence + change – we mean not only interaction in a multi-generation environment, but also cooperating, having mutual influence, and generating changes together. To face the challenges of our society at a time when everything is changing rapidly and constantly, we need new and more inclusive approaches.

Currently, our societies have become more liquid, companies more horizontal, and relationships freer and more flexible, so again we have the opportunity to explore new horizons. We must re-think new ways to participate and to cooperate, getting out of those 'silos' that we have been generating with our segregated policies. We need a comprehensive and systemic approach on the three levels, public, private, and personal.

---

[3] Oldushka – Senior model agency in Russia.

Regarding the public sector, but also the third sector in Spain, the demographics, social, and economic changes have caught us unawares. Our products and services are still focused on solving the problems of the older generations, because we still dedicate more attention to the 'older people of yesterday.' But the senior citizens of today are very different. We need to look beyond assistance and paternalistic support in order to reach today's 'young older adults.'

* * *

As an example, let us have a look at the centres for the elderly. In Madrid, the City Hall manages eighty-nine centres dedicated to older people. The actual model, which was designed in the past century, is open only for those who meet these requirements: users must be aged 60 years old or over, or be retired. In short, the centres for the elderly in Madrid are reserved solely for elderly citizens.

Does this model still make sense today? Does it make sense to continue segregating by age? Could not those eighty-nine centres be intergenerational centres? Or could they not be simply cultural centres where everyone can enjoy activities together, perhaps with different entry passes? In order to answer these questions, a research project has been designed for the Madrid City Hall, scheduled to last six months, the aim of which is to investigate the four possible scenarios for the future.

The first scenario preserves the same conditions as today: the elderly centre maintains exclusivity for older people. In the second scenario, the model of the centre still maintains the main characteristics of today, but it starts to open the space to some specific activities that involve persons of other age groups. The third model contemplates a substantial opening of the centre, introducing intergenerational activities as an essential part of the centre, while the centre is maintained, conceptually, for elderly people. Finally, the fourth scenario is the more futuristic one, because it contemplates the possibility of completely changing the model and dismissing an isolated centre that is exclusively at the disposition of elderly people.

During the process, there will be four phases: information, participation, action, and dissemination. In these phases, different kinds of interviews, workshops, and focus groups will be combined in order to achieve two main objectives: on the one hand, to understand the needs and the desires of older people, both inside and outside the centre and, on the other hand, to identify all those needs and opportunities that are not currently met in the neighbourhood by the present model.

With regard to those elderly persons who do not enjoy the centre, special attention will be dedicated to these in order to understand why they do not use the equipment. Finally, we will have a sort of map of talent – inside the centre – and a map of needs – outside the centre – with the intention of identifying the forces that are moving from the first scenario to the last one, with details about ages, what kind of training they choose, skills and abilities, the type of intergenerational project and subject they prefer – environment; job; security; gender; groups at risk of social exclusion; education; health inclusion; culture; the arts – and so on.

Will the older people who actually enjoy the centre inform that they are quite happy about the services and the equipment? Do they perceive the centre as a property that they have won as compensation over the years of work? And why are the older people who are not using the centre today not willing to enjoy it?

At the present time, the generations are changing very fast, so the questions are relevant. If we do not change the models and the way we use the equipment and make them more relevant for participation in society, who are being excluded? And what are the consequences? In ten years' time, might there not be eighty-nine centres in Madrid, but serving only 40% of the elderly in the city?

* * *

Moreover, regarding the private sector, the reality in Spain is similar to the rest of the Mediterranean area; the private sector is very good at many things, but not so good at anticipating the future!

It is true that the terms "Age-Management" and "Generational Diversity" are beginning to appear in a lot of newspapers, congress agendas, conferences, workshops, and so on. In the last six months, there has been an appreciable acceleration of interest in these topics but, in the end, companies are not willing to start thinking about the challenges and opportunities of an aged workforce, and re-designing processes and policies seriously. Only 29% of Spanish companies have policies related to the recruitment and retention of older workers, compared with 52% on average in Europe and other countries, like the United States of America, Canada, and Australia, countries which are also much more advanced in terms of age-management.[4] There are plenty of studies, reports, recommendations, and alerts, but no serious Spanish approach in the direction of introducing age-management into the strategic planning of companies. Beyond mentoring and training,

---

[4] Source: Top Employers Institute (2015).

best practices in intergenerational innovation have not yet been identified and described, and much less has the Spanish private sector been able to articulate the concern to consider the mature workforce as an opportunity and not as a problem.

Companies love millennials. Ageism is still very powerful in our environment, and the people still have a lot of prejudices. In reality, older workers are no longer off sick; nor do they suffer more accidents; nor are they less productive; nor have they lost their ability to learn. On the contrary, elderly workers have high adaptability, greater awareness of quality and, of course, more experience.

The question is: if you remain twenty-five years sitting in the same chair, doing the same job, looking at the same landscape, and interacting with the same group of people, can you imagine how to maintain your productivity high? Poor conditions in the workplace affect worker performance, so employees accumulate stress and can develop diseases or simply exhaustion. A lack of flexibility and stagnation of the organizational structure in many companies inhibit task- and function-rotation that are necessary in order to have a global vision of the business and, thereby, feel committed to the company. Moreover, the rigid design of jobs is not compatible with the permanent transformation of businesses and customers. These are the main reasons for the lower employability and productivity of older workers, not their relatively-advanced age.

And again, if we try to look at the issue in a systemic way, who are we excluding or including? Is ageist management policy favourable for the greater inclusion of younger people? Is it advantageous for the economy and the profitability of companies? Rapid retirements deprive companies of critical experience and knowledge, which undermines productivity across the entire economy:

> An older worker's experience increases not only his own productivity but also the productivity of those who work with him. One study found that productivity peaks at age 50, when productivity is 60% higher than for the average 20-year-old. (...) A journeyman carpenter doesn't just work faster than an apprentice; he also helps the apprentice learn the tricks of the trade. New doctors diagnose patients more accurately under the tutelage of experienced practitioners.[5]

---

[5] See Nicole Maestas, Kathleen J. Mullen, and David Powell. *The Effect of Population Aging on Economic Growth, the Labor Force and Productivity*. The National Bureau of Economic

So, seniors help the working environment to develop faster, and Age-Management helps companies to transform diversity towards a competitive advantage. Once again, it seems necessary to develop measures to increment participation of the older workers, both within and outside companies.

In this sense, before turning to the level of the individual, it is relevant to highlight the responsibility of organizations to accompany people in the transition towards retirement, especially because of the importance of planning their post-retirement. Regrettably only 4% of Spanish companies support a worker to plan his or her retirement period, according to a study conducted by GFK consulting which surveyed about four-hundred Spanish companies in 2015.[6]

* * *

At the personal, individual level, in general, when a person retires, 80% of the possibilities for enjoying and participating in the society depends on consuming – consuming training, consuming travel, consuming culture, consuming food, consuming leisure, and so on. Here again, a huge percentage of the market has yet to be invented and exploited. Fortunately, and looking deeper and beyond consuming, there are other opportunities: the possibility for volunteering, perhaps teaching something about professional expertise; for becoming a senior entrepreneur; and, finally, for mentoring younger entrepreneurs. These are the three main possibilities that value experience and guarantee active participation for older people.

Can we test other possibilities? At "memory in motion between Young and Old" (mYmO), the power of cooperation between generations is seen as a means by which to have a systemic view of the problems, and by which to try to co-create 'societies for all ages.' The question is, how to value the 'senior experience' and, at the same time, to help solve problems collaboratively, in such a way that a culture centred on solutions might be generated for the long term. The answer will surely involve combining the critical expertise of older adults with the aspirations of young people to learn, a mix that might well take place in varieties of Social Business Incubators and Citizens' Laboratories.

Research, July 2016. [NBER Working Paper Nº 22452] Nicole Maestas is affiliated to Harvard University, and Kathleen Mullen and David Powell to the Rand Corporation.

[6] GFK consulting. *Previsión Social Empresarial para la Jubilación en España: empleados y empresas* (2015). This report was elaborated by GFK consulting for Nationale-Nederlanden.

A momentary look back to review the unemployment data reveals that both young and old people are being constantly discriminated against, for different reasons, irrespective of the fact that, ultimately, a retired man or woman has a lot in common with a young, unemployed man or woman. For this reason, the practice proposed here brings together senior people – persons who probably do not want to head up businesses – with young people who are looking for opportunities to learn and to work. Together, the two generations will work together to generate ideas and convert them into projects, using the Service Design Methodology and problems-solving approach.

The intergenerational groups work around a concern, a challenge, or an interest. The process passes through the three steps of service design – Inspiration-Ideation-Implementation – in order that those persons who enter the Citizens' Laboratories undergo a process of training and working at the same time. This is necessary because Service Design Methodology is focused on solving real problems and, ultimately, on designing a project that can be offered to other entities, both in the private and public sectors. Working on such a project, this kind of Laboratory may be able to facilitate solutions and employment for all ages and, at the same time, generate more long-term, sustainable communities.

* * *

This leads to the reflection: Who we are excluding if we continue in the same direction of segregating by age? No answer to this has been forthcoming yet, but one of the clear needs, for instance, in the Mediterranean area, is to deepen our awareness in respect of what it means to discriminate against elderly persons. Spanish society in general has not even begun to understand this point. Without first passing through a profound campaign of awareness, people, organisations, and public authorities in Spain will not be in a position to confront a serious process of re-designing policies, products, and services. How, then, can companies, citizens, and employees inoculate Spanish organisations with this message?

Moreover, if there is a need to mix ages and work in an 'intergenerational' way, then responsibilities and frames of influence should also be mixed. When envisaging a more integrated system, it is not only companies that are responsible for generating economic wealth, but also Non-Governmental Organisations (NGOs); it is not only public authorities that should be looking after the common good, but also the citizens themselves; and there is not only corporate social responsibility, but also individual social responsibility. Once again, the 'intergenerational' approach would appear to be part of the solution.

Within the concept of the Citizens' Laboratories lies a potential solution to foster employment and give to senior people new opportunities to stay active in society. The model works only by boosting cooperation across the generations, and by activating community networks that are currently disconnected. Senior people would be able not only to mentor younger entrepreneurs, but also to test and invent new products, to help investigate new opportunities in the field of the silver economy, and to invent other services. The possibilities are endless; the search for innovation has only just started.

There is a need to encourage dialogue and facilitate quality relationships in order to generate greater impact. Also, attempts should be made to investigate new models of intervention and participation for all people because, in the end, who are being excluded if we 'retire' or ignore elderly people? Obviously, it is elderly persons who are being excluded, but in fact the entire system is being damaged because young adults and children forfeit their role models and mentors. All future development is seriously limited. If you are a senior and planning to retire soon, please reconsider your decision; we all need you more than you can imagine.

Works Cited

Dubois, Hans, Georgiana Runceanu, and Robert Anderson. *Extending working lives through flexible retirement schemes: Partial retirement*. Eurofound, 2016.

GFK consulting. Previsión Social Empresarial para la Jubilación en España: empleados y empresas (2015). [Report commissioned by Nationale-Nederlanden]

Maestas, Nicole, Kathleen J. Mullen, and David Powell. *The Effect of Population Aging on Economic Growth, the Labor Force and Productivity*. The National Bureau of Economic Research, July 2016. [NBER Working Paper Nº 22452]

Ministerio de Sanidad, Servicios Sociales e Igualdad / Fundación para la Diversidad / Unión Europea. *Gestión de la Diversidad en la Empresa, Casos de éxito y difusión pública de buenas prácticas*. 2015.

UK Department for Work and Pensions. *Attitudes of the over 50s to Fuller Working Lives*, 2015.

'Intergenerational Solidarity' in Community Practice[1]

Baiba Bela, Liga Rasnaca, and Anna Stepcenko
University of Latvia

This chapter is dedicated to discussing the role of 'intergenerational solidarity'[2] in the practical implementation of an Active and Healthy Ageing (AHA) policy. The topicality of this theme relates to population aging as a global phenomenon that is manifest, especially, in European Union member states, including Latvia. The subject provides not just new opportunities, but also new challenges. In this regard, aging is no longer associated with physical helplessness and passive retirement; instead, new forms and ways are sought to continue an active life after retirement. The 'active ageing' policy is a social response to challenges caused by demographic and social changes. It aims to provide opportunities for older persons to maintain independence and autonomy, continue participation in social, economic, cultural, and civic life, living a life of fulfilment. Mutual support and Intergenerational Solidarity (IS) implemented in families, communities, and society is one way of ensuring 'active ageing.'

By studying social innovation for Active and Healthy Ageing (AHA), community-level action is shown to be vital in the creation of 'a society for all ages,' and 'intergenerational solidarity' to play a particularly important role in a number of activities. However, it has also to be acknowledged that, at the mezzo-level – in communities, groups, and

[1] Acknowledgments: The authors are grateful to Dirk Jarré, EURAG president, for reviewing this chapter and for his generous advice. We also acknowledge the generous support of the funding scheme "Collaborative Project" of the European Union's "Research, Technological Development, and Demonstration Activities" (7th Framework Programme).
[2] For the purposes of this study, the following definition of 'intergenerational solidarity,' as presented by AGE Platform Europe, is used:

> Intergenerational solidarity refers to the mutual support and cooperation between different age groups in order to achieve a society where people of all ages have a role to play in line with their needs and capacities and can benefit from their community's economic and social progress on an equal basis." (Age Platform Europe 2012)

organizations – in the scientific literature, 'intergenerational solidarity' has received the least attention. The aim here, therefore, is to establish how mezzo-level, innovative activities contribute to 'intergenerational solidarity,' stimulating 'active ageing' and social-inclusion for persons of all ages at the community level. Such an objective includes the development of an appropriate methodology for exploring 'intergenerational solidarity' at the mezzo-level, for identifying boundaries of 'intergenerational solidarity' that might be strengthened, and for defining those areas at the community level in which the full potential of the elderly individual can be promoted.

The research for this study was carried out within the framework of The SIforAGE Project.[3] Based on a mixed-methods approach, forty-three case studies from the SIforAGE 'good practice' database were analysed. At least three dimensions of 'intergenerational solidarity' were analysed in each example of 'good practice,' both theoretical and data-based analyses being applied. For the 'intergenerational solidarity' mezzo-level analysis, the six-dimensional model of solidarity proposed by Vern Bengtson and Robert Roberts (1991) was adopted.[4]

'Active ageing' and 'intergenerational solidarity'
In order to carry out an in-depth analysis of the successful implementation of 'active ageing' in relation to 'intergenerational solidarity' at the community level, the nature of 'active ageing' itself and the role of solidarity between generations possible therein must be reviewed. In this vein, an insight into previous research on 'intergenerational solidarity' is provided.

The ageing process and character undergo changes.[5] Long and healthy life is seen as an important social achievement.[6] On the other hand, the increase in the proportion of elderly people is seen as a risk to the

---

[3] Amongst other objectives, "Social Innovation on Active and Healthy Aging for sustainable economic growth" (SIforAGE), a European Union research project (7th Framework Programme), which commenced in November 2012 and ended in October 2016, also addressed 'intergenerational solidarity' as an important element in building 'a society for all ages.'

[4] See Vern L. Bengtson, and Robert E.L. Roberts. "Intergenerational Solidarity in Aging Families: An Example of Formal Theory Construction." *Journal of Marriage and Family*. 53. 4, 1991. 856-870.

[5] See Hans-Werner Wahl, Dorly J.H. Deeg, Howard Litwin. "Successful ageing as a persistent priority in ageing research." *European Journal of Ageing*. 13. 1, March 2016. 1-3.

[6] See World Health Organization (WHO). *Active Ageing: A Policy Framework*. (Geneva: World Health Organization, 2002).

sustainability of social security systems.[7] Moreover, social and health services in the conditions of economic crisis and reduced funding are faced with increasing pressure.[8] Therefore, 'active ageing' and longer years of healthy life are seen not only as a humanistic value, but also as a pragmatic one, since 'active ageing,' which presupposes relatively 'healthy ageing,' brings with it proportionally-reduced expenditure on social security and health care systems.

Swiss researcher Marion Repetti has noted that, in the middle of the twentieth century, public perception formed a specific social image of the "deserving pensioner."[9] Since the end of the twentieth century, there appears the image of the 'active senior,' whereby a person is expected to retain an active involvement in public life at an advanced age. The World Health Organization (WHO) explains 'active ageing' extensively as a means of optimizing health, participation, and security in order to improve quality-of-life as people age.[10] The explanation is based on a multidimensional perspective on 'active ageing,' which includes economically- and socially-productive, as well as leisure activities, including hobbies, travel, and a variety of creative activities.[11]

It is widely recognised that an active lifestyle is an important factor for better social integration. In building the database containing the examples of good practice, special attention has been focused on strategies for overcoming isolation and for promoting integration. Previous research has concentrated on a variety of factors promoting or hindering integration at the individual level, factors associated with personal resources such as social and cultural capital, and health condition.[12] Voluntary work as an integration tool

---

[7] See Henrike Galenkamp, and Dorly J.H. Deeg. "Increasing social participation of older people: are there different barriers for those in poor health? Introduction to the special section." *European Journal of Ageing.* 13. 2, June 2016. 87–90.

[8] See Laura Jones, and Jesse Heley. "Practices of Participation and Voluntarism among Older People in Rural Wales: Choice, Obligation and Constraints to Active Ageing." *Sociologia Ruralis.* 56. 2, April 2016. 176-196.

[9] Marion Repetti. "Du retraité méritant au senior actif: genèse et actualité d'une figure sociale en Suisse." ["From the deserving pensioner to the active senior: The then and now of a social figure in Switzerland"] *Retraite et Société.* 71. 2, 2015. 15-33.

[10] See World Health Organization (WHO). *Active Ageing: A Policy Framework.* (Geneva: World Health Organization, 2002).

[11] See Kim Boudiny. "'Active ageing': from empty rhetoric to effective policy tool." *Ageing and Society.* 33. 6, August 2013. 1077–1098.

[12] See Axel Börsch-Supan, Martina Brandt, Howard Litwin, and Guglielmo Weber. Eds. *Active Ageing and Solidarity between Generations in Europe: First Results from SHARE after the Economic Crisis.* (Berlin: DeGruyter, 2013); and Henrike Galenkamp, and Dorly J.H.

and its positive impact on 'good' ageing and quality-of-life is also extensively reviewed,[13] and so is the elderly person's motivation to engage in voluntary work.[14] However, 'intergenerational solidarity' as a factor promoting social inclusion has received little attention to date.

* * *

Formerly, 'intergenerational solidarity' from a sociological perspective has been analysed mostly on two levels.[15] On the macro level, it is predominantly directed at social policy issues in society, and on the micro level, families and individuals are studied.

Social solidarity from the perspective of social policy on the macro level is linked to the definition of a social, minimum income:

> the solidarity of those who pay with those in need. The most far-reaching idea of solidarity is to introduce a basic income for all citizens, ensuring an income independent of contributions, employment, or any other condition. (Widerquist *et al.* 2005)[16]

There has been a paradigm shift in policy goals from passive to active social policy. Insofar as the ageing population is concerned, this shift transforms into an "active ageing" policy,[17] the concept "active ageing" being rooted in

---

Deeg. "Increasing social participation of older people: are there different barriers for those in poor health? Introduction to the special section." *European Journal of Ageing*. 13. 2, June 2016. 87–90.

[13] See Andrea Principi, Robert Lindley, Jolanta Perek-Bialas, and Konrad Turek. "Volunteering in older age: an organizational perspective." *International Journal of Manpower*. 33. 6, 2012. 685-703; and Jason S. Ulsperger, Jericho McElroy, Haley Robertson, and Kristen Ulsperger. "Senior Companion Program Volunteers: Exploring Experiences, Transformative Rituals, and Recruitment/Retention Issues." *The Qualitative Report*. 20. 9, September 2015. 1458-1475.

[14] See Laura Jones, and Jesse Heley. "Practices of Participation and Voluntarism among Older People in Rural Wales: Choice, Obligation and Constraints to Active Ageing." *Sociologia Ruralis*. 56. 2, April 2016. 176-196.

[15] See Vern L. Bengtson, and Petrice S. Oyama. "Intergenerational Solidarity and Conflict." María Amparo Cruz-Saco, and Sergei Zelenev. Eds. *Intergenerational Solidarity. Strengthening Economic and Social Ties*. (New York: Palgrave Macmillan, 2010). 35-52.

[16] Karl Widerquist, Michael Lewis, and Steven Pressman. *The Ethics and Economics of the Basic Income Guarantee*. (Aldershot: Ashgate, 2005).

[17] See Thomas Bahle, Thomas, Michaela Pfeifer, and Claus Wendt. "Social Assistance." Francis G. Castles, Stephan Leibfried, Jane Lewis, Herbert Obinger, and Christopher Pierson. Eds. *The Oxford Handbook of the Welfare State*. (Oxford: Oxford University Press, 2010). 448–461.

an "active employment" policy, which, in turn, is intended to promote social inclusion. However, an 'active ageing' policy, unlike an 'active employment' policy, encompasses not only inclusion in the labour market, but also 'social inclusion' in its broadest sense, that is, in civil society, in sporting events, in cultural activities, and so on. Having said that, the theoretical foundations of an "active employment" policy are similar, in some cases, to those of an 'active ageing' policy, a point made in the works of Austrian researcher Marie Jahoda and American sociologist William Julius Wilson.[18] In their respective books, both Jahoda and Wilson emphasise the idea that lack of employment should, where possible, be replaced with other forms of activity that ensure social interaction, contacts, public significance, status, and temporal parameters. Whenever people find themselves living in an inactive zone, segregated from the labour market, and in which the economically-active population of other generations is absent, then social-exclusion appears, brought about by endemic inactivity and a lack of exposure to other generations. Thus, active social policy, in relation to social solidarity, is not just about income redistribution, but also, more broadly, about diversified social interaction and successful inclusion in society, specifically at a personal, individual level.

Paul Spicker defines solidarity as,

> (...) mutual responsibility; responsibilities to others in society, which are the basis for collective social action; policy built on a complex range of overlapping networks. (Spicker 2008: 299)

In his book *Social Policy. Themes and Approaches,*[19] Paul Spicker emphasizes solidarity as a mutual responsibility at the level of society, but it can also be expressed on the level of community – based on territory or shared interests – and organisation. Social work researcher Malcolm Payne emphasizes group solidarity and its multiple facets.[20] Spicker's conclusions about solidarity as mutual responsibility and Payne's acknowledgment of the diverse character of group solidarity can certainly be also attributed to 'intergenerational solidarity' on the community level, thus supplementing the definition provided by Age Platform Europe.

---

[18] Marie Jahoda. *Employment and Unemployment: A Social-Psychological Analysis.* (Cambridge: Cambridge University Press, 1982); and William Julius Wilson. *When Work Disappears. The World of the New Urban Poor.* (New York: Alfred A. Knopf, 1996).

[19] Paul Spicker. *Social Policy. Themes and Approaches.* (Bristol: Policy Press, 2008).

[20] See Malcolm Payne. *Modern Social Work Theory.* (New York: Palgrave Macmillan, 2005).

Researching 'intergenerational solidarity' on the micro level, attention is focused primarily on the adult-child relationship with ageing parents,[21] and social support networks at the individual level,[22] basically using quantitative research methods. Nienke Moor and Aafke Komter (2008) have studied Intergenerational Solidarity (IS) within the family and have found that, in Europe, this type of solidarity within nuclear families does not decrease, although the significance of its diverse dimensions differs from country to country.[23] Other researchers reject this finding, stressing that,

> [w]ith heightened geographic mobility, later marriage, and increased divorce, neighbourhood and family ties have been dissipating (…). (Kenworthy 2010: 437)[24]

Publications focussing on 'intergenerational solidarity' discuss various aspects of *de facto* relationships between members of different generations, mostly on the micro level and quantitatively, in family and the individual's social networks.

However, surprisingly-little attention has been paid to changes in intergenerational relationships in conjunction with lifestyle changes in today's society. Most notably, there has been a dearth of studies on the technology literacy gap between generations. The Great Digital Transformation encompasses a wide spectrum of issues, and it has changed the way people live and work. As with any change, it has created 'winners'

---

[21] See, for example, Eva-Maria Merz, Hans-Joachim Schulze, and Carlo Schuengel. "Consequences of Filial Support for Two Generations: A Narrative and Quantitative Review." *Journal of Family Issues*. 31. 11, 2010. 1530–1554; and Axel Börsch-Supan, Martina Brandt, Howard Litwin, and Guglielmo Weber. Eds. *Active Ageing and Solidarity between Generations in Europe: First Results from SHARE after the Economic Crisis*. (Berlin: DeGruyter, 2013).

[22] See, for example, Valentina Hlebec, Milivoja Šircelj, and Maja Mrzel. "How to Monitor Intergenerational Solidarity in Social Support Networks?" *Teorija in Praksa*. 47. 6, 2010. 1127–1149; and Axel Börsch-Supan, Martina Brandt, Howard Litwin, and Guglielmo Weber. Eds. *Active Ageing and Solidarity between Generations in Europe: First Results from SHARE after the Economic Crisis*. (Berlin: DeGruyter, 2013).

[23] See Nienke Moor, and Aafke Komter. "Demographic changes, intergenerational solidarity and well-being in Europe: a comparative approach." *MULTILINKS Position Paper*, April 2008.

[24] Lane Kenworthy. "Labour Market Activation." Francis G. Castles, Stephan Leibfried, Jane Lewis, Herbert Obinger, and Christopher Pierson. Eds. *The Oxford Handbook of the Welfare State*. (Oxford: Oxford University Press, 2010). 435-437.

and 'losers.'[25] Technology-driven developments are certain to further increase existing inequalities and to create new ones. If the digital and intergenerational gaps converge, the barriers to be surmounted in intergenerational relationships become higher.[26] The most significant changes in intergenerational relations are brought about by Information Technology (IT) and increased mobility, innovations that can transform interpersonal communication channels and the spatial positioning of family, respectively. Due to these factors, the ageing process of most people today is different from that experienced by their predecessors. For example, active involvement in public life is not only expected, but is a prerequisite of persons making up the older generation. In research carried out within the remit of The SIforAGE Project, special attention has been given to those social innovations for which bridging the digital gap is an important goal of intergenerational activity.

Methodology for researching role of 'intergenerational solidarity' in 'active ageing'

Within the framework provided by The SIforAGE Project, research into 'intergenerational solidarity' was undertaken using the triangulation of complementary qualitative and quantitative methodologies. This work involved the review of examples of good practice, and the organisation of focus groups, intergenerational interventions, and workshops that brought together elderly persons, decision-makers, and the researchers themselves.

The focus here is exclusively upon the analysis of examples of good practice, examples accumulated in the case-study database, which,

> focused on fundamental aspects of participation and integration of older persons in European society – including a close look at the obstacles and barriers that might prevent these processes from being effective, as well as the necessary enabling environment to allow, encourage, and support participation and integration of older persons in society.[27]

---

[25] See Marc Saxer. "Shaping the Great Digital Transformation." *Social Europe Journal.* 9, 2015.

[26] See Henning Meyer. "The Work and Inequality Challenge of the Digital Revolution: How Should Governments Respond?" *Social Europe Journal.* 9, 2015. 20-22.

[27] SIforAGE. Recommendations guide to increase the involvement of older persons and civil society organizations in research. 2015. 11.

The SIforAGE Consortium Partners provided one hundred and twelve case studies from nineteen countries. Of these, one hundred examples of good practice were from twelve European Union countries, and twelve examples were from seven other countries.

Descriptions of case studies were structured according to uniform methodology. The criteria for selection of cases were defined sufficiently widely to encompass activities of various spheres, scales, and significance, namely, innovative praxis on participation and integration of older persons into European society, contributing to healthy and active ageing. This analysis of the compiled data is intended to retrieve opinions, attitudes, and ideas as far as possible 'off the beaten track,' and to dig out unconventional views, strategies, and actions that have produced successful results and, thereby, have helped to create more enabling environments. For the purposes of the analysis, forty-three case descriptions were selected in conformity with the following criteria: a) it represents a country of the European Union; b) it contains intergenerational dialogue and solidarity as a goal or an important component of the activity; and c) it contains at least three 'intergenerational solidarity' dimensions. The analysis combines approaches based on theory and data.

* * *

The dimensions of 'intergenerational solidarity' have been adapted from Nienke Moore and Aafke Komter (2008)[28] who, in turn, use the six-dimensional model proposed by Vern Bengston and Robert Roberts (1991),[29] as they analyse 'intergenerational solidarity' in families. These dimensions are:

> associational integration (the level of contact between members of different generations), affectional integration (the degree of positive feelings), consensual integration (the degree of consensus in beliefs and attitudes), functional integration (the exchanged help), normative integration (the norms of familism), and structural

---

[28] See Nienke Moor, and Aafke Komter. "Demographic changes, intergenerational solidarity and well-being in Europe: a comparative approach." *MULTILINKS Position Paper*, April 2008.

[29] See Vern L. Bengtson, and Robert E.L. Roberts. "Intergenerational Solidarity in Aging Families: An Example of Formal Theory Construction." *Journal of Marriage and Family*. 53. 4, 1991. 856-870.

integration (geographical proximity). (Bengston, and Roberts 1991, in Moor, and Komter 2008: 12)[30]

The analysis does not address two of the dimensions specifically. The dimension of normative integration – the norms of familism – was not adapted for community or group norms' analysis, because case descriptions did not provide sufficient information for a more profound analysis thereof. The dimension of structural integration – geographical proximity – was not viewed separately, since at a mezzo-level this dimension is a mandatory precondition of the activity.

The research addressed dimensions, which include communication between the generations (also within the IT environment), positive feelings and attitudes, as well as mutual assistance (both direct and mediated). The dimension of consensual integration – the degree of consensus in beliefs and attitudes – was adapted as a dimension reducing stereotypes, strengthening shared values and mutual respect. The authors believe that mutual respect is a key element of 'intergenerational solidarity' and, in the dimension at the community level, the most important is not solely the consensus of opinions, but also tolerance and respect towards different beliefs and views held by people of another generation.

Additionally, it is proposed here that the civic and political dimension of solidarity in the analysis of 'intergenerational solidarity' be introduced at a mezzo-level. This dimension emerged as an important aspect during the analysis of the data. This can be interpreted both as advancing Active and Healthy Ageing (AHA) policy objectives in the community, organization, and administrative territory – there are sufficient examples of that – as well as 'bottom-up' movement to implement an all-age-friendly society.

'Intergenerational solidarity' in examples of good practice
The database of examples of good practice[31] reveals diverse activities of various scales that include 'intergenerational solidarity' and its dimensions. For this reason, the analysis of 'intergenerational solidarity' ought to include the dimension of the content of the activities in order to explore whether

---

[30] See Nienke Moor, and Aafke Komter. "Demographic changes, intergenerational solidarity and well-being in Europe: a comparative approach." *MULTILINKS Position Paper*, April 2008. 12.
[31] This database of examples of good practice was compiled during the European Union research project "Social Innovation on Active and Healthy Aging for sustainable economic growth" (SIforAGE), November 2012-October 2016.

intergenerational meetings and encounters between people of different generations are mutually enriching, stimulating activities.[32] Hence, the content dimension of these activities will be addressed first and, subsequently, the nature of the solidarity dimensions and the ways in which they are being strengthened will be identified, thereby determining how 'active ageing' and 'a better society for all' are being promoted.

The range of innovative activities, including 'intergenerational solidarity' on the mezzo-level, is very wide. Dimensions with various content are covered, from lifelong learning to services for the mitigation of loneliness. Also, the activities are on different scales – national, regional, and local – and their operation may be long-term or short-term – several years or just one day. Furthermore, the activities may be implemented by a consortium incorporating a wide variety of agents, or by an individual enthusiast. According to the action-content dimension, all activities can be grouped into five broad categories: a) lifelong learning; b) joint creative work; c) healthcare; d) assistance; and e) policy-making.

Community-level activities related to lifelong learning included collective learning: whereby older persons learn together with students or their grandchildren; or whereby older persons teach children skills and knowledge, for example, craftsmanship, growing vegetables, crafts, and culinary; or whereby older persons help children to learn, for example, help immigrant children to learn host country's language and culture after their lessons at school or in day-care centres; or whereby children teach older persons computer skills. Some of the learning-related activities include acquisition of new technology, thereby reducing the intergenerational digital divide.

Moreover, many common creative-engagement activities overlap with lifelong learning. For example, passing on crafts and culinary skills to the younger generation, growing vegetables together, and handicrafts include both learning and shared creative activity. Less frequently represented are those activities which are primarily focused on the creative process and creativity. An example of one such activity were the older persons and schoolchildren "Slam" poetry sessions, held in Reims during the French National Week, which was dedicated to Active and Healthy Ageing (AHA).[33] Another example was the filming of *Luna de Miel* for participation

---

[32] See Cara N. Gilbert, and Kristina G. Ricketts. "Children's Attitudes Toward Older Adults and Aging: A Synthesis of Research." *Educational Gerontology*. 34. 7, 2008. 570-586.
[33] "Ateliers Slam intergénérationels / Intergenerational Slam workshops" (France).

in the Spanish National Contest of Videos by Agers, an event which was attended by nursing home residents, employees, and the creative group.[34]

Learning and creative-engagement activities contribute to forming new social ties, which are particularly important for elderly persons living far from their family or alone. Activities in which elderly persons transfer their knowledge to the middle and younger generations allow the older people to feel useful. The acquisition of new skills together makes one feel included and in step with the times. An outstanding example of this is the Experimental University of Grandparents and Grandchildren in the Czech Republic, where each year, since the academic year 2004-2005, members of the youngest and the oldest generation of the family jointly acquire another topic, thus both expanding their knowledge and strengthening mutual relationships.[35] In all the reviewed examples, 'intergenerational solidarity' dimensions support reduction of stereotypes, formation of reciprocal positive feelings, and mutual respect, as well as formation of intergenerational social bonds and intensification of interaction.

Mutual assistance, in addition to support and services-related activities for elderly persons, included a wide variety of initiatives, whereby members of every generation shared their resources with each other. There were initiatives aimed at giving elderly persons assistance, services, and support for Active and Healthy Ageing (AHA), as well as help and support in cases of illness and disability, or a need to lessen loneliness. In the project "Abitare solidale. Pensare alla casa per una Comunità più Solidale," which has been implemented in the Italian region of Tuscany, municipality of Florence, older people shared their living space with troubled young people, who, in turn, assisted in the home cleaning, shopping, and making online payments, and so on.[36] Support and training for caregivers was also included in this category. The project "House of Memories," which was implemented in the United Kingdom, supplied support and training to dementia caregivers, increasing the dementia patients' quality-of-life through better care.[37]

In many cases, assistance- and support-activities overlapped with activities focussing on Active and Healthy Ageing (AHA) policy and civic solidarity. They served to provide a broader basket of social services in an informal and innovative way. The political and civic dimensions of

---

[34] Participation in "Premios NICO 2014 / NICO Prizes 2014" (Spain).

[35] "Experimental University for Grandparents and Grandchildren" (Czech Republic).

[36] "Abitare solidale. Pensare alla casa per una Comunità più Solidale / Fair living. Thinking on home for a more supportive community" (Italy).

[37] "House of Memories" (United Kingdom)

'intergenerational solidarity' were found to be encompassed within two types of activities. One of these activities included an elderly persons' political support for other generations. In an example implemented in Spain, "@iaioflautas," older persons were shown to support young persons' fight against the dismantling of the Welfare State.[38] A second of these activities targeted the implementation and making of the Active and Healthy Ageing (AHA) policy. The project "Development of policy for active and healthy aging," which was implemented in Latvia, covered a variety of policy-makers and included a wide representation of the older generation.[39] These activities strengthened the civic solidarity dimension, mutual accountability, respect, and support, and increased mutual, positive feelings. They also contributed to building intergenerational social bonds and intensifying contacts.

'Intergenerational solidarity' in Latvia
Three examples of 'intergenerational solidarity' projects from Latvia are provided:

1."Pieslēdzies, Latvija" / "Connect, Latvia," illustrating lifelong learning activity related to a company's social responsibility;

2. Vecmāmiņu birža" / "Grandmother Exchange," with the community's offer to replace the family intergenerational support activity; and

3. "Development of policy for active and healthy aging" (Latvia), aiming a political solidarity initiative toward developing Active and Healthy Ageing (AHA) policy.[40]

1. "Pieslēdzies, Latvija" / "Connect, Latvia": 'Intergenerational solidarity' promoted by a company's social responsibility
An example of good practice of 'intergenerational solidarity' implemented at mezzo-level of local communities, but available throughout the territory of Latvia, is a public-private co-operation project "Connect, Latvia!"[41] implemented and financed entirely by the communication company Lattelecom. Informative support was provided by the Ministry of Welfare,

---

[38] "@iaioflautas" (Spain).
[39] "Development of policy for active and healthy aging" (Latvia).
[40] "Development of policy for active and healthy aging" (Latvia).
[41] "Pieslēdzies, Latvija" / "Connect, Latvia" (Latvia).

the Ministry of Education and Science, the Ministry of Culture, and the State Employment Agency. The project was launched in 2008. Since 2011, the only target group has comprised recipients of 'old-age' pensions. 6,680 persons were trained in 2012, and 10,130 persons in 2013. The project will be implemented until 2018, the centenary of the Latvian state.

"Connect, Latvia!" has been made possible thanks to the previously-implemented digitization of all Latvian public libraries. The material base has been established, but the digital skills have been lacking among generations who had been educated at a time when IT was not an everyday reality. Most Latvian pensioners' material conditions preclude them from buying a computer, obtaining an Internet connection, and affording to pay for training. The project provides free digital literacy training and is motivated by social responsibility. Undoubtedly, this motive can be supplemented by a goal to build a good company reputation and customer retention tactics in competition with other communications' companies. In this case, the company's interests and common benefit form a synergy.[42]

The training in Information Technology (IT) is organized on three levels of expertise over three days, four academic hours per day, from May to November, in groups of no larger than fourteen persons. Applications for training in the regions is organized by Pensioners' Associations and, electronically, through the Lattelecom portal.[43] It is useful to compare the Latvian examples of good practice in this area with examples of good practice in the Irish lifelong learning programme "Getting Started." In the Irish lifelong learning programme, digital skills are taught to older persons on a one-to-one basis.[44] The common feature in both countries is the recruitment of voluntary teaching staff.[45]

The main benefits of the programme indicated by project participants have been manifested in an interest in continuing to use the computer and the Internet, raised self-esteem and more successful integration into society, and the rise of social activity, as well as the feeling that digital skills improve communication with younger generations. In short, it has become evident that "Connect, Latvia!" strengthens 'intergenerational solidarity,' helping to connect the living space of older persons and with that

---

[42] More information and electronic self-study course materials are available on the website <www.piesledzieslatvija.lv>

[43] "Interview with L. Bite," interviewed by Anna Stepcenko (29th January 2014). "Pieslēdzies, Latvija" / "Connect, Latvia" (Latvia).

[44] The civic society, the Irish lifelong learning programme "Getting Started," was initiated in 2006, and receives financial support from the Irish Government.

[45] "Age Action's 'Getting Started' Programme" (Ireland).

of the younger generations, spaces which, in IT application, have until now been parallel worlds.

2. *"Vecmāmiņu birža" / "Grandmother Exchange": community solutions for intergenerational support*

An example of mezzo-level 'intergenerational solidarity,' "Grandmother Exchange," shows the replacement of the traditional role of grandmother with a solution offered by the community. "Grandmother Exchange" is an activity of a non-governmental organization (NGO), "Riga Active Seniors' Alliance" (RASA), which was launched in 2012. This RASA sub-programme is headed by Dr Rita Sprūža, who substantiates the motivation for such an initiative with the interest of the different generations and social groups:

> The only foundation for creating grandmother exchange is the opportunity for young families to return to the labour market and for retired women who retire to overcome a-socialisation, the isolation in their homes, which leads to physical and psychological degradation. For example, a woman who started out dressed recklessly, with dirty hair, turns into a coiffed woman, dressed in a suit. A similar practice exists in Germany and Norway, where older ladies aid young families as volunteers because they have large old-age pensions. In Latvia, a family pays for this service 1·5 lats per hour [since 2014, €2·13]. The proceeds enable the purchase of medicine and the payment of water, electricity, and heating bills, because poverty is widespread among old-age pensioners.[46]

The potential grandmothers are trained in groups of twenty for three weeks, a total of ninety academic hours. Training on a voluntary basis or for a small fee is given by highly-qualified professionals. The training covers biological, psychological, and legal aspects of communication, ethics, conflict prevention and resolution, emergency assistance, alternative pedagogical methods, communication in a multicultural environment, and changes in society.

---

[46] "Interview with R. Sprūža." Rita Sprūža was interviewed by Anna Stepcenko on 15th July 2013. "Vecmāmiņu birža" / "Grandmother Exchange (Grandmothers' Contact Bureau Exchange in Riga City)."

In June 2013, fifty-nine host grandmothers prepared in the previously-described training programme worked at "Grandmother Exchange." "Leased grandmother" duties include looking after children during their parents' working hours, if necessary, also at night and at weekends, accompanying children to extracurricular activities, meeting after lessons, and helping with studies. The demand for these "leased grandmothers" exceeded the supply.

It is clear from these experiences that community 'intergenerational solidarity' has both social and economic benefits. For the younger generation, individuals are freer to function more effectively in the labour market and obtain more free time, while for the representatives of the older generation, they become better integrated into the social environment and may even slightly improve their economic situation.

3. "Development of policy for active and healthy aging" (Latvia). 'Intergenerational solidarity' for building Active and Healthy Ageing (AHA) policy

This project was initiated by policy-makers from the Latvian Parliament and scientists. It was carried out in 2013, receiving financial support from the Parliamentary Sub-commission on Demography.[47] The goal was to achieve better coordination of "Silver policy" development between the national (ministerial), regional, and local levels. There are three groups of organizations engaged in the project. First, the Cross-sectoral Coordination Centre of the Republic of Latvia, Ministries, and national-level NGOs; second, regional planning administrations; and third, local NGOs, municipalities, and initiative groups. The outcomes include development of national-level documents for Active and Healthy Ageing (AHA).

A survey of municipalities was implemented about initiatives undertaken pertaining to elderly persons, and five regional-level discussions took place in Latvian planning regions. The discussed issues included: 1. income and living conditions; 2. health and health-care; and 3. social space – social inclusion, and intergenerational relationships in family and society. The project involved policy-makers, administrators, representatives of different level seniors' organizations, and active elderly people. The innovative features of the project were: 1. the effort to aggregate information about local and regional initiatives regarding Active and Healthy Ageing (AHA); and 2. the coordination of policy on horizontal and vertical levels. The discussed policy initiatives covered three directions: 1. policy initiatives

---

[47] "Development of policy for active and healthy aging" (Latvia).

at local, regional, and national levels, and their coordination; 2. intergenerational cooperation in policy-making; and 3. health care reforms for healthy ageing.

The project created an opportunity to raise the question of launching national and regional support for local initiatives promoting Active and Healthy Ageing (AHA). The project encompassed the entire one hundred and nineteen local governments of Latvia, and the regional discussions involved approximately eight hundred elderly persons, making it one of the most extensive initiatives of involvement in policy-making in Latvia. The project was testament to the Government's care for the older generation, and to the high degree of activity of elderly persons when it comes to participation in making decisions concerning themselves.

Conclusions

For the purposes of this study, 'intergenerational solidarity' has been interpreted as mutual support and cooperation of different age groups, as well as mutual accountability on group and community levels. A deeper insight into the mezzo-level examples of strengthening 'intergenerational solidarity' showed their performance in different content dimensions, namely, lifelong learning, joint creative work, health-care, assistance, and policy-making. Each of these dimensions, in its way, encourages 'active ageing' and supports the social inclusion of elderly persons.

For a more in-depth analysis of examples of good practice compiled for The SIforAGE Project, the six-dimension model of 'intergenerational solidarity' was adapted, adjusting it for mezzo-level research. The geographical proximity dimension was considered important in all cases of community activities. Due to lack of data, the normative integration dimension was not analysed. Three dimensions – level of contacts between the generations; positive feelings and attitudes; and mutual assistance – were adapted with slight adjustments. The consensual integration dimension was adapted as mutual respect and reduction of stereotypes. Additionally, the authors advanced political and civic dimensions of solidarity, which is particularly important for implementing an Active and Healthy Ageing (AHA) policy at the community level.

By implementing community-level activities, all the 'intergenerational solidarity' dimensions were strengthened, especially communication between generations, increasing mutually-positive feelings, reducing stereotypes, reinforcing mutual respect and common values, as well as boosting civic solidarity. These dimensions mutually interact, and an activity in one dimension also positively affects the others.

The study confirms that 'intergenerational solidarity' has a significant potential to ensure Active and Healthy Ageing (AHA) at the community level. The mezzo-level activities showed both top-down- and bottom-up-initiated political and civic initiatives, well-adapted to local contexts. To ensure the sustainability of the activities, macro-level policy and financial support at European Union (EU) and national levels are crucial. 'Intergenerational solidarity,' as a part of diverse solidarity expression, is a value to be kept in mind as opposed to egocentrism and individualism, both of which lead to social corrosion and distancing from the preferred model of society.

Works Cited

AGE Platform Europe. European Year for Active Ageing and Solidarity between Generations. Everyone has a role to play! 2012. <ec.europa.eu/social/BlobServlet?docId=6773&langId=ne>

Bahle, Thomas, Michaela Pfeifer, and Claus Wendt. "Social Assistance." Francis G. Castles, Stephan Leibfried, Jane Lewis, Herbert Obinger, and Christopher Pierson. Eds. *The Oxford Handbook of the Welfare State*. Oxford: Oxford University Press, 2010. 448–461.

Bengtson Vern L., and Petrice S. Oyama. "Intergenerational Solidarity and Conflict." María Amparo Cruz-Saco, and Sergei Zelenev. Eds. *Intergenerational Solidarity. Strengthening Economic and Social Ties*. New York: Palgrave Macmillan, 2010. 35-52. <www.un.org/esa/socdev/unyin/documents/egm_unhq_oct07_bengtson.pdf>

Bengtson Vern L., and Robert E.L. Roberts. "Intergenerational Solidarity in Aging Families: An Example of Formal Theory Construction." *Journal of Marriage and Family*. 53. 4, 1991. 856-870. [doi: 10.2307/352993]

Boudiny, Kim. "'Active ageing': from empty rhetoric to effective policy tool." *Ageing and Society*. 33. 6, August 2013. 1077–1098. [doi: 10.1017/S0144686X1200030X] <www.ncbi.nlm.nih.gov/pmc/articles/PMC3728916/>

Börsch-Supan, Axel., Martina Brandt, Howard Litwin, and Guglielmo Weber. Eds. Active Ageing and Solidarity between Generations in Europe: First Results from SHARE after the Economic Crisis. Berlin: DeGruyter, 2013.

Galenkamp, Henrike, and Dorly J.H. Deeg. (2016) "Increasing social participation of older people: are there different barriers for those in

poor health? Introduction to the special section." *European Journal of Ageing*. 13. 2, June 2016. 87-90.
<link.springer.com/article/10.1007/s10433-016-0379-y>

Gilbert, Cara N., and Kristina G. Ricketts. "Children's Attitudes Toward Older Adults and Aging: A Synthesis of Research." *Educational Gerontology*. 34. 7, 2008. 570-586. [doi 10.1080/03601270801900420]

Hlebec, Valentina, Milivoja Šircelj, and Maja Mrzel. "How to Monitor Intergenerational Solidarity in Social Support Networks?" *Teorija in Praksa*. 47. 6, 2010. 1127–1149.
<dk.fdv.uni-lj.si/db/pdfs/tip20106_hlebec_sircelj_mrzel.pdf>

Jahoda, Marie. *Employment and Unemployment: A Social-Psychological Analysis*. Cambridge: Cambridge University Press, 1982.

Jones, Laura, and Jesse Heley. "Practices of Participation and Voluntarism among Older People in Rural Wales: Choice, Obligation and Constraints to Active Ageing." *Sociologia Ruralis*. 56. 2, April 2016. 176-196. [doi: 10.1111/soru.12073]

Kenworthy, Lane. "Labour Market Activation." Francis G. Castles, Stephan Leibfried, Jane Lewis, Herbert Obinger, and Christopher Pierson. Eds. *The Oxford Handbook of the Welfare State*. Oxford: Oxford University Press, 2010. 435-437.
<lanekenworthy.files.wordpress.com/2014/07/2010labormarketacti vation.pdf>

Merz, Eva-Maria, Hans-Joachim Schulze, and Carlo Schuengel. "Consequences of Filial Support for Two Generations: A Narrative and Quantitative Review." *Journal of Family Issues*. 31. 11, 2010. 1530–1554. [doi 10.1177/0192513X10365116]
<s3.amazonaws.com/academia.edu.documents/39189722/5489a9ae 0cf2d1800d7a9d3c.pdf?AWSAccessKeyId=AKIAIWOWYYGZ2 Y53UL3A&Expires=1496605324&Signature=kL0CpVuzaDf5Xhq F4%2BLJuKhkGAU%3D&response-content-disposition=inline%3B%20filename%3DConsequences_of_Filial_ Support_for_Two_G.pdf>

Meyer, Henning. "The Work and Inequality Challenge Of The Digital Revolution: How Should Governments Respond?" *Social Europe Journal*. 9, 2015. 20-22.
<www.socialeurope.eu/2015/08/the-work-and-inequality-challenge-of-the-digital-revolution-how-should-governments-respond/>

Moor, Nienke, and Aafke Komter. "Demographic changes, intergenerational solidarity and well-being in Europe: a comparative approach." *MULTILINKS Position Paper*, April 2008. <www.multilinks-project.eu/wp-content/uploads/2014/01/Demographic_changes_intergenerational_solidarity_and_well-being_in_Europe_final__Moor___Komter_1.pdf>

Payne, Malcolm. *Modern Social Work Theory.* New York: Palgrave Macmillan, 2005. [Third edition]

Principi, Andrea, Robert Lindley, Jolanta Perek-Bialas, and Konrad Turek. "Volunteering in older age: an organizational perspective." *International Journal of Manpower.* 33. 6, 2012. 685-703. [doi: 10.1108/01437721211261822]

Repetti, Marion. "Du retraité méritant au senior actif: genèse et actualité d'une figure sociale en Suisse." ["From the deserving pensioner to the active senior: The then and now of a social figure in Switzerland"] *Retraite et Société.* 71. 2, 2015. 15-33.

Saxer, Marc. "Shaping the Great Digital Transformation." *Social Europe Journal.* 9, 2015. 5-8. <www.socialeurope.eu/2015/05/shaping-great-digital-transformation/> <medium.com/@marc_saxer/shaping-the-great-digital-transformation-76e56403d0c3>

SIforAGE. Recommendations guide to increase the involvement of older persons and civil society organizations in research, 2015. <www.siforage.eu/eotools_files/files/Deliverable%203.5%20-%20SIforAGE.pdf>

Spicker, Paul. *Social Policy. Themes and Approaches.* Bristol: Policy Press, 2008.

Ulsperger, Jason S., Jericho McElroy, Haley Robertson, and Kristen Ulsperger. "Senior Companion Program Volunteers: Exploring Experiences, Transformative Rituals, and Recruitment/Retention Issues." *The Qualitative Report.* 20. 9, 2015. 1458-1475. <nsuworks.nova.edu/tqr/vol20/iss9/9>

Wahl, Hans-Werner, Dorly J.H. Deeg, Howard Litwin. "Successful ageing as a persistent priority in ageing research." *European Journal of Ageing.* 13. 1, March 2016. 1-3. <link.springer.com/article/10.1007/s10433-016-0364-5>

Widerquist, Karl, Michael Lewis, and Steven Pressman. *The Ethics and Economics of the Basic Income Guarantee*. Aldershot: Ashgate, 2005.

Wilson, William Julius. *When Work Disappears. The World of the New Urban Poor*. New York: Alfred A. Knopf, 1996.

World Health Organization (WHO). *Active Ageing: A Policy Framework*. Geneva: World Health Organization, 2002. <apps.who.int/iris/bitstream/10665/67215/1/WHO_NMH_NPH_02.8.pdf>

Social Participation of the Elderly Through Intergenerational Programmes (IPs) in the Region of Murcia

Pedro Moreno-Abellán, Silvia Martínez de Miguel-López, and Andrés Escarbajal-de Haro

Faculty of Education. University of Murcia (Spain)

In society, there are numerous factors of change that are inseparable from the human being. Significant factors to be taken into consideration are the influence of the cultural, the educational, the political, and a deep demographic transformation – these in addition to conditions of life in a Welfare State and the exponential increase in life expectancy. There are new factors that are appearing which make a new social structure yet to be developed. Overall, it is about a phenomenon represented in the twenty-first century, surrounded by a tendency of larger proportions that are a challenge for all European countries.

The world is witnessing 'demographic ageing,' taking forward the concept of 'active ageing,' a concept that was presented and highlighted by the World Health Organization (WHO) at the "World Assembly on Ageing," held in Madrid in April 2002. This is why physical, social, and mental wellness opportunities are optimized with the aim of extending the quality of peoples' lives in their declining years. Nowadays, compared with previous generations, there is an increase in the number of people with improved quality-of-life and augmented life-expectancy. Today, elderly people are generally more prepared for and demanding of social participation. This situation invites reflection on the utilization of new tools and specific guidelines to enable participation in social and educational services in a more systematic and practical way. From here on, it will become increasingly necessary to encourage and to tailor the equity of social participation to fit the collective group of elderly people, taking into account the rest of the age groups at all their stages.

It is essential, therefore, for a new concept of participation for individual spaces to be created. Nevertheless, such spaces should not be exclusively physical spaces, but places of participation in which, different cohorts of the social sphere come together. The need for spaces of participation, known as 'interactive spaces,' with the elderly as the main group, is an implicit demand on all institutions, both administrative and technical, to provide for and expand new ways of motivation for this group. In today's society, the promotion of such 'active participation' is a priority. Moreover, the projected educational conception of the social sciences can be both inseparable and vital to teaching and learning throughout the process. Accordingly, a focus on Intergenerational Relationships (IRs) constitutes a clear example of what has been expressed so far. As a result, the programmes presented here have a strong character of 'social innovation.'

In general, the Intergenerational Programmes (IPs) are understood as an extending line of participation for elder and younger generations in society. The Intergenerational Programmes (IPs) provide a source of study that shows great interest today for the improvement of quality-of-life, self-esteem, and dignity, especially in instances when the elderly are fundamental pillars for their families and communities. To get a sense of their own merit, the elderly remain active, experiencing significant social contact, and feeling respected and useful in terms of their socio-personal contribution.

Theoretical framework

From the second half of the twentieth century, the concept of the "Welfare State" appears to respond to a new model of society. For the elderly population, it does not have to be questioned, nor do the different mechanisms existing in social security need to be undervalued. In this respect, Marta Gutiérrez-Sánchez and G. Herráiz (2009) declared that the mechanisms of the Welfare State comprise,

> the combination of instruments and remedies provided in favour of social groups, in order to protect their needs through various ideas of performance...[1]

that is, 'ideas of performance' such as the impulse of participation, integration, and approach to citizens. All such mechanisms also relate to the psychological well-being studied by Ángel De-Juanas-Oliva, María Rosario

---

[1] Marta Gutiérrez-Sánchez., and G. Herráiz, "La sinergia intergeneracional." (Valencia: *EsPAi sOciAl*. 9, 2009). 21.

Limón-Mendizábal, and Enrique Navarro-Asencio (2013) with the aim of achieving healthy ageing and an increase in the quality-of-life.[2]

This basis, transferred to the elderly population in the knowledge of their diversity, is, today, a space yet to be developed that requires the development of new tools and guidelines in order to intervene in an even more specific, systematic, and practical way. Many older people reach the age of retirement with optimism, ready to enjoy and take advantage of those activities and objectives that previously they were not in a position to pursue, attempting to get together as a human resource to be encouraged to participate in an active way and employ favourably their leisure time.

Directly in response to the factor of social participation, the community of education still needs to face a challenge of huge social consequence. From the landmass gerontology of the Educational Sciences originates a different definition for educating in its "theoretical-practical" field. According to Mariano Sánchez and Juan Sáez-Carreras (2007),[3] in respect of elderly people, the "theoretical-practical" field must focus mainly on education for the individual, putting aside not only the features of the phase in the life-cycle to which he or she belongs, but also the discreet experience of elderly people and their relationships with one another, understanding it as a social education. Being old does not mean that you are not knowledgeable. Therefore, the value of personal, cultural, social, and communal development provided by education is shared, while rescuing the essential and beneficial mechanisms that prevail throughout all stages of life.

Participation of the elderly in society

It is known that the idea of participation has already been approved in the report published by the United Nations at the World Assembly on Ageing in Madrid. In the report, the U.N. policy statement (Article 10) highlights the contribution of the elderly through their knowledge and experience, encouraging their active participation in society. Also, this report set down a number of recommendations (second paragraph) on their active participation in society and development, recommendations which include the following observations of significance:

---

[2] See Ángel De-Juanas-Oliva, María Rosario Limón-Mendizábal, and Enrique Navarro-Asencio. "Análisis del bienestar psicológico, estado de salud percibido y calidad de vida en personas adultas mayores." *Pedagogía Social. Revista Interuniversitaria.* 22, 2013.

[3] See Mariano Sánchez, and Juan Sáez-Carreras. "Bases pedagógicas de la educación de las personas mayores." Andrés Escarbajal-de Haro. Ed. *Educación y personas mayores.* (Murcia: Diego Marín, 2007). 13-63. 34-37.

— participation in social, economic, cultural, sporting, recreational, and volunteer activities also contributes to increasing and maintaining personal well-being;

— organizations of elderly compose a way for the development and interaction between generations;

— provide opportunities, programmes, and support to encourage the elderly to continue to participate in learning throughout their lives;

— provide information and access to help with the participation of the elderly in intergenerational community groups, and mutual help, and to provide opportunities to help realize their full potential;

— create an environment that provides voluntary services for all ages, including public recognition, and facilitate the participation of older people whose access to be engaging voluntary activities may be limited or none;

— promote civil and cultural participation as strategies to combat social isolation and support empowerment. To ensure the enablement of full and equal participation of elderly people, especially older women, in taking decisions at all levels.

The literalness of the preceding paragraphs reflects credible reasons for the promotion and the establishment of equity in social participation for elderly people. This is compared to other age groups at all stages. If the aim is to reinforce the need for participation spaces, called 'interactive spaces,' for the elderly as the main group, then it is desirable that all institutions, both administrative and technical, provide and expand new models of motivation for this group. This will be the clearest way to promote active participation into today's society.

All these ideas, in which reside a commitment to citizenship through social coexistence, to social relationships for psychological well-being, and to the construction of quality social networks, can be developed through the implementation of Intergenerational Programmes (IPs). The concept of the Intergenerational Programme (IP) must undoubtedly be reflected in this new conception of participation with the aim of creating discreet personal spaces. Nevertheless, such spaces will not be exclusively physical spaces, but interactive learning spaces in which different cohorts converge, both directly and indirectly.

* * *

Another standard, supported by several authors,[4] covers the "critical and conceptual education" to break with traditional styles that classify elders as unproductive or, in another way, use their leisure time without concrete objectives. This socio-critical standard aims to achieve the participation of the elderly based more on their skills rather than on what they lack. For this proposal to help by way of critical reflection, consider this group as builders of knowledge.[5] From this perspective, the authors claim that elderly people understand their limitations and implement, *on their own*, a process of transformation on aspects such as their social environment, for personal growth and development. To give significance to this standard, María Esther Alcalá-Mangas shares a beneficial agreement for the elderly:[6]

— if elderly people stay active they will enjoy greater physical and mental wellbeing;
— also, they will feel useful which will increase their self-esteem by offering contributions to society;
— if they get involved socially, they need not perceive any social exclusion;
— if the elderly have freedom to choose according to their needs and concerns, they will have various alternatives of participation;
— through active participation, elderly people can be responsible for their actions and not be exclusively passive receivers.

With the above benefits of this educational ideal, another benchmark can be clearly adhered to as a social integration strategy regarding the greater collective. Elaborating on this concept, it is understood that there is a need for a new culture of ageing, in which the protagonists acquire a participatory predisposition, with both their peer group as with other generations. The emergence of this new culture of ageing must ensure a crescendo in healthy longevity and must satisfy the elderly individual's knowledge and concerns

---

[4] See Andrés Escarbajal-de Haro. "Fomentando la reflexión crítica en las personas mayores" (1998); J. García-Mínguez. "Introducción: una aproximación al concepto de educación intergeneracional" (2002); José Alberto Yuni, Claudio Ariel Urbano, and Liliana Tarditi. *Educación de adultos mayores: teoría, investigación e intervenciones.* (Córdoba, Argentina: Editorial Brujas, 2005); and Silvia Martínez de Miguel-López, and Andrés Escarbajal-de Haro. *Alternativas socioeducativas para las personas mayores.* (Madrid: Dykinson, 2009).
[5] See Juan Antonio Salmerón-Aroca, Silvia Martínez de Miguel-López, and Andrés Escarbajal-de Haro. *Vejez, mujer y educación. Un enfoque cualitativo de trabajo socioeducativo.* (Madrid: Dykinson, 2014).
[6] See María Esther Alcalá-Mangas. "La participación como estrategia de integración social." María Esther Alcalá-Mangas, and E. Valenzuela-Sánchez. Eds. *El aprendizaje de los mayores ante los retos del nuevo milenio.* (Madrid: Dykinson, 2000). 275-315.

for personal growth. Indeed, all elderly can contribute in many ways to modern society. Furthermore, the message of Ban Ki-moon, eighth United Nations Secretary-General, on the occasion of the International Day of Older Persons,[7] should not be overlooked. His message recalls overcoming prejudices related to discrimination and social exclusion to make way for an active and protected ability to age in a healthy population – all this under the slogan "Do not leave anyone behind: promoting a society for all."

In a similar vein, in *Active Ageing: A Policy Framework in Response to the Longevity Revolution*, published by the International Longevity Centre Brazil (ILC-Brazil), the research data on active longevity presented in Section III presents "participation" as a main pillar of Active and Healthy Ageing (AHA).[8] This concept translates as any kind of social, civil, recreational, and cultural activity giving a sense of belonging to a social group. In this case, as highlighted by Concepción Sánchez-Palacios (2004), the idea of participation in social activities must be understood as "a wide range of relationships with people who are not necessarily linked with bonding,"[9] leading to community values that give rise to the turning of a scale of voluntary and selfless action.

To conclude the above, it is necessary to direct this argument towards the Intergenerational Programme (IP) again, as an instrument of great viability and social innovation, both in respect of the participation of elderly people – so that their voices can be heard – as of the younger generations, which, in turn, receive experiences, build knowledge, and enhance their perception of the older collective. As Juan Antonio Salmerón-Aroca, Silvia Martinez de Miguel-López, and Andrés Escarbajal-de Haro (2014) point out, it is essential that "information on older people also reach young people, and you get free of social biases, imposition, preconceived ideas,"[10] in order to understand that the longevity process is not a constant in terms of human behaviour. In short, through these kinds of programmes an intergenerational dialogue can be guaranteed, whereby influential subjects

---

[7] UN Secretary-General Ban Ki-moon's address. International Day of Older Persons (1st October 2014). <www.un.org/press/en/2014/sgsm16217.doc.htm>

[8] See International Longevity Centre Brazil (ILC-Brazil). *Active Ageing: A Policy Framework in Response to the Longevity Revolution.* (Rio de Janeiro, July 2015). 39-48.

[9] Concepción Sánchez-Palacios. *Estereotipos negativos hacia la vejez y su relación con variables sociodemográficas, psicosociales y psicológicas.* (Málaga, 2004). 66-67. [PhD thesis]

[10] Juan Antonio Salmerón-Aroca, Silvia Martínez de Miguel-López, and Andrés Escarbajal-de Haro. *Vejez, mujer y educación. Un enfoque cualitativo de trabajo socioeducativo.* (Madrid: Dykinson, 2014). 152.

can talk about the kind of social inclusion that brings about a progressive stage in active participation and an extension of social networks for everyone.

Research objectives

For the present investigation, the objectives listed below were raised:

— to study the experiential process of the established intergenerational relationships between older people and children in order to optimize the relationship between both generations;
— to know the functions and features of the main agents involved in intergenerational action: older people and other generations according to the context where they live and act.

Methodology

In the latest gerontological literature, educational intervention with older people is gaining ground toward the reflective area in its most qualitative aspect, where their different personal views can be extracted to fit a more direct reality.[11] Hence, a qualitative methodology has been adopted, since the idea is posited that the best way to achieve a better understanding of the world which surrounds the elderly is through their own voices as protagonists. In this light, they will be able to reflect and communicate their beliefs, experiences, needs, and knowledge.[12]

Participants

The study population is distributed in a balanced way throughout the Murcian region, where those social centres belonging to the Murcian Institute for Social Action (IMAS) have been considered the principal stage.

---

[11] See Carmen Serdio-Sánchez, Begoña Díaz-Rincón, and Purificación Cifuentes-Vicente. "Envejecer activamente, aprender activamente. Apuntes para una propuesta educativa en el ámbito universitario." *International Journal of Developmental and Educational Psychology INFAD*. 2. 1, 2014. 91-98.

[12] See Silvia Martínez de Miguel-López, Andrés Escarbajal-de Haro, and Pedro Moreno-Abellán. "El rol de los abuelos en la relación con sus nietos. Una aproximación cualitativa desde el punto de vista socioeducativo." María Gloria Pérez-Serrano. Ed. *I Simposio Internacional de Envejecimiento Activo y Solidaridad Intergeneracional.* (Madrid: Universidad Nacional de Educación a Distancia - UNED, 2012).

These social centres are developing a higher number of Intergenerational Programmes (IPs) that are framed within the area of social and educational activities. Together with the capital city of Murcia (Murcia II), the towns of Alcantarilla, San Javier, and Puerto de Mazarrón are locations in which the participants of the intergenerational activity are the older people of the social centres themselves. In total, there were twenty-eight elderly citizens selected – fourteen men and fourteen women – who eventually formed four discussion groups of seven components for each social centre. As for the selection criteria, it was intended that the selected elderly had been actively involved throughout the whole development process of the Intergenerational Programmes (IPs), in order to obtain different viewpoints in the most valuable way possible. Regarding the age of the people finally interviewed, it ranges between 66 and 89 years old, where most individuals (39%) are between 70 and 74 years old. Almost half of them (43%) have a history of involvement in Intergenerational Programmes (IPs) of between six and ten years. A high proportion of them (83%) spend three hours per week on direct involvement in the Intergenerational Programme (IP). Another factor reveals that the vast majority (85%) have primary education. Similarly, seniors close to the previous percentage (79%) are professionally grouped in either the tertiary or services sector.

The instruments used for research were participant observation and the discussion group. Also, and as a complementary process of gathering information, a field notebook was used in order to enable the collection of relevant issues that may sometimes be left behind in that course of the process for which there is no procedural strategy.

Results: reasons for their participation

This category is intended primarily to discover the reasons and motives that have driven older people to participate in this model of Intergenerational Programmes (IPs). Initially, it has been found that, for the majority of older people, the main reasons for participating in the Intergenerational Programme (IP) correspond to their satisfaction and personal initiative–

> "Because you feel proud of having those conversations with other generations, of course."

Secondly, following this majority opinion, the elderly express the important fact that children and young people somehow know their world, while also transmitting their knowledge–

"It is rather..., that the children can have some understanding of our world because there is a gap between the mentality that they (have) with our seventy years."

On the other hand, half of the participants believe that the fact of taking part in such programmes makes them remain active. One way to feel useful to themselves, to be renewed, and to be able to share their experience with their peers or other generations–

"… mostly for active ageing. For being active."

To the same extent, new ways of involving older people directly related are discovered. In this sense, four types of answers can be distinguished: specifically, from the agents and technical coordinators of the Intergenerational Programmes (IPs) themselves; from the degrees of motivation of other older individuals who had previously participated; from the informative-community offer of the day-centre; and from other uninvolved professionals who recommend their participation. On its own, all this representation may seek an alternative to the traditional activities that the elderly participants have been performing by demanding their attention as new participants. To a lesser extent, although directly related to the motivation to keep active, statements may be added to the above on the pretext that represents for some seniors the fact of keeping learning–

"We are still in age to learn."

Finally, there was a small group of people who expressed their interest in participation as the best way to spend their leisure time after retirement–

"And I have discovered after retirement that free time exists."

Moreover, it is also identified that, during their active working period, they did not have the same availability as now. One can say that it is during this new stage, when they have time and provided that they do not have duties, they organize themselves and are interested and feel strong to undertake further activities–

"That time exists, while working I had no time for anything before, and I had no time for anything."

Intergenerational Relationships (IRs)

a) Social dimension

The first approach offered by most of the participants, related to their social contribution to the Intergenerational Programmes (IPs), expresses concerns such as instilling social values in children, given that it is a contribution that may influence the use and inclusion of positive social values in the long run. The concern is, in itself, to help children become better people–

"To teach them to be better people. Precisely."

Moreover, taking into consideration the shortcomings that the elderly had in the past society, they attempt to generate from their personal experience a value for their socio-personal present and future–

"For them to see that life has not been as easy as they have now."

A further significant group of responses lies in the approach to find out the importance that older people place on the *rapprochement* between different generations, emphasizing the Intergenerational Programme (IP) and the Intergenerational Relationships (IRs) in general, to subtract differences at certain barriers of social distancing, and to produce this important synergy as a projection of each group–

"To connect with them."

"Living together with a number of people whom you have not previously had a relationship with, but this binds you to a common cause."

There exists the necessity to live with other generations, being the latter an aspect that society will demand as that *rapprochement* between generations is increasing.

As a last observation, some participants emphasize, more concretely, the social aspect within the Intergenerational Relationship (IR), as an essential binding value that refers to any generational group within the social ensemble, and for its importance for social media.

* * *

Related to the latter aspect, almost half the participants showed that, through the Intergenerational Relationship (IR), continuity to the programmes can be given, in the sense that exchange continues to be produced and it does not disappear, becoming an adaptation process for the current and future society–

> "I think that if, in that experience, the intergenerational factor is not present, they would be lost."

They underline that the Intergenerational Relationship (IR) will improve over time, causing a greater proximity between both generations. They also insist that both generations should embrace each other continuously and search for strategies in an attempt to gradually change the image from one generation to another for a greater proximity to occur.

In conclusion, another objective of this study should be highlighted whereby a significant number of the elderly consider the Intergenerational Programme (IP) useful to rebuild and transform their image as an elderly person, eliminating negative stereotypes of both the two generations mainly involved and the ensemble and social community in general–

> "This means that not only children see us better, but parents and everyone in general."

b) Personal dimension
The importance that this subcategory acquires comes from the personal opinion that older people show regarding their work as participants, taking down those factors that are predominant and give meaning to the Intergenerational Relationship (IR). At first, there exists the coincidence that all elderly participants believe that, through the Intergenerational Programme (IP) itself, using the intergenerational setting, they are able to transmit experiences, knowledge, and a set of positive values acquired throughout their lives–

> "Because it implies a transmission of experiences."

They also see it as a way to make children aware through those personally-experienced values themselves–

> "To raise a bit awareness about how we were."
> "What I transmit is what I've lived, what I've been."

The elderly participants emphasize that there must be another generation eager to learn and listen to those life experiences from older people – at the same time, leading the younger persons with their extensive experience; with the fact that they could not enjoy themselves in the past; and, for the value of the things that children must handle nowadays–

> "When you communicate with someone, you're giving what you are, and that you are, your life, your experience; that you transmit to the other."

Furthermore, the elderly participants regard the elderly themselves to be the most suitable group to provide first-hand experience, because they have undergone it in more depth and for longer than anyone else–

> "You cannot tell them our experience. You are a teacher, but you cannot tell him the experience of a person."

A further example is observed of that set of values and experiences, which is aimed at allowing younger generations to enter and understand better the socio-personal nature of the elderly, constituted as a group. In turn, any possibility of separation between the two generations is denied. Following from this majority, it is shown that almost all the elderly participants feel enriched and satisfied by the action they develop through the Intergenerational Programme (IP), in addition to the relational process established between both generations–

> "Besides, because that satisfies you to have those conversations with other generations, of course."

The elderly participants see the relational process as the fusion of various satisfactions, coming from the involvement of each and every one of them. It makes them very happy and fills them with self-esteem. Moreover, older people also feel valued by other components of the Centre, whatever the generation involved–

> "We are greatly valued, even from here, by the Centre."

In conclusion, in the same way as it is proved that older people feel satisfied and enriched by the action they accomplish, the members of the younger generations also qualify almost to the same extent: they are excited, enjoying themselves, and satisfied. A positive response by the younger individuals is generally observed.

Discussion

In the relatively near future, almost a third of the population will be elderly persons over 65 years old, with children newly-retired, or about to be so. This situation will require new relational and supportive guidelines, many of them quite opposed to the customs of the past.[13] It will be a trigger that evidences the renewal, enhancement, and innovation of intergenerational processes, of new challenges for participation, of solidarity and social cohesion viewed from the reality of increased life-expectancy and of the demographic changes expected – hence the importance of fulfilling the Intergenerational Programme (IP) in the region of Murcia from the perspective of the elderly, conducting a study of their discourses as actors directly involved in the process.

Regarding the reasons for the participation of older people, their personal satisfaction becomes evident, as well as their capacity to feel useful by continuing to learn, coinciding with the pedagogical approach of personal development studied by Concepción Aparicio-Alonso (2013),[14] and the aspect of the necessity to keep learning and acquire new knowledge, expressed by Juan Agustín Morón-Marchena (2014).[15] From this perspective, it makes sense that the socio-critical model break with traditional styles that pigeonhole the older as non-productive, leading to their active participation, and taking into consideration their abilities, as other research has recommended.[16]

---

[13] See Juan López-Doblas, and María del Pilar Díaz-Conde. "XIV. Aspectos sociológicos del envejecimiento." Madrid: Portal Mayores, *Informes Portal Mayores.* 73. *Lecciones de Gerontología,* 2007.

[14] See Concepción Aparicio-Alonso. *Educación y envejecimiento activo. Una experiencia comunitaria.* (Alcalá de Henares: Departamento de Ciencias de la Educación. Universidad de Alcalá, 2013). [PhD thesis]

[15] Juan Agustín Morón-Marchena. "Educación y personas mayores." *Revista Electrónica Interuniversitaria de Formación del Profesorado.* 17. 1, 2014. 107-121.

[16] See J. García-Mínguez. "Introducción: una aproximación al concepto de educación intergeneracional." J. García-Mínguez, and M. Bedmar. Eds. *Hacia la educación intergeneracional.* (Madrid: Dykinson, 2002). 11-22; and Silvia Martínez de Miguel-López, and Andrés Escarbajal-de Haro. *Alternativas socioeducativas para las personas mayores.* (Madrid: Dykinson, 2009).

The main function of social participation is the transmission of knowledge to the children, to the older group itself, and to the rest of the generations. These results converge with clear transmission processes of learning and experience instilled by José Antonio Caride-Gómez (2013).[17] Similarly, and conforming to the perspective of José Alberto Yuni, Claudio Ariel Urbano, and Liliana Tarditi (2005),[18] the elderly consider their role as protagonist with an active attitude, rejecting the idea of passivity. The contributions described connect directly with the studies on the theory of generativity maintained by James M. McCrea and Thomas B. Smith (1997),[19] whereby the older people who acquire a wealth of knowledge and values from their own society throughout life feel the need to transfer them to younger generations. This observation is supported by the contribution of Feliciano Villar-Posada, Olatz López-Fernández, and Montserrat Celdrán-Castro (2013) that is related to welfare.[20]

As for the Intergenerational Relationships (IRs) that occurred in the Intergenerational Programme (IP), there emerges a very positive outlook from the full set of protagonists. A vision of sharing values and life experiences feedbacks into learning processes among all generations. Coinciding with the prospect of Pratt (2013),[21] the results show a commitment to learn, to hear, and to be heard from the younger generations. Similarly, these results acquire a special concomitance with the work of Sandra Huenchuan (2013), when she reaffirms the transmission of knowledge and skills with younger generations, sharing different facts and ideas in a reciprocal manner.[22]

---

[17] See José Antonio Caride-Gómez. "La Educación Social en el Siglo XXI como instrumento para la construcción de una nueva ciudadanía." *Jornadas: Influencia de la educación y la sensibilización social en la construcción de una sociedad para todas las edades*. Madrid. 1st and 2nd October 2013. [Opening lecture]

[18] See José Alberto Yuni, Claudio Ariel Urbano, and Liliana Tarditi. *Educación de adultos mayores: teoría, investigación e intervenciones*. (Córdoba, Argentina: Editorial Brujas, 2005).

[19] See James M. McCrea, and Thomas B. Smith. "Social Issues Addressed by Intergenerational Programs." Sally Newman, Christopher R. Ward, Thomas B. Smith, Janet O. Wilson, and James M. McCrea. Eds. *Intergenerational Programs. Past, Present and Future*. (Washington: Taylor & Francis. 1997). 37-51.

[20] See Feliciano Villar-Posada, Olatz López-Fernández, and Montserrat Celdrán-Castro. "La generatividad en la vejez y su relación con el bienestar: ¿Quién más contribuye es quien más se beneficia?" *Anales de Psicología*, 29. 3, 2013. 897-906.

[21] See Michael W. Pratt. "Erikson's Seventh Stage: Fostering Adults' Generativity Through Intergenerational Programs." *Journal of Intergenerational Relationships*. 11. 1, 2013. 97-100.

[22] See Sandra Huenchuan. *Los derechos de las personas mayores. Materiales avanzados de estudio y aprendizaje. Módulo 2 Los derechos de las personas mayores en el ámbito*

Within the intergenerational literature, these findings are related to previous research, such as the outstanding contributions of Judith MacCallum *et al.* (2006), and like those of Sally Newman and Mariano Sánchez-Martínez (2007), Sacramento Pinazo-Hernandis (2009), and Marta Gutiérrez-Sánchez (2011).[23] In the same way, the contribution of the study of María del Carmen Orte-Socías, *et al.* (2015)[24] entails equality with another of the benefits identified, since this type of experience serves as a motivation gateway to continue conducting other kinds of activities and, in addition, the feeling that they are serving society.[25]

Conclusions

From the specific aims contemplated in the present study, the main conclusions from the obtained results in the empirical exploration are intended to be exposed in detail.

First, focusing on the processes of the Intergenerational Relationships (IRs) between older people and children, it should be noted that the motives and reasons that have prompted the elderly to participate in

---

internacional. (Santiago de Chile: United Nations. Comisión Económica para América Latina y el Caribe (CEPAL), November 2013).

[23] Judith MacCallum, David Palmer, Peter Wright, Wendy Cumming-Potvin, Jeremy Northcote, Michelle Brooker, and Cameron Tero. *Community building through intergenerational exchange programs.* (Australia: Australian Government Department of Families, Community Services and Indigenous Affairs (FaCSIA). National Youth Affairs Research Scheme - NYARS, 2006); Sally Newman, and Mariano Sánchez-Martínez. "Los programas intergeneracionales: concepto, historia y modelos." Mariano Sánchez-Martínez. Dir. *Programas intergeneracionales. Hacia una sociedad para todas las edades.* Colección Estudios Sociales. 23. (Barcelona: Fundación "la Caixa," 2007. 37-69); Sacramento Pinazo-Hernandis, "Beneficios de los programas intergeneracionales. Espai Social." *Revista del Colegio Oficial d'Educadores i Educators Socials de la Comunitat Valenciana.* 9, 2009. 13-16; and Marta Gutiérrez-Sánchez. *Programas intergeneracionales. Teoría, política y práctica.* (Saarbrücken, Germany: Editorial Académica Española, 2011).

[24] See María del Carmen Orte-Socías, María Belén Pascual-Barrio, Marga Vives-Barceló, Rosario Pozo-Gordaliza, Maria Antònia Gomila-Grau, and Joan Alfred Amer-Fernández. "Educación intergeneracional: el programa Sharing Childhood - Compartir la infancia." Ángel De-Juanas-Alonso, and Ana Fernández-García. Eds. *Pedagogía social, universidad y sociedad.* (Madrid: Universidad Nacional de Educación a Distancia - UNED, 2015). 151-164.

[25] See Sally Newman, and Barbara Larimer. *Senior Citizen School Volunteer Program: Report on Cumulative Data. 1988-1995.* (Pittsburgh, PA: Generations Together, 1995); and Mariano Sánchez-Martínez, Pilar Díaz-Conde, Juan López-Doblas, Sacramento Pinazo-Hernandis, and Juan Sáez-Carreras. "Proyecto I+D+I Descripción, análisis y evaluación de los programas intergeneracionales en España. Modelos y buenas prácticas (Expte. 172/06)," 2008.

the Intergenerational Programme (IP) are due, mainly, to both their satisfaction and personal initiative, and to the enthusiasm and affection they feel towards children, taking into consideration that they are at a stage in their lives during which they consider their training important for the future. They also offer young persons the opportunity to know their world, and they seize the opportunity to transmit their knowledge to the younger generation. Therefore, a way to feel useful is discovered – a way to be able to renew themselves and share their own experience with the community of seniors itself and the rest of the generations. Everything seems to indicate the importance they attach to the processes of 'intergenerational solidarity' and 'active ageing,' either for the 'pretext' which entails, for many of them, to continue learning, even if compared to a reduced availability of participation before retirement or because, after retirement, they enjoy more free time. As long as they do not have duties and other commitments, they organize themselves, and the conducting of new activities arouses some interest in them.

To these results, related to the reasons for participation, are added, in a coincidental way, viewpoints on the elderly of the professionals, in the sense of experiencing a sense of usefulness, motivation, and growth of self-esteem, because the professionals see the elderly individuals immersed in spaces where they are able to contribute and share their experience. Despite this, it is proved that elderly people come to be involved in the Intergenerational Programme (IP) not only in *motu propio*; there appear different motivations, such as the example of other seniors involved in previous editions, the influence of the coordinators themselves, the offer of the Social Centre itself, and even the recommendation by other professionals unconnected to these experiences who regard participation in Intergenerational Programmes (IPs) as positive for the elderly person's personal welfare.

Second, reference is made to the specific target raised about knowing the functions and characteristics regarding all the participants involved – elderly and other generations, according to the context in which they reside. In particular, considering the role of the elderly in the Intergenerational Programme (IP), it is verified that the main function expressed is to transmit their gathered knowledge to the children with whom they share the programme and, more especially, to serve as a positive experience so that the children acquire a sense of responsibility throughout their lives. The elderly feel themselves to be the protagonists, and they believe that the role they play is active, rejecting the idea of passivity at all costs.

In general, the active role played by older people when participating in Intergenerational Programmes (IPs) gives consistency to the fact of transferring their vast experience, their value of autonomy and personal initiative, their capacity for decision-making and selection, their freedom of action, and the preparation of numerous activities on their own initiative. With all this, the elderly participants feel valued by the rest of the people involved and, undoubtedly, they perceive a climate of mutual learning in the sense of bi-directional knowledge. They are really satisfied, happy, proud, and full of self-esteem, both for the work they perform, and for their influence in the development of relational processes in the context of the Intergenerational Programme (IP).

Concerning the social contribution of the Intergenerational Programme (IP), the efficiency offered by the elderly is demonstrated in an overwhelming way. They show the benefit of instilling positive social values in children – an influence that may serve them in the present and in the future by helping the young individuals become better people in their personal lives; the young persons are able to extract values from those deficiencies that older people had in the past society – knowledge to be used in the socio-personal field.

Intergenerational Relationships (IRs) play a key role, in that they can bring about the binding of groups. According to the importance of intensifying the intergenerational *rapprochement*, it can be verified from the perspective of the elderly that this fact must be used to lessen differences, abolish certain barriers of social distancing, thereby giving way to the concept of synergy among all age groups. Although it seems obvious, if the Intergenerational Programmes (IPs) are amplified, with their effect, cohabitation between an augmented number of generations can be implemented, and a greater impact will be recognized for the community, such that it will give rise to an increasing demand for the Intergenerational Programme (IP) as a valuable tool for generational balance and social diffusion.

Works Cited

Alcalá-Mangas, María Esther. "La participación como estrategia de integración social." María Esther Alcalá-Mangas, and E. Valenzuela-Sánchez. Eds. *El aprendizaje de los mayores ante los retos del nuevo milenio.* Madrid: Dykinson, 2000. 275-315.

Aparicio-Alonso, Concepción. *Educación y envejecimiento activo. Una experiencia comunitaria.* Alcalá de Henares: Departamento de Ciencias de la Educación. Universidad de Alcalá, 2013. [PhD thesis] <dspace.uah.es/dspace/bitstream/handle/10017/20295/Tesis%20Concepci%F3n%20Aparicio.pdf?sequence=1>

Caride-Gómez, José Antonio. "La Educación Social en el Siglo XXI como instrumento para la construcción de una nueva ciudadanía." *Jornadas: Influencia de la educación y la sensibilización social en la construcción de una sociedad para todas las edades.* Madrid. 1st and 2nd October 2013. [Opening lecture]

De-Juanas-Oliva, Ángel, María Rosario Limón-Mendizábal, and Enrique Navarro-Asencio. "Análisis del bienestar psicológico, estado de salud percibido y calidad de vida en personas adultas mayores." *Pedagogía Social. Revista Interuniversitaria.* 22, 2013. 153-168. <www.redalyc.org/pdf/1350/135031394011.pdf>

Escarbajal-de Haro, Andrés. "Fomentando la reflexión crítica en las personas mayores." Juan Sáez-Carreras, and Andrés Escarbajal-de Haro. Eds. *La educación de personas adultas: en defensa de la reflexividad crítica.* Salamanca: Amarú, 1998. 143-202.

García-Mínguez, J. "Introducción: una aproximación al concepto de educación intergeneracional." J. García-Mínguez, and M. Bedmar. Eds. *Hacia la educación intergeneracional.* Madrid: Dykinson, 2002. 11-22.

Gutiérrez-Sánchez, Marta. *Programas intergeneracionales. Teoría, política y práctica.* Saarbrücken, Germany: Editorial Académica Española, 2011.

Gutiérrez-Sànchez, Marta., and G. Herráiz, "La sinergia intergeneracional." Valencia: *EsPAi sOciAl.* 9, 2009. <www.espaisocial.net/docs/revistas/espai_social_09.pdf>

—. "Programa Intergeneracional Escuela de Abuelos. Espai Social." Revista del Colegio Oficial d'Educadores i Educadors Socials de la Comunitat Valenciana. 9, 2009. 41-44.

Huenchuan, Sandra. *Los derechos de las personas mayores. Materiales avanzados de estudio y aprendizaje. Módulo 2 Los derechos de las personas mayores en el ámbito internacional.* Santiago de Chile: United Nations. Comisión Económica para América Latina y el Caribe (CEPAL), November 2013. <www.cepal.org/celade/noticias/documentosdetrabajo/8/51618/Derechos_PMayores_M2.pdf>

International Longevity Centre Brazil (ILC-Brazil). *Active Ageing: A Policy Framework in Response to the Longevity Revolution*. Rio de Janeiro, July 2015. [Executive Summary]
<www.ilcbrazil.org/wp-content/uploads/2015/07/Executive_Summary_20150714.pdf>

López-Doblas, Juan, and María del Pilar Díaz-Conde. "XIV. Aspectos sociológicos del envejecimiento." Madrid: Portal Mayores, *Informes Portal Mayores*. 73. *Lecciones de Gerontología*, 2007.
<envejecimiento.csic.es/documentos/documentos/lopez-aspectos-01.pdf>
<www.imsersomayores.csic.es/documentos/documentos/documentos/lopez-aspectos-01.pdf>

MacCallum, Judith, David Palmer, Peter Wright, Wendy Cumming-Potvin, Jeremy Northcote, Michelle Brooker, and Cameron Tero. *Community building through intergenerational exchange programs*. Australia: Australian Government Department of Families, Community Services and Indigenous Affairs (FaCSIA). National Youth Affairs Research Scheme (NYARS), 2006.
<docs.education.gov.au/system/files/doc/other/community_building_through_intergenerational_exchange_programs.pdf>

Martínez de Miguel-López, Silvia, and Andrés Escarbajal-de Haro. *Alternativas socioeducativas para las personas mayores*. Madrid: Dykinson, 2009.

Martínez de Miguel-López, Silvia., Andrés Escarbajal-de Haro, and Pedro Moreno-Abellán. "El rol de los abuelos en la relación con sus nietos. Una aproximación cualitativa desde el punto de vista socioeducativo." María Gloria Pérez-Serrano. Ed. *I Simposio Internacional de Envejecimiento Activo y Solidaridad Intergeneracional*. Madrid: Universidad Nacional de Educación a Distancia (UNED), 2012. [CD-ROM]

McCrea, James M., and Thomas B. Smith. "Social Issues Addressed by Intergenerational Programs." Sally Newman, Christopher R. Ward, Thomas B. Smith, Janet O. Wilson, and James M. McCrea. Eds. *Intergenerational Programs. Past, Present and Future*. Washington: Taylor & Francis. 1997. 37-51.

Morón-Marchena, Juan Agustín. "Educación y personas mayores." *Revista Electrónica Interuniversitaria de Formación del Profesorado*. 17. 1, 2014. 107-121.
<www.redalyc.org/pdf/2170/217030664008.pdf>

Newman, Sally, and Barbara Larimer. *Senior Citizen School Volunteer Program: Report on Cumulative Data. 1988-1995*. Pittsburgh, PA: Generations Together, 1995.

Newman, Sally, and Mariano Sánchez-Martínez. "Los programas intergeneracionales: concepto, historia y modelos." Mariano Sánchez-Martínez. Dir. *Programas intergeneracionales. Hacia una sociedad para todas las edades*. Colección Estudios Sociales. 23. Barcelona: Fundación "la Caixa," 2007. 37-69.
<www.aepumayores.org/sites/default/files/Programas_Intergeneracionales_Coleccion_Estudios_Sociales_vol23_es.pdf>

Orte-Socías, María del Carmen, María Belén Pascual-Barrio, Marga Vives-Barceló, Rosario Pozo-Gordaliza, Maria Antònia Gomila-Grau, and Joan Alfred Amer-Fernández. "Educación intergeneracional: el programa Sharing Childhood - Compartir la infancia." Ángel De-Juanas-Alonso, and Ana Fernández-García. Eds. *Pedagogía social, universidad y sociedad*. Madrid: Universidad Nacional de Educación a Distancia (UNED), 2015. 151-164.
<SIPS-15_SACHI.pdf>

Pinazo-Hernandis, Sacramento. "Beneficios de los programas intergeneracionales. Espai Social." *Revista del Colegio Oficial d'Educadors i Educadors Socials de la Comunitat Valenciana*. 9, 2009. 13-16.

Pratt, Michael W. "Erikson's Seventh Stage: Fostering Adults' Generativity Through Intergenerational Programs." *Journal of Intergenerational Relationships*. 11. 1, 2013. 97-100.
<www.tandfonline.com/doi/full/10.1080/15350770.2013.754700?scroll=top&needAccess=true>

Salmerón-Aroca, Juan Antonio, Silvia Martínez de Miguel-López, and Andrés Escarbajal-de Haro. *Vejez, mujer y educación. Un enfoque cualitativo de trabajo socioeducativo*. Madrid: Dykinson, 2014.

Sánchez-Martínez, Mariano, Pilar Díaz-Conde, Juan López-Doblas, Sacramento Pinazo-Hernandis, and Juan Sáez-Carreras. (2008). "Proyecto I+D+I Descripción, análisis y evaluación de los programas intergeneracionales en España. Modelos y buenas prácticas (Expte. 172/06)." [Executive summary]
<www.imserso.es/InterPresent1/groups/imserso/documents/binario/idi172_06ugranada.pdf>

Sánchez-Palacios, Concepción. Estereotipos negativos hacia la vejez y su relación con variables sociodemográficas, psicosociales y psicológicas. Málaga, 2004. [PhD thesis]

<www.biblioteca.uma.es/bbldoc/tesisuma/16704046.pdf>

Sánchez-Martínez, Mariano, and Juan Sáez-Carreras. "Bases pedagógicas de la educación de las personas mayores." Andrés Escarbajal-de Haro. Ed. *Educación y personas mayores*. Murcia: Diego Marín, 2007. 13-63. 34-37.

Serdio-Sánchez, Carmen, Begoña Díaz-Rincón, and Purificación Cifuentes-Vicente. "Envejecer activamente, aprender activamente. Apuntes para una propuesta educativa en el ámbito universitario." *International Journal of Developmental and Educational Psychology INFAD*. 2. 1, 2014. 91-98. <infad.eu/RevistaINFAD/2013/n2/volumen1/0214-9877_2013_2_1_91.pdf>

United Nations (UN) *Plan de acción internacional de Madrid sobre el Envejecimiento. Informe de la II Asamblea Mundial sobre el Envejecimiento. Madrid, 8th-12th April 2002*. New York: United Nations, 2002. <www.imsersomayores.csic.es/documentos/documentos/onu-informe01.pdf>

Villar-Posada, Feliciano, Olatz López-Fernández, and Montserrat Celdrán-Castro. "La generatividad en la vejez y su relación con el bienestar: ¿Quién más contribuye es quien más se beneficia?" *Anales de Psicología*, 29. 3, 2013. 897-906. <www.redalyc.org/articulo.oa?id=16728244029>

World Health Organization (WHO) *Active Ageing: A Policy Framework*. Geneva: World Health Organization. 2002. <www.who.int/ageing/publications/active_ageing/en/> <apps.who.int/iris/bitstream/10665/67215/1/WHO_NMH_NPH_02.8.pdf>

Yuni, José Alberto, Claudio Ariel Urbano, and Liliana Tarditi. *Educación de adultos mayores: teoría, investigación e intervenciones*. Córdoba, Argentina: Editorial Brujas, 2005.

Social Gatherings and Healthy Breakfasts. New Strategies for Participation: an 'Intergenerational Education' (IE) Project at the University of Murcia (UMU)[1]

Juan Antonio Salmerón-Aroca, Antonia María Sánchez-Lázaro, and Gema Belchi-Romero

University of Murcia

First initiatives in Intergenerational Education (IE) started in Spain in 1993, European Year of the Elderly and Solidarity among Generations, during which the importance of carrying out programmes which reinforced social coexistence among young persons at university and elderly people in order to foment communication among the generations was highlighted.[2] Later on, there were some exchange generational meetings involving elderly people in schools – Secondary Education Centres, and Centres of Baccalaureate and Professional Education – most of which were promoted in 1999, the International Year of Elderly People. In fact, at the Second World Assembly of Ageing,[3] there was a Plan of Action that set down the need to improve 'intergenerational solidarity' which would be asserted throughout the Plan of Action for Elderly People, 2003-2007. Furthermore, 'intergenerational solidarity' is a topic which is taken up in a report of the Third National

---

[1] The authors express their gratitude to the Principal Researcher of the project, Dr Silvia Martínez de Miguel-López, to the teaching group of Searching "Education, Quality-of-Life, and Development" of the Faculty of Education (FE) at the University of Murcia (UMU), to the Institute in Murcia for Social Action (IMAS), and to the Official School of Social Educators in the Region of Murcia.

[2] See José-Luis Vega-Vega, and Belén Bueno-Martínez. "Los programas intergeneracionales." Víctor Alba, and José Buendía-Vidal. (Comps.). *Envejecimiento y psicología de la salud.* (Madrid: Siglo XXI, 1998). 399-429.

[3] The "United Nations Second World Assembly on Ageing" took place in Madrid (Spain) in April 2002.

Congress for Elderly People[4] in which the dynamic idea of the concept of generation and the importance of interaction among generations is propounded. In the same way, the year 2012 was declared "European Year of Active Ageing and Intergenerational Solidarity," taking as principal objective the creation of Active and Healthy Ageing (AHA), within a framework for any age. Taking this into account, one of the proposed aspects for the improvement of 'intergenerational solidarity' was, precisely, to favour intergenerational relationships not just with an educative objective, but with a social one as well, encouraging considerations for an 'intergenerational education.' To this end, it is necessary to approach the educational space of one's own institution and create relationships between members of the younger generations and elderly people in order to facilitate the exchange of knowledge. As Antoni Petrus-Rotger states:

> Nowadays, it is more and more necessary to open the doors of Schools, and Education, to Elderly people. It is this fact of coexistence of Educational Generations in different domains of society, including educative institutions which allows us to affirm that 'We Are All Society.' (Petrus-Rotger 2002: 642)[5]

* * *

In line with the definition proposed by Maria Lourdes Pérez-González (2007),[6] for the purposes of this "'Intergenerational Education' Project at the University of Murcia," Intergenerational Education (IE) is conceived of as being based on a mutually-agreed meeting between members of two or more generations, being elderly people one of these generations. In order to approach the elderly persons, it is necessary to create an exchange of communication between the participants by favouring cultural proximity

---

[4] Third National Congress for Elderly People – El Instituto de Mayores y Servicios Sociales (IMSERSO). *Relaciones Intergeneracionales*. (Madrid: Ministerio de Sanidad, Política Social e Igualdad, 2009).

[5] Antoni Petrus-Rotger. "Nuevas experiencias de intervención socioeducativa hacia las personas mayores" Antoni Joan Colom-Cañellas, and Carmen Orte-Socías. (Coords.) *Gerontología educativa y social. Pedagogía social y personas mayores*. (Palma: Universitat de les Illes Balears, 2001). 611-649.

[6] See Maria Lourdes Pérez-González. "La educación intergeneracional: necesidad de la sociedad actual." CEOMA. Aplicación y Seguimiento del Plan de Acción Internacional, Asamblea Mundial sobre el Envejecimiento, Madrid, 2002. Actas del VIII Congreso Nacional de Organizaciones de Mayores, 22-23 abril de 2007. (Madrid: Confederación Española de Organizaciones de Mayores – CEOMA, 2007). 295-297.

between members of different age groups. Different motivations and common objectives are sought so that this communication can be effective, constitute a common meeting point, and lead to an exchange of knowledge, values, feelings, perceptions, and cultures. Likewise, a relationship of equality between generations is created, based on respect and the difference of varied values, customs, individual and collective identities, competences, and different societal levels.

The final objective of this "'Intergenerational Education' Project at the University of Murcia" is mutually-exchanged knowledge and the acceptance of different generation groups.[7] Within this Project, this objective relates to the University of Murcia (UMU) of which the Faculty of Education (FE) and the Council for Family and Equality of Opportunities has made possible, from the year 2009, the development of the "'Intergenerational Education' Project at the University of Murcia."[8]

Justification

As has been stated, this research presupposes a precedent when referring to the intergeneration meetings within the university area, and it involves the formation of future professionals when dealing with Intergenerational Education (IE) and the reinforcement of interest within this area aimed at offering opportunities to keep in touch with a socially-contextualized reality regarding elderly people.

The proposals which are planned as a result of this project are inspired by the recommendations which, at all levels of administration, have been carried out over the past few years. Such recommendations have highlighted 'Intergenerational Relationships' (IRs) as an important area to be developed and to be paid attention to. With the purpose of trying to eliminate stereotypes, prejudices, untrue, and negative images, administrations have tried to promote social participation and active ageing.

---

[7] See Jesús García-Mínguez. "Una aproximación al concepto de educación intergeneracional." Jesús García-Mínguez, and Matías Bedmar-Moreno. (Coords.) *Hacia la educación intergeneracional.* (Madrid: Dykinson, 2002); and Ronald J. Manheimer. "Promesas y políticas de la educación de personas mayores." Juan Sáez-Carreras. (Coord.) *Pedagogía social y programas intergeneracionales: educación de personas mayores.* (Archidona, Málaga: Aljibe, 2002).

[8] In this endeavour, the Faculty of Education and the Council for Family and Equality of Opportunities (*Consejería de Familia e Igualdad de Oportunidades*) at the University of Murcia have been aided by the Institute in Murcia for Social Action (IMAS), and the Official School of Social Education, in the Region of Murcia.

They have also tried to prepare future professionals in Social Education for them to be able to develop and put into practice their knowledge, abilities, and skills. Here follows, therefore, a description of some of the innovations that have been carried out as part of the "'Intergenerational Education' Project at the University of Murcia" during the academic course 2015-2016. The findings of the project derive from the following proposed specific objectives:

– acknowledgement of the benefits of educational experiences that have been incorporated throughout collaboration with The SIforAGE Project,[9] in a sustained dialogue about quality-of-life, and cooperation between elderly and young people;

– evaluation of the sustainability of those activities which have been set up for the above reasons, as well as to promote Active and Healthy Ageing (AHA);

– identification of ways in which not only to improve the general project, but also the specific research developed by the students at the University of Murcia (UMU) and the elderly participants in the obtainment of benefits from their own institutions.

Method

1. Description of the project

The "'Intergenerational Education' Project at the University of Murcia" is based on a model of socio-educative action which favours the leadership of the participants and their active participation. This is achieved by promoting the interaction of equality-based, generational interdependence which exists in order to obtain 'a full life' for people, without age-discrimination, by allowing the acquisition of knowledge, habits, abilities, and skills which, in turn, enable elderly persons to obtain a meaningful experience, contributing to the personal and social development of all participants.

---

[9] Amongst other objectives, "Social Innovation on Active and Healthy Aging for sustainable economic growth" (SIforAGE), a European Union research project (7th Framework Programme), which commenced in November 2012 and ended in October 2016, addressed Intergenerational Relationships (IRs) as an important element in building 'intergenerational solidarity.'

Several contributions have been carried out in different participative centres at the Institute in Murcia for Social Action (IMAS), and within the same University of Murcia (UMU). These contributions set up specific activities involving the collaboration of teachers at the Official School of Social Education,[10] of assistants at centres for elderly people, of students from the Faculty of Education (FE-UMU), of the Council for Family and Equality of Opportunities (UMU), and of annual General Conferences held in the Faculty of Education (FE-UMU) where centres of elderly people from the Institute in Murcia for Social Action (IMAS) are concentrated, together with future professionals of Social Education.

During the academic course 2015-2016, the incorporation of two more subjects in the field of Social Education, apart from Education for Elderly People, led to some experiences of collaboration between the elderly people and the students, strengthening the intergenerational dialogue, bringing about greater interaction between members of the different generations due to closer interaction among the project participants, and providing opportunities for lively exchanges of experiences, beliefs, thoughts, and values.

2. Development of the research

2.1. Beginning of the activities and participants

Several meetings were attended, on the one hand, by the lecturers of the University of Murcia (UMU), who are responsible for planning the course for the centres of the Institute in Murcia for Social Action (IMAS), for designing activities, and for the preparation of materials, and, on the other hand, by students taking the programme for Social Education and Elderly People. The final tally of participants at the meetings was as follows:

– ninety-five participants in all, of these;

– sixty-two students aged between 20 and 27 years old, from the Official School of Social Education;

– thirty-three elderly people aged between 65 and 88 years old, from the social centre Santa María de Gracia, in Murcia;

---

[10] Specifically, in the programme for the subject Education for the Elderly.

– two lecturers from the University of Murcia (UMU) who give classes in the subjects "Education for Health" and "Sociocultural Entertainment and Community Developments;"

– one tutor from the Centre for Elderly People;

– one tutor-appraiser; and

– the Coordinator of the whole project.

All participants worked with no kind of financial benefit, and with their consent to be part of the project.

2.2. Temporality

The activities took place over a period of twelve months, from July 2015 until July 2016. The main aim was to achieve continuity and confluence within the subjects to be incorporated into the new projects: Sociocultural Animation and Community Development, and Education for Health. These subjects are in addition to Education for Elderly People, the subject in which all the activities had been developed.

2.3. Procedure

Four work sessions with the lecturers of the University of Murcia (UMU) and those persons responsible for the Institute in Murcia for Social Action (IMAS) were carried out. In the same way, ten sessions were attended by students and elderly people: two sessions for preparation; one session for the elaboration of materials; six sessions for intergenerational work; and one final session, with closure. All ten sessions were supported by a tutor – a university lecturer or tutor from the Centre for Elderly People – who supervised and guided all working sessions. The most important role of the tutor was to invigorate the meetings, as well as solving doubts, motivating for the elaboration of materials, and collecting information. In this way, different research documents were elaborated within the subjects – materials such as photographs, panels, videos, dossiers, and so on.

Hereafter follows a more specific description of the way in which the work was carried out in these subjects over the course of the development of the project.

2.3.1. "Sociocultural Animation and Community Development"

In the course 2015-2016, Sociocultural Animation and Community Development was the obligatory subject taken by students of Social Education during the third level of their degree programme at the University of Murcia (UMU). The subject involves various aspects within the field of Social Education, aspects which are further developed in the social arena relating to Community Development. In this sense, the principal models of socio-educative supervision are acknowledged, not only for Community Development, but also for evaluation by professionals working in Social Education. The purpose is to try to offer other alternative models which serve to improve the socio-educative praxis and, thereby, solve those social problems which are faced by the different communities.[11]

The reason for the incorporation of a new subject[12] derives from a perceived need to claim Sociocultural Animation as an important factor in Community Development pertaining to elderly people. The students of Sociocultural Animation were offered theoretical content that was subsequently transformed into practice. Special attention was given to community development, socio-educative supervision, research-action, and socio-cultural animation as tools for enhancing community development, qualitative techniques, and communication. At the same time, students were given a work plan and a guideline for socio-educative supervision, a guideline which recommends a classical process of evaluation and social action, namely, the analysis of the real situation, the perception of problems and needs, problem-solving, planning, and the development of this kind of area. The project plan was revised throughout the research period and reviewed weekly, in order to pick up on the strengths and weaknesses of the plan once the work with elderly people had started.

As set out in the Social Education programme, an educational experience, "Social Conversations," was established to confront stereotypes and prejudices on immigration. The aim of this was to promote discussion on education for intercultural values and respect for cultural diversity without discrimination, both with regard to students and to the elderly. To achieve this, the following procedure was followed:

---

[11] See Andrés Escarbajal-de Haro. *Guía Docente de la asignatura Animación Sociocultural y Desarrollo Comunitario del Grado de Educación Social.* (Murcia: Universidad de Murcia. 2015).

[12] The new subject "Sociocultural Animation and Community Development" was introduced at the University of Murcia (UMU) within the programme of The SIforAGE Project.

a) In the first instance, work was undertaken to create cohesion and group solidarity in the class, taking into account the perceptions and needs of intergenerational dependence manifested by members of both generations.

b) A complete analysis of the real situation was carried out within the social centre.

c) In class, an educative proposal was set up by following the considerations of the PAS method – thinking, acting, and feeling – which was developed by the Colectivo Amani[13] in order to establish objectives and plan activities.

d) In a second phase, at the Centre for elderly people, all participants were asked to write a narration, poem, or describe an event about their experience with immigration. Moreover, if they wanted to, they could accompany that text with any photograph related to their script so that they could transmit their emotions in a better way.

e) Following this, there was a dialogical and thoughtful session with emotional expression referring to the photographs and the texts.

f) Finally, in a third phase, a brief cinema shoot was carried out by the students and teachers, a cut which formed part of the film *Spain in a day* (Dir. Isabel Coixet, 2015).[14] This enterprise was developed on the 24th October 2015 in the Centre for Elderly People "Santa María de Gracia" in Murcia. Throughout the filming, positive intergenerational friendships developed which allowed for the exchange of experiences about immigration among elderly people, and for reflection about the present-day situation, in particular about immigrants who are searching for employment in a foreign country which, these days, is the domain of young people.

2.3.2. Education and promotion of health

The more active elderly people are, the more they can contribute to society. It represents a meaningful change whenever they appreciate ageing, and,

---

[13] See Beatriz Aguilera-Reija, Juan Gómez-Lara, Mar Morollón-Pardo, and Juan de Vicente-Abad. *Educación intercultural. Análisis y resolución de conflictos.* (Madrid: Editorial Popular, 2006).

[14] Isabel Coixet (Dir.) *Spain in a day*, 2015. [Film]

instead of being represented as a 'problem,' a positive attitude towards ageing is, in itself, a potential solution for a lot of problems.[15]

It is significant to make this point since, within this project, both students and elderly people worked together when determining health. This intergenerational experience is named "Intergenerational Healthy Breakfasts: Referring to determinants of Health."[16] During the 'breakfasts,' discussions revolved around the promotion of styles of healthy living and measures to be taken which, as part of everyday life, have been considered essential guarantees of quality-of-life for elderly people,[17] measures such as a healthy and balanced food-intake, and exercising, among other determinants. Moreover, these measures are shared by students at university, a factor which enables all participants to work together and exchange group experiences.

The 'breakfasts' and joint checking of the results were carried out in a participative, practical way. Participation was an experience which incorporated both the task of historical construction and the dimension of living practice. In this case, the participation of elderly people in class was solid and voluntary.[18] So, participation was a starting point for the elaboration of determinant areas for health, which involved the improvement in quality-of-life of both groups, elderly and students, at the University of Murcia (UMU).

Consequently, the description of the activity remained as follows:

a) By way of an introduction, and with the intention of having a first intergenerational contact, a healthy breakfast was shared between students and elderly people, welcoming the older persons to this space, that is, the

[15] See Alfonso García-Martínez, and Antonia María Sánchez-Lázaro. "La Calidad de Vida y la Personas Mayores." Alfonso García-Martínez, and Juan Benito-Martínez. (Coords.) *Educación para la salud y Personas Mayores.* Murcia: Ayuntamiento de San Pedro de Pinatar, 2003; and World Health Organisation (WHO). *World report on ageing and health.* (Geneva: World Health Organisation, 2015).

[16] The activity "Intergenerational Healthy Breakfasts: Referring to determinants of Health" was developed as part of The SIforAGE Project in the field of the subject Education and Promotion of Health in the fourth course of Social Education, in the Faculty of Education (FE) at the University of Murcia (UMU).

[17] See Alfonso García-Martínez, Juan Agustín Morón-Marchena, and Antonia María Sánchez-Lázaro, and María Lourdes Cobacho-Inglés. *Educación y Promoción de la Salud. Una mirada contextual.* (Murcia: DM, 2009).

[18] See Purificación Causapié-Lopesino, Antonio Balbontín-López-Cerón, Manuel Porras-Muñoz, and Adela Mateo-Echanagorría. *Envejecimiento activo. Libro Blanco.* (Madrid: Ministerio de Sanidad, Política Social e Igualdad, 2011).

classroom. This activity was developed through introduction techniques such that both groups brainstormed their own interests.

b) In a second phase, determinants of health were established, from the point-of-view of both the elderly participants and that of the students. This part was carried out in groups which generated debates about the cultural norms which focus on the lifestyles of the students and the elderly individuals. The mixed groups dealt with determinants of health, and all groups developed a discussion to promote mutual learning through the transmission of customs. The discussions were guided by interviews about those determinants of health which some of the students had carried out with the elderly persons, and *vice versa*, and that the students had prepared previously in class. The team worked with a specific group of determinants. As the intention was to draw up a list of 'good,' healthy habits by way of a conclusion, a list which reflected healthy habits which both the elderly participants and the students could subscribe to relating to those determinants of health that had been identified.

c) Finally, a letter on intergenerational health was written, a letter which listed the most meaningful contributions of the groups and their representatives, by obtaining a series of intergenerational proposals which favour the healthiest lifestyle based on the determinants of health.

3. Evaluation

A mixed, quantitative and qualitative methodology was employed in order to evaluate all the activities. The results presented here were obtained throughout this qualitative technique, with an evaluation meeting, as described by Silvia Martínez de Miguel-López and Andrés Escarbajal-de Haro.[19] The findings generated during the sessions of intergenerational work were analysed in the same way.

Two evaluation meetings were carried out with students and, at the end of the project, two other meetings took place with thirty selected elderly participants. The topics which were dealt with in these meetings were:

a) organizational aspects – different means by which these activities were carried out, timing, and spaces in which they were developed;

---

[19] See Silvia Margarita Martínez de Miguel-López, and Andrés Escarbajal-de Haro. *Alternativas socioeducativas para las personas mayores.* (Madrid: Dykinson, 2009). 229.

b) activities which were carried out – topics dealt with in the sessions;

c) fulfilment of the expectations – breaking down stereotypes, creation of spaces and intergenerational knowledge, professionalization; and

d) degree of general satisfaction with the activities carried out – exchange of opinions, methodology used, dynamics of the sessions, and proposals for improvement.

The data collected in these meetings were filtered according to their relevance and significance for the project and, later, all data were analysed, using a matrix of SWOT codes, into various categories, following the procedure described by Rosa María Sisamón-Gil (2012).[20] The SWOT categories are as follows:

– weaknesses, which are mal-functional aspects of the participants in the Project which are placed in the area for improvement;

– threats, which are aspects outside the Project, but which do not favour its development;

– strengths, which are functional elements of the participants or the projects, which give them more relevance; and

– opportunities, which are elements which can have a positive effect, or can help in the developments of such a project.

The reliability of the collected data was measured in concurrence between observers who were using the Cohen's *Kappa* coefficient.[21] Only those indicators which obtained concordance between observers and *Kappa* values 0·81-1 were taken into account.

---

[20] Rosa María Sisamón-Gil. "El análisis 'DAFO' aplicado a la intervención en casos de personas en situación de exclusión social." *Revista de trabajo y acción social.* 51, 2012. 469-487.

[21] Richard Landis, and Gary Koch. "The measurement of observer agreement for categorical data." *Biometrics.* 33, 1977. 159-174.

Analysis and discussion of results

From here onwards, the results obtained in each category were shown to the students at the University of Murcia (UMU) and to the elderly people. The researchers concurred to a high degree with the results.

Strengths
The category of 'Strengths' in the SWOT analysis revealed the following:

– development of new competences, acquired by the students for their future professional job, with the different activities which were proposed in both subjects;

– acquisition of meaningful experiences which can contribute to the personal and social development of both groups;

– longer period of curricular practices by the students, which makes it easier for the individual student to acknowledge her/his own characteristics in the field of elderly people;

– intergenerational contact through those actions which were developed with the elderly in the social centres, an aspect which was valued in a very positive way;

– breaking stereotypes and favouring communication and the exchange of opinions through qualitative strategies during the meetings;

– involvement and support by the teachers for an adequate development of the activity.

Weaknesses
The category of 'Weaknesses' in the SWOT analysis revealed the following:

– lack of time to develop the activities in an effective way due to the need for compatibility with other activities and subjects undertaken by the students;

– elderly people show a lack of time dedicated to activities with an intergenerational character;

– lack of previous experience in this work with elderly people on the part of the students, which slows down the learning process, and which generated, at first, some uncertainty when carrying out these activities;

– some of the sessions were carried out outside the timetable of the classes, so it was impossible for some participants to take part in the sessions which had been planned beforehand;

– on some occasions, a lack of definition about work expectations and different levels of involvement, can generate variations in the results of learning;

– no knowledge of the professional figure of social educator on the part of elderly people in the centres, where there is no practice within the area of Social Education, tends to lead to confusion with other professional figures.

Opportunities
The category of 'Opportunities' in the SWOT analysis revealed the following:

– students face important work in their personal development, all the time the presence of Social Educators in the Institute in Murcia for Social Action (IMAS) centres is not recognised;

– the new needs, which elderly people show within the culture of Active and Healthy Ageing (AHA), favour the intervention within a socio-educative field;

– elderly people refer to new spaces of participation emerging around Active and Healthy Ageing (AHA) which, traditionally, have not been considered as "usual" for the success of elderly people;

– some elderly people demand the figure of Social Educator as an integral part of a professional team, considering this profile to be necessary to lifelong learning.

Threats
The category of 'Threats' in the SWOT analysis revealed the following:

– several activities were being carried out at the same time by other professionals present in the Social Centres for Elderly People;

– lack of rules which regulate the figure of the Social Educator in these institutions;

– the transition of old "Pensioner Homes" into Social Centres for elderly people is not accompanied by the renewal of professionals which make this change real;

– the absence of Social Educators in centres for elderly people make this professional figure unknown to them, causing them to suppose that there is no need for the Social Educator and that such a figure will have no repercussion when answering their needs.

Conclusions

With regard to the first proposed objective of the "'Intergenerational Education' Project at the University of Murcia," the experiences presented here such as 'Healthy Breakfasts' and 'Social Conversations,' which are based on Intergenerational Education (IE), generated many benefits. Through these experiences, students and elderly people established theoretical and practical frameworks within which to develop active and healthy lifestyles, linked to basic conditions in daily life which relate to nutrition and intercultural processes, and which were incorporated into present-day lifestyles by students at the University.

Along these lines, certain strengths within the Project which favoured the prosecution of the objectives can be highlighted. On the one hand, elderly people were able to give continuity to cultural values, being, collectively, a fountain of transmission of experiences and past knowledge. In the same way, they could participate in social and educative activities, thereby contributing to 'active ageing' which develops their capacity to continue learning and to making the concept of 'Permanent Education' real. Likewise, the experiences provided opportunities for bringing individuals together and getting to know members of other generations, thereby building a space which favoured social integration. On the other hand, these activities helped members of the young generations and future professionals to learn with and from elderly people through experiences, knowledge, and skills with which they collaborated. In this way, negative stereotypes about ageing were eliminated, and the students' professional qualifications enhanced.

These findings have made it possible to propose some concrete actions based on the experience and needs of the students and older people, having carried out an accessible plan within the community framework.[22] On the basis of the results presented, it is possible to confirm that all activities fulfilled the objectives proposed initially:

1. to design strategies of performance in those areas of Social Education that are related to 'Active and Healthy Ageing' (AHA), by applying several points-of-view, methodologies, and search techniques, and action and improvement relating to this paradigm; and, finally,

2. to encourage the participation of elderly people in the centres, fulfilling, in this way, the second objective of this research which refers to the suitability of the activities developed, and the opportunities offered by the centres for elderly persons in the Region of Murcia.

In order to fulfil the third objective planned for this research, some aspects have to borne in mind regarding the improvement of the developed Project itself. Above all, there is a need to focus on correcting the detected 'weaknesses' and confront the 'threats' which the SWOT analysis identified. In this sense, there are several aspects that require attention, aspects which involve the existence of logistical barriers and limits for the development of intergenerational meetings. With such improvements, the participants felt that the topics could have been dealt with in more depth. In a similar vein, the participants expressed their dissatisfaction with the temporality of the activities; it was generally agreed that the intergenerational sessions could have been longer and scheduled so as to render them compatible with other programmed commitments. Equally, it was proposed that the aims of the activities could be divided into less ambitious ones, to be attained in a shorter time, an improvement which would encourage the carrying out of such activities.

It is contended, therefore, that the types of activities for Intergenerational Education (IE) under study here develop a framework for 'Active and Healthy Ageing' (AHA) through educative and qualitative views of collaboration, cooperation, and learning. Intergenerational Education (IE) offers other broad-based alternatives for breaking down the intergenerational

---

[22] These findings and recommended actions are included in the documentation of the European Union research project "Social Innovation on Active and Healthy Ageing for sustainable economic growth" (SIforAGE), November 2012-October 2016.

distances, which still exist in our society, by changing negative conceptions which members of each one of the generations possess about members of the others. At the same time, Intergenerational Education (IE) favours a kind of education rooted in greater solidarity between members of the different generations, and a more democratic form of education whereby the social integration of these groups would become a social reality and not simply a political proclamation of human rights which might never be put into practice.

Works Cited

Aguilera-Reija, Beatriz, Juan Gómez-Lara, Mar Morollón-Pardo, and Juan de Vicente-Abad. *Educación intercultural. Análisis y resolución de conflictos*. Madrid: Editorial Popular, 2006.

Causapié-Lopesino, Purificación., Antonio Balbontín-López-Cerón, Manuel Porras-Muñoz, and Adela Mateo-Echanagorría. *Envejecimiento activo. Libro Blanco*. Madrid: Ministerio de Sanidad, Política Social e Igualdad, 2011.

Coixet, Isabel (Dir.) *Spain in a day*, 2015. <www.rtve.es/television/20150904/rtve-presenta-spain-in-day-historia-dia-espanoles-rodada-ellos-dirigida-isabel-coixet/1211800.shtml>

Escarbajal-de Haro, Andrés. *Guía Docente de la asignatura Animación Sociocultural y Desarrollo Comunitario del Grado de Educación Social*. Murcia: Universidad de Murcia, 2015.

García-Martínez, Alfonso, and Antonia María Sánchez-Lázaro. "La Calidad de Vida y la Personas Mayores." Alfonso García-Martínez, and Juan Benito-Martínez. (Coords.) *Educación para la salud y Personas Mayores*. Murcia: Ayuntamiento de San Pedro de Pinatar, 2003.

García-Martínez, Alfonso, Juan Agustín Morón-Marchena, Antonia María Sánchez-Lázaro, and María Lourdes Cobacho-Inglés. *Educación y Promoción de la Salud. Una mirada contextual*. Murcia: DM, 2009.

García-Mínguez, Jesús. "Una aproximación al concepto de educación intergeneracional." Jesús García-Mínguez, and Matías Bedmar-Moreno. (Coords.) *Hacia la educación intergeneracional*. Madrid: Dykinson, 2002.

Instituto de Mayores y Servicios Sociales, El (IMSERSO). *Plan de Acción para las Personas Mayores 2003-2007*. Madrid: Ministerio de Trabajo y Asuntos Sociales, 2003.

Instituto de Mayores y Servicios Sociales, El (IMSERSO). *Año europeo del envejecimiento activo y de la solidaridad intergeneracional. Resultados del programa de actividades en España. Informe final.* Madrid: Ministerio de Sanidad, Servicios Sociales e Igualdad, 2012.

Landis, Richard, and Gary Koch. "The measurement of observer agreement for categorical data." *Biometrics.* 33, 1977. 159-174.

Manheimer, Ronald J. "Promesas y políticas de la educación de personas mayores." Juan Sáez-Carreras. (Coord.) *Pedagogía social y programas intergeneracionales: educación de personas mayores.* Archidona, Málaga: Aljibe, 2002.

Martínez de Miguel-López, Silvia Margarita. "La educación de personas mayores como derecho social: diferencias con otras generaciones y posibilidades de encuentro." Matías Bedmar-Moreno, and Inmaculada Montero-García. (Coords.) *La Educación Intergeneracional: un nuevo ámbito educativo.* Madrid: Dykinson, 2003.

Martínez de Miguel-López, Silvia Margarita, and Andrés Escarbajal-de Haro. *Alternativas socioeducativas para las personas mayores.* Madrid: Dykinson, 2009.

Pérez-González, Maria Lourdes. "La educación intergeneracional: necesidad de la sociedad actual." *Aplicación y Seguimiento del Plan de Acción Internacional, Asamblea Mundial sobre el Envejecimiento.* Madrid, 2002. Actas del VIII Congreso Nacional de Organizaciones de Mayores, 22-23 abril de 2007. Madrid: Confederación Española de Organizaciones de Mayores (CEOMA), 2007. 295-297.
<ceoma.org/wp-content/uploads/2014/07/LIBRO_8_Congreso_DEF.pdf>

Petrus-Rotger, Antoni. "Nuevas experiencias de intervención socioeducativa hacia las personas mayors." Antoni Joan Colom-Cañellas, and Carmen Orte-Socías. (Coords.) *Gerontología educativa y social. Pedagogía social y personas mayores.* Palma: Universitat de les Illes Balears, 2001. 611-649.

Sisamón-Gil, Rosa María. "El análisis 'DAFO' aplicado a la intervención en casos de personas en situación de exclusión social." *Revista de trabajo y acción social.* 51, 2012. 469-487.
<Dialnet-ElAnalisisDAFOAplicadoALaIntervencionEnCasosDePers-4640569.pdf>

United Nations (UN) *Report of the Second World Assembly on Ageing.* Madrid, 8-12 April 2002. New York: United Nations, 2002.

<<u>www.un.org/en/ga/search/view_doc.asp?symbol=A/CONF.197/9</u>

Vega-Vega, José-Luis, and Belén Bueno-Martínez. "Los programas intergeneracionales." José Buendía-Vidal (Comp.) *Envejecimiento y psicología de la salud.* Madrid: Siglo XXI, 1998. 399-409.

World Health Organisation (WHO). *World report on ageing and health.* Geneva: World Health Organisation, 2015.

A Space to Grow Old In

Place Identity in Doris Lessing's *The Diary of a Good Neighbour* (1983)

María del Rocío González-Torres
University of Málaga (Spain)

The field of British fiction over the last years has addressed old age in order to show the reader a reality that is not foreign to any of us. Indeed, our experiences of old age are not reduced to our own coming-of-age, but they also comprise the interaction with members of our family, beloved ones, and people we know. As much as social structures diminish the role of the elder in society and relegate them to be passive members, it is of vital importance to give voice to the process of ageing that every person experiences from the moment we are born. Ageism has spread a negative discourse in the field of ageing narrative, where old peoples' narratives are oriented towards rememorizing their past instead of either living their present or reimagining their future. Therefore, ageing is feared instead of accepted, and much of the context that surrounds the elderly individual is neglected. However, attention to the process of ageing has proliferated over the past few decades, and revised perceptions and attitudes are starting to have an impact on the image and identity of the elderly person, not only in terms of its inherent susceptibility to frailty, but also in terms of its potential to salve the dilemmas of those individuals of the more youthful generations who live with the anxiety of their own process of growing old.

It is interesting to observe that most of the writers who nowadays address ageing in their narratives are women, probably because, as Tavengwa M. Nhongo observes,

> (a)n ageing world is predominantly a woman's world. Research has shown that as populations continue to age, women are the survivors, outliving their male counterparts who are more likely to suffer from specific deadly conditions such as lung and prostate cancers, heart diseases, and strokes.[1]

---

[1] Tavengwa M. Nhongo. "Preface." Brian J. Worsfold. Ed. *Women Ageing Through Literature and Experience*. (Lleida: Edicions i Publicacions de la Universitat de Lleida, 2005). viii.

Besides, women are not only outliving the male ageing population, but also face the challenges of social- and economic-injustice which affect lower-class women. Cynthia Port observes that longevity is…

> problematic for women, who generally live longer and are usually poorer, having been paid less for their work and often employed in the unpaid labour of caretaking and housekeeping.[2]

However, the main object of discontent is most frequently to be found in the body, which remains the troubling spot for cultures that emphasise an idealization of it.

* * *

Novels that delve into the realms of old age are divided into two different kinds of narratives. Age-critic Margaret Morganroth Gullette has labelled these 'narratives of decline' and 'narratives of progress.'[3] The main contribution of these fictionalisations is to construct new ageing identities that, in some cases, break the stereotypes proposed by society, or contribute to raising reader-awareness towards issues that were previously unconsidered.

Margaret Gullette states that "once you've lived long enough, an identity story is always a story of aging."[4] This idea fits in with William Randall and Gary Kenyon's statement when they say that,

> making stories is how we make meaning, which means that it is central to how we learn, how we interact with others, how we experience our gender and culture, and most important for our purposes here, how we grow old.[5]

---

[2] Cynthia Port. "None of it adds up: Economies of Aging in Doris Lessing's *The Diary of a Good Neighbor*." Brian J. Worsfold. Ed. *The Art of Ageing: Textualizing the Phases of Life*. (Lleida: Edicions i Publicacions de la Universitat de Lleida, 2005). 116.

[3] See Margaret Morganroth Gullette. *Aged by Culture*. (London: University of Chicago Press, 2004).

[4] Margaret Morganroth Gullette. *Aged by Culture*. (London: University of Chicago Press, 2004). 122.

[5] William L. Randall, and Gary M. Kenyon. "Time Story, and Wisdom: Emerging Themes in Narrative Gerontology." *Canadian Journal on Aging*. 23. 4, 2004. 334.

In most of the cases, the elderly person is deprived of the opportunity to explore later life due to the powerful influence culture has on us. Therefore, in the development of ageing identities there is a need to realise that individuals have the capacity to reformulate old age, change the narratives of their lives, and "tell about one's self, to self and others, whether informally in conversation or written for archival purposes."[6]

Along with this idea of ageing identity that recapitulates former selves in dynamic and fluid processes, the role of *the house* is of great value in the narrative representation of elderly persons, since it is in *the home* where they dwell and store most of their precious memories. Nonetheless, recent fiction about ageing tends to portray the home of the elderly individual simply as a location, but not as a reflection of the owner's sense of identity in the world. Indeed, the symbolism of *the house* reflects the persona. Clare Cooper Marcus states that,

> a home fulfils many needs: a place of self-expression, a vessel of memories, a refuge from the world, a cocoon where we can feel nurtured and let down our guard.[7]

Therefore, just as there is a need to reaffirm age identity in the memory of loved ones and in important events, attention must also be given to geographical location as provider of identity. As has been explored in the field of environmental psychology, phenomenology of space, and architecture, the way a person transforms 'space' into 'place' is closely related to that individual's capacity to give sense to her or his experience, such that raw space evolves into a defined structure that meets the human need for the substantiation of what is unknown and indefinite into more concrete forms. Yi-Fu Tuan asserts how, even though...

> space and place are basic components of the lived world; we take them for granted. When we think about them, however, [we] may assume unexpected meanings and raise questions we have not thought to ask.[8]

---

[6] Margaret Morganroth Gullette. *Aged by Culture.* (London: University of Chicago Press, 2004). 124.

[7] Clare Cooper Marcus. *House as a Mirror of the Self: Exploring the Deeper Meaning of Home.* (Berwick, Maine: Nicolas-Hays, 1995). 2.

[8] Yi-Fu Tuan. *Space and Place: The Perspective of Experience.* (Minnesota: University of Minnesota Press, 2001). 3.

The meaning of 'place' is bound in most cases to a person's capacity to engage emotionally with the material world. Thus, as Gerald Kyle, Alan Graefe, Robert Manning, and James Bacon state, there is a need to take into consideration that,

> places are more than geographic settings with definitive physical and textual characteristics; they are fluid, changeable, dynamic contexts of social interaction and memory.[9]

The aim of this paper, therefore, is to analyse place-identity in the persona of Maudie Fowler, a 90-year-old woman who lives alone in a rented apartment, the elderly protagonist of the novel *The Diary of a Good Neighbour* (1983) by the British novelist Doris Lessing.

* * *

Judging from her own words spoken in an interview with Thomas Frick and published in *The Paris Review*, Doris Lessing "sees every book as a problem that you have to solve."[10] Ageing is viewed in her narrative from a feminist standpoint, where the world is deconstructed from "female subjectivity, an issue that is foundational to much feminist theory," and which still needs to be dealt with.[11] As Debrah Raschke, Phyllis Sternberg Perrakis, and Sandra Singer assert,

> Lessing's fiction and nonfiction demand a reformulation of some of our most taken-for-granted assumptions about the contemporary world and how we relate to that world.[12]

Doris Lessing presents the topic of old age in *The Diary of a Good Neighbour* (1983) as a reality that the reader needs to reflect upon.[13] Certainly, this

---

[9] Gerard Kyle, Alan Graefe, Robert Manning, and James Bacon. "Effects of Place Attachment on Users' Perceptions of Social and Environmental Conditions in a Natural Setting." *Journal of Environmental Psychology*. 24. 2, 2004. 213.

[10] Thomas Frick. "Doris Lessing, The Art of Fiction No. 102." *The Paris Review*. 106, 1988. 7.

[11] Debrah Raschke, Phyllis Sternberg Perrakis, and Sandra Singer. Eds. *Doris Lessing: Interrogating the Times*. (Ohio: Ohio State University Press, 2010). 2.

[12] Debrah Raschke, Phyllis Sternberg Perrakis, and Sandra Singer. Eds. *Doris Lessing: Interrogating the Times*. (Ohio: Ohio State University Press, 2010). 1.

[13] Doris Lessing (1919-2013) was 64 years old when *The Diary of a Good Neighbour* (1983) was first published.

process of reflection on the coming-of-age, the politics of care, and the role of the elderly individual in socio-economic structures that leave persons like Maudie Fowler unprotected and vulnerable, is made possible through the character of Janna, a successful attractive woman who is into fashion and comfort, a character with whom the reader can connect emotionally and empathise with the fears and insecurities of a person like her. However, Janna has learnt to look at the world through eyes that see its beauty and are blind to its ugliness. When she decides to befriend Maudie Fowler, this friendship will instigate a change in the moral growth of Janna, such that she will learn to look at the world differently:

> Before a few weeks ago, I did not see old people at all. My eyes were pulled towards, and I saw, the young, the attractive, the well-dressed and handsome. And now it is as if a transparency has been drawn across that former picture and there, all at once, are the old, the infirm. (*The Diary of a Good Neighbour* 1983: 20)

The visibility of Maudie Fowler is perceived in its fullness when Janna enters Maudie's house. Essentially, this is because elderly persons tend to develop a strong connection with their *home*. Doris Lessing grasps the complexity of this relationship, and she uses the metaphor of domestic space to reflect upon the role of the *house* in the construction of ageing identities.

* * *

In 1978, Harold M. Proshansky coined the term *place identity*.[14] In a subsequent article in *Journal of Environmental Psychology* (1996), Clare L. Twigger-Ross and David L. Uzzell analyse how Proshansky's theory...

> proposes that place identity is another aspect of identity comparable to social identity that describes the person's socialization with the physical world.[15]

Harold M. Proshansky, Abbe K. Fabian, and Robert Kaminoff consider that *place identity* is not founded uniquely on the ground of routine, but that it is also based on past memories, in particular 'the environmental past' of the

---

[14] See Harold M. Proshansky, Abbe K. Fabian, and Robert Kaminoff. "Place-Identity: Physical World Socialization of the Self." *Journal of Environmental Psychology*. 3. 1, 1983. 57-83.

[15] Clare L. Twigger-Ross, and David L. Uzzell. "Place and Identity Processes." *Journal of Environmental Psychology*. 16. 3, 1996. 206.

person – a past consisting of places, spaces, and their properties which have served instrumentally in the satisfaction of the person's biological, psychological, social, and cultural needs.[16] For this reason, Maudie Fowler's sense of identity is based not only on the physical occupation of her house, which is the result of years of saving up to pay her rent, but also on a past of scarcity and struggles. So, the *house* is not valued merely on the basis of the comfort it brings, which in Maudie's circumstances is limited owing to her low income:

> She is cold now, summer or not. She sits in that old chair of hers, by the cold grate and feels the heat leaking out of her. She has to get the fire made. Should she plug in the heater? But it takes so much electricity, she is only just balancing her needs with her pension. (*The Diary of a Good Neighbour* 1983: 120)

In his article "Accumulated Lives: Metaphor, Materiality, and the Homes of the Elderly," James Krasner observes that,

> gerontologists who study place attachment among the elderly address the complex relationships between self, space, and habit when elders identify with their homes.[17]

Furthermore, it has been argued that the house functions as 'a container of accumulated experiences,' and 'a shelter for private and personal retreat,' which, in most cases, is associated with a restriction in mobility that ends in what Krasner refers to as "environmental centralization" (Krasner 2005: 215). This centralization occurs when…

> the elder often establishes a central location, such as the kitchen table or living room sofa, and cease to utilize more peripheral rooms of the house.[18]

---

[16] See Harold M. Proshansky, Abbe K. Fabian, and Robert Kaminoff. "Place-Identity: Physical World Socialization of the Self." *Journal of Environmental Psychology*. 3. 1, 1983. 59.

[17] James Krasner. "Accumulated Lives: Metaphor, Materiality, and the Homes of the Elderly." *Literature and Medicine*. 24. 2, 2005. 210.

[18] James Krasner. "Accumulated Lives: Metaphor, Materiality, and the Homes of the Elderly." *Literature and Medicine*. 24. 2, 2005. 215.

Maudie Fowler's behaviour exemplifies this centralization, as she uses only those parts of the house that are necessary for her daily routine of eating, warming up, and sleeping. Janna observes this centralization not only through Maudie's use of space, but also through the alteration of Maudie's cleaning routine:

> Even now she does her own chimney once a week, and then scrubs the grate, brushes up the dust and cinders – though less and less thoroughly. She wasn't feeling well, and didn't bother, once, twice – and then her room was not really cleaned, only the floor in the middle of the room sometimes, and she learned not to look around the edges or under the bed. (*The Diary of a Good Neighbour* 1983: 55)

Consequently, as Juan I. Aragonés, María Amérigo, and Raquel Pérez-López state in their article "Perception of Personal Identity at Home,"

> the home is conceived as an affirmation of identity through a common symbolic language and as a vehicle to express identity through the manipulation of its outward appearance.[19]

Maudie Fowler's *place identity* has strengthened over the years, and it reaches a high level of attachment when Maudie keeps hold of her apartment despite its inhospitality and the worsening of her health. As Janna describes, "it was all so dirty and dingy and grim and awful" (*The Diary of a Good Neighbour* 1983: 12) that it is hard to believe that someone could live in those conditions in a city like London.

* * *

The idea of leaving her apartment is recurrent and appealing to Maudie Fowler. She considers the possibility of living with Janna. Often, Maudie "drifts off into a dream that Janna has taken her into her own home and is looking after her" (*The Diary of a Good Neighbour* 1983: 120), but this is not what she really desires. Therefore, the idea of leaving her apartment is not lasting in her mind. As she reinforces the idea of owning one's own space over and over again, it turns into a kind of mantra she cannot get rid of: "Get yourself your own place and never let go of" (*The Diary of a Good*

---

[19] Juan I. Aragonés, María Amérigo, and Raquel Pérez-López. "Perception of Personal Identity at Home." *Psicothema*. 22. 4, 2010. 873.

Neighbour 1983: 120). Clare Cooper Marcus suggests that "the places themselves have a powerful effect on our journey to wholeness" (Marcus 1995: 8). They not only function as indicators of who we are or may become, but spaces contain deeper meanings of 'the self.'

In this analysis, it is Maudie Fowler's willingness to open her house to a stranger that allows the character to experience the warming embrace of a society that so often has turned its back on her. The political and social instability of England at the time has left a mark on her. The death of her mother when she was a child, and an unfortunate marriage to an abusive husband together are reinforcements for Maudie's attachment to her place and the development of an identity of being someone in the world by being in her own place. Partly for these reasons, Maudie's possessions, all contained in her rented apartment, are of great value to her. She is well acquainted with most of the things she has accumulated. The story behind every item of clothing – even dirty or unusable – are dear to her and convey a meaningful part of her bio-profile. Indeed,

> [when] faced with an unintentional loss of treasurable possessions, most people experience a profound sense of diminishing the self. Thus, when possessions are lost to theft, burglary, or natural disaster, many people go through an experience of grief, similar to losing a loved one.[20]

Moreover, it can be added that the house in the novel *The Diary of a Good Neighbour* (1983) not only symbolizes material possession in itself, but a prolongation of 'the self.' As mentioned above, Janna often establishes comparisons between two occurrences – the deterioration of the house and the progressive physical decline of Maudie. Along with its occupant, the place has aged as well and, compared with new constructions, it is obsolete and ready to be demolished. Janna reads Maudie's physical environment and the non-verbal symbols of Maudie's place, and compares them with the comfort of her own apartment. She also observes Maudie's body and foresees in it the destiny of her own. In fact, 'the young' *fear* 'the old' because any comparison tends towards raising awareness of their own process of ageing. Recognition of the role of location for the elderly person as a projection of her or his identity is essential in order to understand that possessions need to be kept in a space that the owner has some control over.

---

[20] Clare Cooper Marcus. *House as a Mirror of the Self: Exploring the Deeper Meaning of Home*. (Berwick, Maine: Nicolas-Hays, 1995). 239.

As Åshild Lappegard Hauge claims, "a 'home' does not simply exist, but is made,"[21] and through this making we project our past and present.

When Doris Lessing is describing Maudie Fowler's place through the eyes of Janna, there is a change in the perception of both 'the house' and 'the elderly person.' As a symbiosis, presented to Janna as a reality that can be overlooked, only if we change the way we look and judge what we see can we start perceiving things differently as we do so. The act of judging 'the old' and their environment is a personal choice, an attitude of aversion to what we do not like, the ugliness of the unknown:

> I sat down in the chair opposite hers and saw the room, with the curtains drawn and the electric light, seemed quite cosy, not so dreadfully dirty and grim. But why do I go on about dirt like this? Why do we judge people like this? She was no worse off for the grime and the dust, and even the smells. I decided not to notice, if I could help it, not to keep judging her. (*The Diary of a Good Neighbour* 1983: 16)

* * *

This analysis of Doris Lessing's novel *The Diary of a Good Neighbour* (1983) focuses on how the ageing identity of the elderly persona is reflected in the place she or he occupies. The symbolisms of the house as explored here are innumerable, but, above all else, the function of conveying the 'meaning' of the elderly inhabitant is the most significant of all. Therefore, "dwelling as an expression of identity"[22] needs to be addressed in further research in the field of ageing studies. In most reviews, 'the house' is compared with a container of possessions, without taking into consideration how the way in which the person forges a bond with 'the space' will result in enhanced identification. This is not, however, to devalue the importance of possessions, a feature that has been extensively studied by Yi-Fu Tuan:

> Personal possessions are perhaps more important for old people. They are too weary to define their sense of self by projects and action: their social world shrinks and with it the opportunities to

---

[21] Åshild Lappegard Hauge. *Housing and Identity: The Meaning of Housing in Communicating Identity and its Influence on Self-Perception.* (Trondheim: Norwegian University of Science and Technology, 2009). 28.

[22] Åshild Lappegard Hauge. "Identity and Place: A Critical Comparison of Three Identity Theories." *Architectural Science Review.* 50. 1, 2007. 44.

proclaim fair deeds; and they may be too fragile to visit places that hold for them fond memories.[23]

As Margaret Moan Rowe asserts, "there are few contemporary writers who have dealt so powerfully with the taboo topic of growing old."[24] Doris Lessing's fictionalisation is a step forward in contemporary literature in that it confers visibility and gives voice to the realities of the vast sector of society that is the ageing population, and evaluates the multiple services that assist the elderly individual, such as "the good neighbour," "meals on wheels," and "home help." In Lessing's narrative, these social services are still "inadequate to the complexity and scope of the problems to be faced" (*The Diary of a Good Neighbour* 1983: 96). In concurrence with this line of thought, Susan L. Flinders asserts that "much of the struggle is culturally stimulated"[25] and that it is by reducing cultural pressure that the ageing person can be freed up to give a more meaningful perspective to her or his own process of ageing. Indeed, there is "often a struggling between a view toward living and a view toward death."[26] As has been exemplified through the characterizations of both women in this analysis, in the elderly Maudie Fowler the reader perceives the struggle of existence through her possessions and her environment, whereas, for the younger woman Janna, there is a process of personal growing that brings light to the shadow of growing old. This duality permeates Lessing's fictionalisation and proves that 'being old' goes well beyond the physical and mental act of having lived for a relatively long time, and is projected, as well, into the physicality of 'the house' – 'my home' – a space that is irrefutably impregnated with memories of a lifetime.

* * *

To conclude, it is relevant to this analysis of Doris Lessing's *The Diary of a Good Neighbour* (1983) to take into consideration that Lessing not only points to the importance of the role of the material environment as reflection of an elderly person's identity, and to how past and present identities converge in a process of coming-to-terms with being old at the present time, but her narrative implies the essential prerequisite of intergenerational

---

[23] Yi-Fu Tuan. *Space and Place: The Perspective of Experience.* (Minnesota: University of Minnesota Press, 2001). 187.

[24] Margaret Moan Rowe. *Doris Lessing.* (London: Palgrave Macmillan, 1994). 96.

[25] Susan L. Flinders. "The Internal Struggles of Aging." *Journal for the Psychoanalysis of Culture and Society.* 8. 2, 2003. 258.

[26] Susan L. Flinders. "The Internal Struggles of Aging." *Journal for the Psychoanalysis of Culture and Society.* 8. 2, 2003. 258.

linkage between middle- and late-age, what Barbara Frey Waxman has identified as a need to "foster linkage between middle age and old age."[27]

Furthermore, the use of domestic space and materiality symbolizes new ways in which generations can communicate with one another. The secret language of things is not foreign to any of us. The tendency to accumulate is almost compulsive in the last decades, but few are aware of the narrative of our acquisitions until we encounter the moment to reflect upon what we have and what part of ourselves echoes. Therefore, the emerging field of literature devoted to old age needs to deepen in issues that are restricted to the privacy of the elderly individual, and to unveil the emotional connections that they establish with their past, family members, and the place they dwell in. This need is rooted mainly in the fact that, if we are able to acknowledge this last stage of life, we will look into the homes of the elderly in full awareness of the conflicting scenario of being old in a culture that praises youth, constantly exalting its virtues. If Doris Lessing's character Janna finds redemption by interacting with an elderly woman as she embraces her own process of growing old, a variety of fictionalisations emerge for innovative representations of elderly persons, variations that provide new identities with which readers can empathise. Neither a negative nor a positive discourse, the realities behind the ageing process remain hidden within the realm of 'one's own home' and, simply by looking at both the person and her or his physical extension, that is, her or his 'space,' more authentic narratives about occurrences that lie ahead in life can be related. Moreover, such narratives are not centred uniquely on gradual physical and mental decline. Rather, they present an opportunity to decide on the nature of the narrative to be passed on to younger generations about what it means to be old, as well as to warn them of the influence that material culture exerts on the way we relate to objects and to our dear ones.

Works Cited

Aragonés, Juan I., María Amérigo, and Raquel Pérez-López. "Perception of Personal Identity at Home." *Psicothema*. 22. 4, 2010. 872-879.

Flinders, Susan L., "The Internal Struggles of Aging." *Journal for the Psychoanalysis of Culture and Society*. 8. 2, 2003. 258-262.

Frick, Thomas. "Doris Lessing, The Art of Fiction No. 102." *The Paris Review*. 106, 1988. [Interview]

---

[27] Barbara Frey Waxman. *From the Hearth to the Open Road: A Feminist Study of Aging in Contemporary Literature*. (Westport, Connecticut: Greenwood Press, 1990). 46.

<www.theparisreview.org/interviews/2537/doris-lessing-the-art-of-fiction-no-102-doris-lessing>

Gullette, Margaret Morganroth. *Aged by Culture*. London: University of Chicago Press, 2004.

Hauge, Åshild Lappegard. "Identity and Place: A Critical Comparison of Three Identity Theories." *Architectural Science Review*. 50. 1, 2007. 44-51.

—. *Housing and Identity: The Meaning of Housing in Communicating Identity and its Influence on Self-Perception*. Trondheim: Norwegian University of Science and Technology, 2009.

Krasner, James. "Accumulated Lives: Metaphor, Materiality, and the Homes of the Elderly." *Literature and Medicine*. 24. 2, 2005. 209-230.

Kyle, Gerard, Alan Graefe, Robert Manning, and James Bacon. "Effects of Place Attachment on Users' Perceptions of Social and Environmental Conditions in a Natural Setting." *Journal of Environmental Psychology*. 24. 2, 2004. 213-225.

Lessing, Doris. *The Diaries of Jane Somers*. London: Flamingo, 1983.

Marcus, Clare Cooper. *House as a Mirror of the Self: Exploring the Deeper Meaning of Home*. Berwick, Maine: Nicolas-Hays, 1995.

Nhongo, Tavengwa M. "Preface." Brian J. Worsfold. Ed. *Women Ageing Through Literature and Experience*. Lleida: Edicions i Publicacions de la Universitat de Lleida, 2005. vii- xii.

Port, Cynthia. "None of it adds up: Economies of Aging in Doris Lessing's *The Diary of a Good Neighbour*." Brian J. Worsfold. Ed. *The Art of Ageing: Textualizing the Phases of Life*. Lleida: Edicions i Publicacions de la Universitat de Lleida, 2005. 115-125.

Proshansky, Harold M., Abbe K. Fabian, and Robert Kaminoff. "Place-Identity: Physical World Socialization of the Self." *Journal of Environmental Psychology*. 3. 1, 1983. 57-83.

Randall, William L., and Gary M. Kenyon. "Time Story, and Wisdom: Emerging Themes in Narrative Gerontology." *Canadian Journal on Aging*. 23. 4, 2004. 333-346.

Raschke, Debrah, Phyllis Sternberg Perrakis, and Sandra Singer. Eds. *Doris Lessing: Interrogating the Times*. Ohio: Ohio State University Press, 2010.

Rowe, Margaret Moan. *Doris Lessing*. Basingstoke: Palgrave Macmillan, 1994.

Tuan, Yi-Fu. *Space and Place: The Perspective of Experience*. Minnesota: University of Minnesota Press, 2001.

Twigger-Ross, Clare L., and David L. Uzzell. "Place and Identity Processes." *Journal of Environmental Psychology*. 16. 3, 1996. 205-220.

Waxman, Barbara Frey. *From the Hearth to the Open Road: A Feminist Study of Aging in Contemporary Literature*. Westport, Connecticut: Greenwood Press, 1990.

Worsfold, Brian J. Ed. *Women Ageing Through Literature and Experience*. Lleida: Edicions i Publicacions de la Universitat de Lleida, 2005.

—. Ed. *The Art of Ageing: Textualizing the Phases of Life*. Lleida: Edicions i Publicacions de la Universitat de Lleida, 2005.

A Language to Age With

Browning's Rabbi, the Gerontologists, and the Aphorism

David Rampton

University of Ottawa

Aphorisms are brief, speculative, slightly subversive miniature works of literary art that simultaneously encourage and resist definition, formulations that readily stand by themselves yet open up large vistas for reflection. Although poetry may have partially ceded the aphoristic field to bestsellers and self-help books, it remains an important resource for propounding and confounding conventional wisdom. In part, this is because as soon as we begin to think of the aphorisms that have become common currency, the ones that give a local habitation and a name to abstractions of various kinds, rhythm and rhyme can make them easier to recall. In *Hamlet*, for example, we are told "This above all – to thine own self be true / …Thou canst not then be false to any man."[1] Here, we feel, is an insight phrased in a drumbeat of monosyllabic inevitability, an aphorism that retains its cutting edge, one that will help us navigate in the world of Shakespeare's play and in our own lives. Wordsworth says in "Tintern Abbey" that "Nature never did betray / The heart that loved her."[2] The idea that we are only a walk in the woods or a ravishing sunset away from the tantalizing sense of the transcendent is always reassuring for those in search of spiritual sustenance. Robert Frost's "Good fences make good neighbours,"[3] cited practically every time someone muses about walling something in or out, signals convincingly our rage for order and need for certain kinds of private space. The forthright, deliberately provocative, somewhat elusive, vaguely admonitory quality of such aphorisms stands out in clear relief.

---

[1] William Shakespeare. *Hamlet*. (The Riverside Shakespeare. Boston: Houghton Mifflin, 1974). 1.3.78-80.

[2] William Wordsworth. "Lines Composed a Few Miles above Tintern Abbey." *The Norton Anthology of English Literature*. 9th ed. (New York and London: Norton, 2012). 291.

[3] Robert Frost. "Mending Wall." Nina Baym, *et al.* Eds. *The Norton Anthology of American Literature*. 8th edition. (New York and London: W.W. Norton, 2013). 1913.

The problems with such sayings, when we go to poetry to find them, or rummage around in the recesses of our brains to recall them, is that they tend to leave out a lot. They offer a quick, inspirational fix to a problem, but no programme the reader might use to resolve the existential dilemmas they hint at. In addition, the ambiguities raised by questions such as who is speaking, who is being addressed, and how are the ideas espoused affected by their context, tend to render difficult our attempts to unpack them.

Look again at the three examples just cited. Quoting Shakespeare's Polonius on how we should conduct ourselves is all very well, we may conclude, but he is a sneak, a windbag, and a scandal-monger – someone who approves of using his daughter as a kind of sexual bait for the play's moody hero. His pompous pronouncements, it might be claimed, are a tedious compendium of attempts to browbeat the younger generation. Likewise, Wordsworth's sentiments are poignant and evocative, but his denial of nature's capacity for betrayal is pure wishful thinking on his part. In his "Intimations Ode," written just a few years after "Tintern Abbey," he devastatingly admits that though "nothing can bring back the hour / Of splendour in the grass, of glory in the flower; / We will grieve not rather find / Strength in what remains behind."[4] That is so gorgeously written we do not want to believe it. Yet the lines make clear that Wordsworth is simply too honest to pretend that nature can function as a source of permanent solace. It is impossible for him to feel as deeply now as he once did, and he sees growing old as a loss of imaginative autonomy.

Inter alia, Wordsworth's poetry is full of insightful and unflinching observations about ageing. So, too, the excerpt from the poem by Robert Frost. As a number of critics have pointed out, the actual energies of "Mending Wall" are directed against the proposition everybody associates with it. The hopelessly-benighted neighbour keeps repeating the crucial phrase like a mantra, but the speaker who narrates the incident cannot stop wondering how wise and how necessary it is to build such barriers, whether or not there are different sorts of "good" at work here. In the process, he characterizes his neighbour as an "old stone savage armed," a throwback to a less civilized world, someone who has grown old, but learned nothing.

So, aphorisms often draw on, contribute to, and sometimes undermine our collective wisdom, particularly concerning the subjects of time passing, human strengths, and human frailties, and the effort to wrest

---

[4] William Wordsworth. "Ode: Intimations of Immortality from Recollections of Early Childhood." *The Norton Anthology of English Literature*. 9th edition. (New York and London: Norton, 2012). 341.

some notion of meaning from the struggle with our mortality, a mortality that often seems to be working hard to deny any such meaning. Moreover, although aphorisms tend to hang out in the literary safe havens mentioned above, it is interesting to note that they got their start in the world of medicine. As John Gross reminds us, the earliest ones "were a collection of brief medical teachings and sayings by Hippocrates, and when the term was revived in the Renaissance it initially looked back to its scientific origins."[5] Ten minutes with his maxims are enough for us to see how often Hippocrates is animated by an urge to say comforting things about the ravages wrought by disease, including time passing. The uneasy aphoristic authority of such observations is bound up with discussions of ageing from the outset.

In this chapter, I argue that, despite their rhetorical usefulness and capacity for synthesis, literary aphorisms, however much we like to invoke them as ultimate authorities on universal questions, are actually better seen as providing an opportunity to reflect further on the complex issues they raise. They should be read as contributions to a discourse, rather than as universal insights for the enlightened. Like other ethical recommendations in the books we read, their cognitive content may be qualified by any number of factors: the dramatic situation of the speaker, ironic gaps between things said and deeds done, uncertainties on the part of the poet, and the messiness of life itself. Furthermore, those complications may be the most essential thing about these texts. The work of art in which such precepts are tested is often quite a bit more interesting than the sum of its wise pronouncements.

* * *

In what follows I have concentrated on the use of a single saying in a poem by Robert Browning (1812-1889). Browning's verse is helpful for our purposes because he is both a distinctive voice and a representative one. A poet with a huge popular following – Browning societies were established in England years before he died and by the end of the nineteenth century numbered in the hundreds – he is someone whose works still belongs definitively to the canon. The problems set, for him and the Victorians, by increasing longevity and the responses it elicited, anticipate our current concerns. A society that was self-consciously building democracy, worrying about the effects of the industrial revolution, debating with science about whither Darwinian insight would take them, defining the terms of the "Woman Question," dealing with the consequences of making education

---

[5] John Gross. "Introduction." John Gross. Ed. *The Oxford Book of Aphorisms*. (Oxford and New York: Oxford University Press, 1983). vii.

obligatory, secular, and free, and contemplating significant increases in longevity – all these make Victorian England the country that first defined in comprehensive fashion the problems that we are still trying to resolve today.

The aphorism in question is from Browning's poem "Rabbi Ben Ezra."[6] The first few lines of the poem read as follows:

> Grow old along with me!
> The best is yet to be,
> The last of life, for which the first was made."[7]

Discussions of ageing include more references to this text than any other. A survey of how it has been invoked will help us see why.

In articles published at the end of the nineteenth century, Browning's lines are sometimes quoted as simply an upbeat antidote to a gloomier view, a hortatory note to sound at the end of an article that may have had a quite specific medical focus. An example: Dr Isaac N. Kerlin, in an 1891 address on the occasion of his retirement, discussed the dangers created by a new American demographic. He announced that there had been "a steady relative increase in the proportion of idiocy and imbecility" in America's population, and more specifically a 228% increase of "imbeciles of foreign birth," notwithstanding limits on immigration and "the efforts to prevent the introduction of defectives from foreign ports."[8] Kerlin went on to become a powerful spokesperson for institutionalizing such people and using eugenics to be rid of them permanently. He concludes his address with the first lines of Browning's poem to exhort his listeners to carry on the great struggle.

Other doctors in America, doubtful about humanity's ability to make good use of the longer lives they were leading, sounded a different sort of cautionary note. As reported in a 1958 article on ageing, a general practitioner named Hazen, is quoted as saying that medicine had "increased the viability of the human carcass," but failed to effect "a corresponding gain for the human spirit." The article's author, a Classics professor named Josiah Partridge, goes on to say that he is unimpressed by Robert Browning's take on ageing in this poem. Partridge cites the famous lines, and says:

---

[6] Robert Browning's "Rabbi Ben Ezra" is a poem from the collection *Dramatis Personae*, published in 1864.

[7] Robert Browning. "Rabbi Ben Ezra." Walter E. Houghton, and G. Robert Stange, Eds. *Victorian Poetry and Poetics*. (Boston: Houghton Mifflin, 1968). 282.

[8] Isaac N. Kerlin. "President's Annual Address." Association of Medical Officers of American Institutions for Idiotic and Feeble-Minded Persons. 274.

This quotation has always been distasteful to me. Browning's sentiment struck me as a piece of cheerleader optimism, artificially worked up in the final stages of a losing game. I much preferred Cicero's calm stoicism in accepting the inevitable, and I mentioned a passage in *De Senectute* in which he says, in substance, 'I feel that I am nearing the end of my stay at an inn and shall soon be continuing my journey.' (Partridge 1958: 607)

Partridge may be right to single out the hortatory quality of the poem, but what is not so certain is the appropriateness of his reference to "final stages of a losing game." Browning was 52 years old when he published "Rabbi Ben Ezra" in 1864 – he was to live another twenty-five years – and his Rabbi wrote his most important work, a full commentary on the Torah, just before he died at the age of seventy-five. The stoicism manifest in the Rabbi's monologue seems as calm as Cicero's, especially in the exploration of its ramifications. They are both champions of intellectual clarity, both aware of death's inevitability, both eager to embrace what life is left to them.

Other semi-sceptical medical reactions to Browning's proposition abound. In his article "Physiological and Clinical Considerations of Geriatric Patient Care,"[9] Dr Robert M. Kaiser, a Washington DC geriatrician, claims that Rabbi Ben Ezra's optimism is a problem:

One might endorse Browning's belief that human relationships become deeper and richer with time, but the inevitability of physiological decline is also a reality that all humans must face as they age" (Kaiser 2015: 32)

For his part, Dr William Kissick, an expert on health policy and the costs of Medicare, insists that "Browning's confidence would be hard to justify today."[10] Along the same lines, a much-cited article by Dr James F. Childress entitled "Ensuring Care, Respect and Fairness for the Elderly," begins by denying the conviction that "the best is yet to be ... in part because of both the success and the failures of medicine and health care."[11] He goes on to

---

[9] Robert M. Kaiser. "Physiological and Clinical Considerations of Geriatric Patient Care." David C. Steffens, Dan G. Blazer, and Mugdha E. Thakur. Eds. *The American Psychiatric Publishing Textbook of Geriatric Psychiatry.* 2015.
[10] Robert Kissick. *Medicine's Dilemmas: Infinite Needs Versus Finite Resources.* (New Haven: Yale University Press, 1994). 14.
[11] James F. Childress. "Ensuring Care, Respect and Fairness for the Elderly." *The Hastings Center Report.* 14. 5 (Oct. 1984). 27.

advocate a renewed interest in fairness, given the temptation to deprive the old of expensive treatments so as to concentrate medical resources on those with longer to live. In a similar spirit, Dr Adair Stuart Mason quotes the first lines of Browning's famous affirmation, saying: "The rest of this somewhat tedious poem does not illuminate the optimism of the first line. The best may come at any age and go and come again."[12]

If the "nay" side is confident, eclectic, mindful of Browning's usefulness but wary of his gratuitous optimism, the "ayes" are equally diverse, convinced, and keen to talk specifics. A cursory look at another, more positive set of responses will help put things into perspective. We can start with R.S. Allison, who in 1952 wrote an article called "Psychiatric Disorders in Later Life" that appeared in the *British Medical Journal*.[13] At the time, Allison was in charge of the Neurological Department at the Royal Victoria Hospital, Belfast. After quoting the poem, he writes:

> As Robert Browning's words imply, it is probable that psychogenic factors causing simple anxiety and hysterical reactions play less part in later life than they do at earlier ages. (Allison 1952: 1286)

It is clear that, in Allison's view, Browning has important psychological insights to convey, that medical practitioners can benefit from thinking about them, and that for him literature must do more than give simple pleasure.

If we turn to the social sciences, it is interesting to note that America's most important twentieth-century philosopher, John Dewey, has interesting things to say about the opening lines of this oft-quoted poem.[14] Dewey proposes a more nuanced view of the Rabbi's pronouncement in his response to the poem's first lines:

> That there should be a gradual wearing down of energies, physical and mental, in the old age period it is reasonable to expect upon biological grounds. That maturing changes, at some particular age, into incapacity for continual growth in every direction is a very different proposition. We may not be able to affirm with the poet…

---

[12] Adair Stuart Mason. *'Wasn't it Exciting!': A Compilation of the Work of A. Stuart Mason.* (Sudbury, Suffolk: Lavenham Press, 2004). 32.

[13] See R.S. Allison. "Psychiatric Disorders in Later Life." *British Medical Journal.* 13 (Dec 1952). 1286-1289.

[14] See Jo Ann Boydston. Ed. *John Dewey. The Later Works, 1925-53: Volume 14, 1929-41.* (Carbondale: Southern Illinois University Press, 1988).

> Grow old along with me
> The best is yet to be,

> But there is something abnormal in the situation if we are obliged to admit that after a certain period nothing *better* in any direction, individual or social, can occur because of the process of growing old. (Boydston. Ed. 1988: 348)

Furthermore, along this more nuanced vein, J. Kenneth Brubaker, a Pennsylvanian gerontologist, uses Browning in the introduction of an article devoted to the rapidly-developing field of geriatric medicine.[15] He not only quotes the poem to strike an uplifting note, but also makes it a central part of his argument. Reminding his readers that life expectancy in America increased dramatically in the nineteenth century, Brubaker uses Browning to draw our attention to the idea that we have already been the beneficiaries of a medical revolution, that the best that is "yet to be" has also already been. Then there is Paola Timiras, a distinguished physician best known for the textbooks he has published in the field of geriatric medicine.[16] He concludes with a similar point, updated for the twenty-first century, about the power of any text that denies despair:

> In this quarter of a new century, we have every reason to rejoice in the vigorous declaration of the nineteenth-century English poet, Robert Browning" (Timiras. Ed. 2007: iii)

He then goes on to quote the lines in question.

Robert Browning's poetic meditation on ageing has also inspired some interesting twenty-first century counterparts. An excellent example is Dr Danielle Ofri's *Singular Intimacies*, in which she records her encounter with Browning's poem in an unusual but very revealing setting, the garden of the Bellevue hospital where she works.[17] One day she reads Browning's aphorism on a sundial that she has passed many times, without ever really looking at it. Ofri says that the makers of this clock, less informative than it was because it has no shadow stick, substituted Browning's "Grow old …"

---

[15] See J. Kenneth Brubaker. "The Birth of a New Speciality: Geriatrics." *The Journal of Lancaster General Hospital.* 3 (Fall 2008).

[16] Paolo Timiras. Ed. *Physiological Basis of Aging and Geriatrics.* 4th edition. (Boca Raton, FL: CRC Press, 2007).

[17] Danielle Ofri. *Singular Intimacies: Becoming a Doctor at Bellevue.* (Boston: Beacon Press, 2003). 240.

for the numbers of the hours that normally adorn the face of the dial. Now an aesthetic object, the sundial puts Ofri into a reverie about time passing. The inclusion of this non-verbal work of art in a verbal one invites us to think about its ekphratic status. Like Keats's urn,[18] this inscription and the sundial slow things down, offer important advice, tell the paradoxical truth about time passing, and remind us in salutary fashion of our own mortality. The point of the episode is Ofri's suggestion that savouring the present can make a future promise realizable in the here and now.

* * *

Such lists could be continued indefinitely, but this brief survey will have performed its task if it has convinced the reader that Browning's aphorism is ubiquitous enough to win the "most frequently used literary allusion in medicine" award, and ambiguous enough to be read in an impressive range of different ways. Now I want to look in detail at an article in which all of the issues discussed above come together.

Reviewing a 2010 collection of essays edited by Janice E. Graham and Peter H. Stephenson entitled *Contesting Aging & Loss*,[19] Dr Mark Clarfield divides up gerontologists into two groups, poets versus pathologists.[20] He argues that the former...

> consider the phenomenon of aging as a part of life, a normal stage in human development, and often portray it as a positive process. For example, those who hold such views will characteristically quote the English poet Robert Browning: "Grow old along with me! The best is yet to be, the last of life, for which the first was made." If the poets tend to be purveyors of the social sciences, for their part the pathologists are usually doctors or biologists. As far as they can see, aging is a negative process resulting in an increase in biological entropy, decreased reserve, a higher chance of illness and ultimately death. That being said, their laureate is of no less distinguished lineage, with Shakespeare outlining "Last scene of all, That ends this strange eventful history. ... Sans teeth, sans eyes, sans taste, sans everything."

---

[18] John Keats. "Ode on a Grecian Urn."

[19] Janice E. Graham, and Peter H. Stephenson. Eds. *Contesting Aging & Loss*. Toronto: University of Toronto Press, 2010.

[20] A. Mark Clarfield. "Grow old along with me! The best is yet to be." *Review of Janice E. Graham, and Peter H. Stephenson. Eds.* Contesting Aging & Loss. *University of Toronto Press. Canadian Medical Association Journal.* (July 12th) 2011. 183 (10).

As we saw at the outset, Shakespeare can be tricky to use as evidence in such an instance. The famous "Seven ages of man" speech, the end of which is quoted here by Clarfield, is taken from Act II of *As You Like It*.[21] It is certainly a gloomy and reductive view of the entire human drama, a body snatcher's view, but is it Shakespeare's? In the same play, we read that "Sweet are the uses of adversity," and that a group of stalwart citizens, unjustly banished to the woods, love their new bucolic surroundings, where they have found "tongues in trees, books in the running brooks, / Sermons in stones and good in everything."[22] It is also worth noting that Jaques, the character who offers this sceptical, materialistic "sans teeth" take on the end of human life, is a perpetual malcontent who manages to alienate himself from everyone. Meanwhile, the other characters are having a great time helping the old and infirm, learning from harsh trials, and banding together for the common good. Venerable adage and represented reality seem to have parted company. There is even a very old man called Adam who makes a cameo appearance. When he is brought on stage, the play makes clear that our society is going to be judged by how we treat old people, by how we understand our mortality and its implications.

Clarfield's larger claim, that one can treat those interested in gerontology as members of two jumbo groups, each "warring" with the other, is equally fraught. Using this capacious binary, where are we going to put multi-faceted figures like Atul Gawande[23] or Tom Kirkwood?[24] Are not they doctors dedicated to medical research, cautiously upbeat proponents of longer and more meaningful life spans, and the human face of medical science and its attempts to understand ageing as a process? What evidence do we see in their work that reveals the "natural tendency to ageism" that

---

[21] See William Shakespeare. *As You Like It* (1599). (The Riverside Shakespeare. Boston: Houghton Mifflin, 1974).

[22] William Shakespeare. *As You Like It*. 2.1.16-17.

[23] Atul Gawande (1965-), writer and public health researcher, is a practicing surgeon at Brigham and Women's Hospital in Boston, Massachusetts. He is also affiliated to the Harvard T.H. Chan School of Public Health and the Harvard Medical School. He is Executive Director of Ariadne Labs, and Chairman of Lifebox, a non-profit organisation that works on reducing deaths in surgery.

[24] Thomas Burton Loram Kirkwood CBE FMedSci (1951-) is a biologist. Now retired, he has been Associate Dean for Ageing at Newcastle University (England), and has directed the Institute for Ageing and Health at the University's School of Clinical Medical Sciences. He is still affiliated currently with the University of Newcastle and the University of Copenhagen (Denmark). He is the author of *Time of Our Lives: The Science of Human Aging* (1999), *The End of Age: Why Everything About Aging Is Changing* (2001), and co-author, with Caleb E. Finch, of *Chance, Development, and Aging* (2000).

Clarfield says typically animates his clinically-minded colleagues? Conversely, how monolithic is the discussion of ageing by those in the humanities? Does Helen Small, for example, the author of *The Long Life*,[25] have a somewhat starry-eyed view of ageing, given her work on ageing from a humanities perspective? But if that is so, why does she conclude her book with a chapter that examines "the evolutionary theory of senescence" to see if we should "revise our assumptions of what is 'natural' for us in old age" (Small 2007: 271)? Her commentary on ethical evolution, cellular biology, and science as an object of satire suggests that Clarfield's characterization of writers interested in ageing runs the risk of becoming a caricature. Karen Chase, who teaches in the English Department at the University of Virginia, discusses in her book on ageing[26] the influence of Charcot's *Clinical Lectures*, cites the *Lancet* and the *British Medical Journal*, and argues that "cultural and scientific representation [of ageing] need to be brought more closely together (Chase 2009: 102)." No yawning culture gaps for her. In *Aging by the Book. The Emergence of Midlife in Victorian Britain*,[27] Kay Heath refuses to accept what she calls the master narrative that "equates deterioration with ageing," yet she worries about a society "rushing with plugged ears to the next new thing in age prevention" (Heath 2009: 202); that is, she refuses to be defined by the biological-social antithesis that Clarfield argues for. And then there are all the nuanced and varied positions taken by the array of authorities these writers include in their bibliographies and indexes, writers convinced that humanity is neither marching avidly towards a far-off divine event that will help us live as long as Lamech,[28] nor doomed to an inexorable decline over a pre-determined time. The literary wisdom cited by Clarfield when he quotes Browning and Shakespeare tempts him to misrepresent the area in which he himself is a specialist.

It would seem that aphoristic poets enjoy playing a range of roles and encouraging a range of responses. When Robert Browning ventriloquizes a 12th-century Hebrew scholar in order to convey a recipe for enlightened longevity, he resorts to aphorisms, in part because in real life Rabbi Abraham ibn Ezra was a grammarian who liked to use them in his own work. But Browning has also structured his poem so that it turns on a paradoxical proverb, namely that life succeeds when it fails. Of course, this

---

[25] Helen Small. *The Long Life*. (Oxford: Oxford University Press, 2007).

[26] Karen Chase. *The Victorians and Old Age*. (Oxford: Oxford University Press, 2009).

[27] Kay Heath. *Aging by the Book: The Emergence of Midlife in Victorian Britain*. (Albany: State University of New York, 2009).

[28] *Genesis* 5: 28-31 records that Lamech, the son of Methuselah and the father of Noah, was 777 years old when he died.

comes from the same language family as "Grow old along with me," but is a more mysterious proposition. For the Rabbi goes on to say:

> What I aspired to be,
> And was not, comforts me:
> A brute I might have been, but would not sink i' the scale."[29]

And he has aspired a lot: anyone who uses astrology's intricate structures to annotate passages in the Bible has his work cut out for him. Teasing out the rational that is intricately bound up with the revelatory means reading the world carefully and incessantly. Setting out to discover God's plan, which the Rabbi announces in the first sentence of the poem, means working a lot of late nights.

Browning's speaker abandons the search for a Pollyanna path to ultimate fulfilment by announcing that there is no such path. On earth, our joys are "three parts pain," particularly now that we are relatively old, but the battle with such pains ennobles us. Losing the battle makes us the *de jure* winner by dint of all our heroic striving. We start to see how the "Grow old along with me" formulation in "Rabbi Ben Ezra" is misleading in more ways than one: it points to what sounds like cosy comfort while it actually announces a period of prolonged engagement with the pain of deterioration. Browning's poem can be read as a paean to the languorous prospects of "Freedom 55"[30] in perpetuity, yet it insists that striving, not relaxing, is the most difficult and the most important thing human beings do. We must, implies Browning, wait for old age and beyond precisely by not waiting, by acting now, and by displaying our energy and our resolve in a world that conflates the future and the past in the present moment. Towards the end of the poem the speaker is particularly scathing about those who advocate some sort of *Carpe diem*, because for him the past is eternally present. Immersing ourselves in the past is a stay against its rushing past us. The moment at which Browning insists that we must opt for the most challenging path not impossible occurs in poem after poem.

This is the paradoxical moral, the hidden aphorism, as it were, not just in "Rabbi Ben Ezra" but in some of Browning's most haunting poems, poems which are in a sense retrospective looks at growing old. They often

---

[29] Walter E. Houghton, and G. Robert Stange, Eds. *Victorian Poetry and Poetics*. (Boston: Houghton Mifflin, 1968). 283.

[30] Freedom 55 Financial inspires Canadians to define freedom on their own terms; whatever that freedom may be. Freedom 55 Financial is a division of London Life Insurance Company.

chronicle worldly successes that constitute moral failures. "The Statue and the Bust"[31] tells the story of a woman on the eve of her wedding who decides to elope with another man, but the couple's cowardice and indecision force them to delay interminably. Violating the sanctity of marriage is a bad thing for Browning; refusing to burn with the intensity of a single-minded passion is worse. In "Youth and Art,"[32] we learn that an aspiring opera singer and a young sculptor dedicated themselves so single-mindedly to their careers that they never get together, dishonouring youthful impulse by settling for a prosperous – read: empty – middle age, resplendent with honours, but devoid of everything that really matters. "Dis Aliter Visum"[33] – the title means "The Gods Willed It Otherwise" – is a more complex exploration of the same idea, an exercise in intense introspection by a woman whose worldly success seems ashes and dust to her now. She and the man she anatomizes in her monologue miscommunicated at a crucial encounter ten years ago, and opted for safe, separate paths as a result. Now she looks back and sees that the gods had nothing to do with it, that the lovers themselves are to blame for their successful failure. In short, all the poems just mentioned treat ageing as a story of critical trials, as studies of crucial moments that constitute parts of a matrix that will help determine the nature of every other moment.

* * *

Such examples should help us to be slightly warier when invoking these sayings, but not so wary that we shun them altogether. Robert Browning in particular seems to have relished such uncertainties. Take, for example, the aphorism on daring to be great that became one of his most popular maxims: "Ah, but a man's reach should exceed his grasp, / Or what's a heaven for?"[34] Browning puts these sentiments in the mouth of Andrea del Sarto, a cuckold whose career as an artist ended in disgrace. The noble appeal seems more poignant because the person who articulates it failed to reach high enough. In Browning's long, early poem "Paracelsus,"[35] we read in the last section:

---

[31] Robert Browning's "The Statue and the Bust" is a poem from the collection *Men and Women*, published in 1855.
[32] Robert Browning's "Youth and Art" is a poem from the collection *Dramatis Personae*, published in 1864.
[33] Robert Browning's "Dis Aliter Visum; or, le Byron de nos jours" is a poem from the collection *Dramatis Personae*, published in 1864.
[34] From "Andrea del Sarto," a poem in the collection *Men and Women*, published in 1855. See Walter E. Houghton, and G. Robert Stange, Eds. *Victorian Poetry and Poetics*. (Boston: Houghton Mifflin, 1968). 246.
[35] Robert Browning's "Paracelsus" was published in 1835.

"Time fleets, youth fades, and life is an empty dream." But does Browning think this or want us to think it? The sentence in quotes is actually a potpourri of sentiments taken from the Anglican Burial Service, Ovid's poem *Fasti*, and Horace's odes, and represents a stage through which Browning's hero can pass before he sees love and life more affirmatively. And then there is the astonishing naïveté of Browning's "God's in His heaven– / All's right with the world!"[36] Once again, though, context is all. For who is being naïve here? We need to remind ourselves that these words are said by an innocent young girl while she wanders the streets of her Italian town, going past houses where adultery is being committed, murder contemplated, and a political assassination planned. Yet this too is a paradox that "comforts while it mocks,"[37] as Browning's rabbi says, because something does manage to keep such evil at bay and all ends happily – well, sort of happily. Poets, pathologists, and general readers, such poems suggest, are right to take the long view if they want to understand how the intricacies of art and science reveal themselves in the work of writers, who are in their turn keen to make formulaic constructions resonate and their extraordinary power reveal itself.

Works Cited

Allison, R.S. "Psychiatric Disorders in Later Life." *British Medical Journal.* 13 (Dec 1952). 1286-1289.

Browning, Robert. "Rabbi Ben Ezra." Walter E. Houghton, and G. Robert Stange, Eds. *Victorian Poetry and Poetics.* Boston: Houghton Mifflin, 1968.

Brubaker, J. Kenneth. "The Birth of a New Speciality: Geriatrics." *The Journal of Lancaster General Hospital.* 3 (Fall 2008). <www.jlgh.org/JLGH/media/Journal-LGH-Media-Library/Past%20Issues/Volume%203%20-%20Issue%203/JLGH_V3n3_p105-107.pdf>

Boydston, Jo Ann. Ed. *John Dewey. The Later Works, 1925-1953: Volume 14, 1929-1941.* Carbondale: Southern Illinois University Press, 1988.

---

[36] These lines are from Robert Browning's *Pippa Passes*, a verse drama published in 1841 as the first volume of his *Bells and Pomegranates* series. See Walter E. Houghton, and G. Robert Stange, Eds. *Victorian Poetry and Poetics.* (Boston: Houghton Mifflin, 1968). 177.

[37] From "Rabbi Ben Ezra." Walter E. Houghton, and G. Robert Stange, Eds. *Victorian Poetry and Poetics.* (Boston: Houghton Mifflin, 1968). 282.

Chase, Karen. *The Victorians and Old Age*. Oxford: Oxford University Press, 2009.

Childress, James F. "Ensuring Care, Respect and Fairness for the Elderly." *The Hastings Center Report*. 14. 5 (Oct. 1984). 27-31. <www.jstor.org/stable/3561094>

Clarfield, A. Mark. "Grow old along with me! The best is yet to be." Review of Janice E. Graham, and Peter H. Stephenson. Eds. *Contesting Aging & Loss*. University of Toronto Press. Canadian Medical Association Journal. (July 12th) 2011. 183 (10). <www.cmaj.ca/content/183/10/E693.full.pdf+html>

Frost, Robert. "Mending Wall." Nina Baym, *et al.* Eds. *The Norton Anthology of American Literature*. 8th edition. New York and London: W.W. Norton, 2013.

Graham, Janice E., and Peter H. Stephenson. Eds. *Contesting Aging & Loss*. Toronto: University of Toronto Press, 2010.

Gross, John. "Introduction." John Gross. Ed. *The Oxford Book of Aphorisms*. Oxford and New York: Oxford University Press, 1983. vii-viii.

Gross, John. Ed. *The Oxford Book of Aphorisms*. Oxford and New York: Oxford University Press, 1983.

Heath, Kay. *Aging by the Book: The Emergence of Midlife in Victorian Britain*. Albany: State University of New York, 2009.

Hippocrates. *Aphorisms*. [Trans. Francis Adams] <en.wikisource.org/wiki/Aphorisms>

Houghton, Walter E., and G. Robert Stange, Eds. *Victorian Poetry and Poetics*. Boston: Houghton Mifflin, 1968.

Kaiser, Robert M. "Physiological and Clinical Considerations of Geriatric Patient Care." David C. Steffens, Dan G. Blazer, and Mugdha E. Thakur. Eds. *The American Psychiatric Publishing Textbook of Geriatric Psychiatry*. 2015. <books.google.ca/books?id=qD22CAAAQBAJ&printsec=frontcover&source=gbs_ge_summary_r&cad=0#v=onepage&q&f=false>

Kerlin, Isaac N. "President's Annual Address." Association of Medical Officers of American Institutions for Idiotic and Feeble-Minded Persons. 274-285. <books.google.ca/books?id=1QVEAQAAMAAJ&pg=PA285&lpg=PA285&dq=browning+%22grow+old+along+with+me%22+medicine&source=bl&ots=JPWS7JJJEo&sig=MBcqXuQrvaAg6tzUlm63lc8Euus&hl=en&sa=X&ved=0ahUKEwiNj7e8vMfRAhWCz4MKHSd1CAUQ6AEILDAD#v=onepage&q=browning%20%22grow%20old%20along%20with%20me%22%20medicine&f=false>

Kissick, Robert. *Medicine's Dilemmas: Infinite Needs Versus Finite Resources*. New Haven: Yale University Press, 1994.

Mason, Adair Stuart. *'Wasn't it Exciting!': A Compilation of the Work of A. Stuart Mason*. Sudbury, Suffolk: Lavenham Press, 2004. 32. <books.google.es/books?isbn=1860162061>

Mangum, Teresa. "Growing Old: Age." Herbert F. Tucker. Ed. *A Companion to Victorian Literature and Culture*. London: Blackwell, 1999. 97-109.

Murphy, Cornelius F., Jr. *Reflections on Old Age: A Study in Christian Humanism*. Eugene, OR: Wipf and Stock, 2015.

Ofri, Danielle. *Singular Intimacies: Becoming a Doctor at Bellevue*. Boston: Beacon Press, 2003.

Partridge, Josiah. "The Man Called 'Ex.'" *American Association of University Professors Bulletin*. 44. 3 (Sept 1958). 604-610.

Shakespeare, William. *As You Like It*. The Riverside Shakespeare. Boston: Houghton Mifflin, 1974.

—. *Hamlet*. The Riverside Shakespeare. Boston: Houghton Mifflin, 1974.

Siegel, Bernard. "Grow Old along with Me the Best is yet to be." *America Holistic Health Association*. <ahha.org/selfhelp-articles/grow-old-along-with-me-the-best-is-yet-to-be/>

Small, Helen. *The Long Life*. Oxford: Oxford University Press, 2007.

Steffens, David C., Dan G. Blazer, and Mugdha E. Thakur. Eds. *The American Psychiatric Publishing Textbook of Geriatric Psychiatry*. 2015. <books.google.ca/books?id=qD22CAAAQBAJ&printsec=frontcover&source=gbs_ge_summary_r&cad=0#v=onepage&q&f=false>

Timiras, Paolo. Ed. *Physiological Basis of Aging and Geriatrics*. 4th ed. Boca Raton, FL: CRC Press, 2007.

Tucker, Herbert F. Ed. *A Companion to Victorian Literature and Culture*. London: Blackwell, 1999.

Wordsworth, William. "Lines Composed a Few Miles above Tintern Abbey." *The Norton Anthology of English Literature*. 9th edition. New York and London: W.W. Norton, 2012.

—. "Ode: Intimations of Immortality from Recollections of Early Childhood." *The Norton Anthology of English Literature*. 9th edition. New York and London: W.W. Norton, 2012.

Part Two

Products

New Technologies and Cultural Difference

Exploring older adults and the use of digital technologies in the context of everyday life in Taiwan

Pei-Wen Chu

University of Bristol, England

The rapid growth of the elderly population in Taiwan is affecting the country's age-structure such that 'lifelong learning' has become crucial to current Taiwanese society, just as it has in the global context. It is essential, therefore, to consider the learning needs of elderly persons in Taiwan. This chapter reports on the findings of an exploratory study, undertaken in 2013, which focused on the use of Information and Communication Technology (ICT) by older adults in a community college in Taiwan. The target participants in the study were elderly individuals – aged between 50 years old and just over 60 years old – who grew up without the Internet. More specifically, this exploratory study aimed to explore the learning processes of older adults using ICT in the digital age, and to gauge their proficiency in the use of digitalised tools.

1. A socio-cultural approach to learning with digital tools

As Lev Vygotsky pointed out, when students become actively involved in a meaningful task, they perform it better when collaborating with other students. From this perspective, learning can be seen as a social practice. More specifically, the learning process can be divided into two levels, the first of which is a social level, which is then integrated into an individual level.[1] On the social level, learning takes place via interaction with other learners, either in pairs or in groups, and the learners then integrate what they

---

[1] See Lev S. Vygotsky. *Mind in Society. The Development of Higher Psychological Processes.* Revised edition. Eds. Michael Cole, Vera John-Steiner, Silvia Scribner, and Ellen Souberman. (Cambridge, MA: Harvard University Press, 1978).

have learned into an individual level. This process of integration is known as internalisation, which takes place in a 'scaffolding' process.[2]

In a school setting, 'scaffolding' evolves from the interaction between teachers and students. The teacher acts as a facilitator to provide 'scaffolding' to students in order to help them strengthen their knowledge and cultivate their skills. The students then develop their potential Zone of Proximal Development (ZPD).[3] From the perspective of informal adult learners, therefore, learning and usage of ICT by older adults in a community college is 'self-directed,' with the students assuming the role of facilitator as well as learner, and with learning achieved through interaction between students on a social level. In addition, the development of new web technology enables teachers and students to work collaboratively online. More and more digital tools are being created to support learner-collaboration in the classroom, outside school settings, and in the online environment.[4]

In a broad sense, the relationship between people and their cultural context is also a kind of 'embodiment' relationship. In this study, the participants are bound by the same culture. However, people with the same culture may have different perspectives of the use of digital technologies, and the way in which they interact with each other might also be different,

---

[2] See Charles Crook. "Theories of formal and informal learning in the world of web 2.0." Economic and Social Research Council (ESRC) *Theorising the benefits of new technology for youth: Controversies of learning and development*. ESRC Seminar series. *The educational and social impact of new technologies on young people in Britain*. Paper 3. (Department of Education. University of Oxford, 2008); Sonia Livingstone. "Seminar introduction. Setting the scene." Economic and Social Research Council (ESRC) *Theorising the benefits of new technology for youth: Controversies of learning and development*. ESRC Seminar series. *The educational and social impact of new technologies on young people in Britain*. (Department of Education. University of Oxford, 2008); UNESCO (2002) *Information and Communication. Technologies in Teacher Education: A Planning Guide*. (Paris: United Nations Educational, Scientific, and Cultural Organisation (UNESCO), 2002); and Lev S. Vygotsky. *Mind in Society. The Development of Higher Psychological Processes*. Revised edition. Eds. Michael Cole, Vera John-Steiner, Silvia Scribner, and Ellen Souberman. (Cambridge, MA: Harvard University Press, 1978).

[3] See UNESCO (2002) *Information and Communication. Technologies in Teacher Education: A Planning Guide*. (Paris: United Nations Educational, Scientific, and Cultural Organisation (UNESCO), 2002); and Lev S. Vygotsky. *Mind in Society. The Development of Higher Psychological Processes*. Revised edition. Eds. Michael Cole, Vera John-Steiner, Silvia Scribner, and Ellen Souberman. (Cambridge, MA: Harvard University Press, 1978).

[4] See UNESCO (2002) *Information and Communication. Technologies in Teacher Education: A Planning Guide*. (Paris: United Nations Educational, Scientific, and Cultural Organisation (UNESCO), 2002).

depending on their personal experience and prior knowledge of evolving digital technologies.

2. 'Lifelong learning' in the international and Taiwanese context

'Lifelong learning' is an on-going aspect of education that covers three learning contexts, namely, formal, non-formal, and informal, as has been clearly pointed out in recent research.[5] This study focuses on informal learning contexts for older adults.

In an international context, the term "lifelong" first appeared in 1972, in the Faure Report by UNESCO, to present the concept of 'lifelong education.' Within the framework of 'lifelong education,' 'lifelong learners' cover all age groups, and the learning process is no longer limited to attending school but is extended to life experiences.[6] From this perspective, everyone can be supposed to be a 'lifelong learner.' Moreover, the definition of 'older adult' may vary. 'Older adults' are defined as individuals aged over 60 years old (Selwyn, 2004; Leander et al. 2010). However, it was evident that, both in the international and in the Taiwanese context, persons aged over 50 years old are considered 'elderly' (Chang, 1998; Millward, 2003; Lin and Chang, 2009). This study considers relevant references and defines 'elderly persons' as individuals aged 50 years old and over.

---

[5] See Carolyn Medel-Añonuevo, Toshio Ohsako, and Werner Mauch. *Revisiting Lifelong Learning for the 21st Century.* (Hamburg: UNESCO Institute for Education, 2001); Somtrakool, Kla. "Lifelong Learning for a Modern Learning Society." Carolyn Medel-Añonuevo. Ed. *Integrating Lifelong Learning Perspectives.* (Hamburg: UNESCO Institute for Education, 2002): 29-36; Peter Sutherland, and Jim Crowther. Eds. *Lifelong Learning: Concepts and Contexts.* (London and New York: Routledge, 2006); UNESCO (1976) *Recommendation on the Development of Adult Education.* (Nairobi: United Nations Educational, Scientific, and Cultural Organisation (UNESCO) General Conference. 19th Session. 26th November 1976); and UNESCO (2009) *Global Report on Adult Learning and Education.* (Hamburg: United Nations Educational, Scientific, and Cultural Organisation (UNESCO) Institute for Lifelong Learning, 2009).

[6] See Carolyn Medel-Añonuevo, Toshio Ohsako, and Werner Mauch. *Revisiting Lifelong Learning for the 21st Century.* (Hamburg: UNESCO Institute for Education, 2001); UNESCO (1976) *Recommendation on the Development of Adult Education.* (Nairobi: United Nations Educational, Scientific, and Cultural Organisation (UNESCO) General Conference. 19th Session. 26th November 1976); and UNESCO (2009) *Global Report on Adult Learning and Education.* (Hamburg: United Nations Educational, Scientific, and Cultural Organisation (UNESCO) Institute for Lifelong Learning, 2009).

3. The exploratory study

This study was undertaken between the 4th and 24th November 2013, with the aim to explore the way in which elderly Taiwanese people re-engage with learning and skills-development using digital technologies, and to test which research methods would be suitable for investigating this area. The location for the exploratory pilot study was a community college in Taiwan which provides non-degree programmes for 'lifelong learning.' The participants in this study were students in an ICT class, whose ages range between 52 and 62 years old.

3.1 Pilot methods

The study used semi-structured interviews and theme-led classroom observation to understand how older Taiwanese people use technologies. The classroom observation focused on three aspects: the surroundings; the activities; and the participants' feelings. First, the *surroundings* in the study referred to physical elements, such as chairs, desks, and computers in the ICT classroom, and more importantly, how they were arranged in the classroom. Second, the *activities* of elderly individuals in the ICT lessons were observed. Observations focused, for instance, on the kind of tasks they undertook and the kind of learning activities they performed during the ICT lessons. Third, the *feelings* of the elderly individuals were observed; for example, their affective responses, emotions, and attitudes in the class.

Moreover, the semi-structured interviews were conducted with the elderly adults on the day following the classroom observation. These interviews focused on their perspective of the experience and the degree of their motivation in the use of digital technologies in their everyday lives and in the community college.

3.2 Access

The ICT course instructor was contacted by phone in order to obtain permission to attend the lessons for the classroom observation in the community college, which had to be carried out within three weeks due to time constraints. Therefore, a theme-led classroom observation was chosen in order to obtain data more specifically for this exploratory pilot study. The community college was contacted by telephone to get permission to visit the ICT instructor to discuss the procedure of the classroom observation. The instructor agreed and allowed photos to be taken and participation in his lesson for observation purposes.

3.3 Course details

The ICT course included sixteen sequential lessons, beginning on the 27th August 2013. Each lesson lasted for two hours every Tuesday evening, from 7 p.m. to 9 p.m. The sixteen-week course began by introducing the ICT equipment – for example, the computer, mouse, and CD/DVD ROM – and was followed by a demonstration of basic ICT skills, such as accessing the Internet, introducing web browsers, browsing webpages, and so on. The next few lessons were more practically oriented, with training sessions, for instance, in how to use email – for example, send, receive, attach text, hyperlink, and send photos – how to find and watch videos with YouTube, and how to use Google maps. The training also involved making use of a social networking site, Facebook. Although the community college provides elderly Taiwanese persons with structured lessons from entry level to the practical stage, the instructor is permitted to modify the structure of the lessons in consequence with participant feedback.

3.4 Participants' profiles

Participant	Age	Gender	Occupation	Experience of using computer
P1	55	Male	Porter	3-4 years
P2	52	Male	IT	More than 10 years
P3	52	Female	Housewife	Around 5 years
P4	58	Female	Housewife	Around 4 years
P5	62	Female	Retired	Around 5 years

3.5 Observation site

The classroom observation was carried out in a community college in central Taiwan. The community college receives a government subsidy to provide an adult learning programme. It offers various courses for older people, including ICT-related courses, cookery classes, digital photography, knitting, and so on. This exploratory pilot study focused particularly on the ICT courses because the aim of the study was to explore how older adults utilise computers and the Internet in their everyday lives.

In terms of the classroom environment, although the community college is subsidised by the Taiwanese government, it still lacks sufficient ICT facilities to run the courses, so it has to cooperate with a local primary school. Because the ICT lessons take place in a primary school ICT classroom, the chairs and desks are designed basically with primary school students aged between 7 and 13 years old in mind, rather than for elderly individuals. (See Figures 1 and 2)

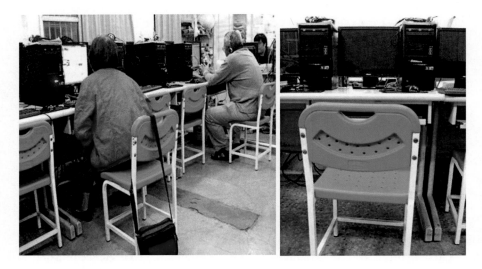

Fig. 1. Surroundings of the ICT classroom in the primary school

Fig. 2. ICT facilities, including desk and chair

4. Discussion

4.1 Classroom observation: Surroundings

As already mentioned, the community college cooperates with a local primarily school. For this reason, the ICT lesson took place in a primary school ICT classroom where all the physical facilities, including the chairs and desks, were designed for primary school students aged between 7 and 13 years old. The first issue to emerge was, therefore, that these seemingly-inadequate facilities may constrain the activities of the elderly adults – in terms of the concept of 'embodiment,' a person's mind and body are considered inseparable when using ICT tools. So, it may have been anticipated that the inappropriateness of the facilities would constitute a constraint for elderly-learner physicality and hinder their adaptation to the usage of desktop computers. However, none of the participants mentioned feelings of either comfort or discomfort while sitting on the primary school chairs. This includes one of the interviewees at the community college who was disabled, suffering from Poliomyelitis. This may have been down to cultural difference. It is a well-known fact that Asian people rarely complain when they are uncomfortable or dissatisfied. For this reason, the school children's chairs and desks seemed not to disrupt the activities of the elderly interviewees under observation to any great extent.

4.2 Classroom observation: Feelings

It was observed that the ICT lesson in the community college was structured and teacher-centred, with a notable lack of interaction between the older adults and the instructor until the lesson involved the use of Facebook. The elderly learners were very quiet in the first and second of the three lessons observed. The objectives of the first and second lessons were to set up an email account, and to attach files or photos and send them to the other elderly learners. However, the participants were observed to have little communication either with the instructor or with each other. They did ask questions sometimes, but not very many. However, the attitudes and feelings of the elderly persons changed when the lesson involved the use of Facebook. They began to ask questions about using Facebook when the instructor was teaching them how to create a Facebook account.

In this study, the findings of classroom observation showed that these elderly learners expressed their intention to participate in social networking, in this case using Facebook. They needed to spend more time in order to adjust to the Facebook interface because the design is probably somewhat complicated for elderly individuals. However, on the plus side, Facebook had the potential to empower them to establish a network *via* the Internet. This might well imply that elderly Taiwanese learners do not want to be socially excluded, and that they are keen to learn how to use digital technologies – computers, the Internet, and social media platforms – because digital exclusion may lead to social-exclusion.

4.3 Semi-structured interviews

In this study, the interview identified confusing questions that the interviewees did not understand, in addition to examining the structure, the questions, and the language used in the interview questions and during the interviews, in order to refine the interview procedure. In respect of the degree of motivation amongst elderly persons in the use of digital technologies, the interviewees expressed the need to learn how to use new technology. The interviewees mentioned especially the use of computers and the Internet, as well as the need to adapt to technological changes. They emphasised that it was essential to learn ICT skills because we are living in a digital age. Moreover, the Internet offered them a new form of communication, since it shortened the distance between them and their friends or children, even those who live overseas. On the one hand, the findings of this exploratory study show that elderly persons have more free time to learn new things in relation to their personal interests and hobbies, something they were not able to do when they were still working. They emphasised that they were able to continue to explore their personal interests after retirement. On the other hand, the elderly learners mentioned that on occasions they became impatient when searching for information online because of their slow typing speed. One elderly female learner was observed to have been attempting to set up her own email account for almost three weeks because the proxy server had a time limit and users had to complete their personal information within three-hundred seconds. This is an automatic mechanism that cannot be changed. The windows close automatically such that elderly users trying to register have to start the same action over and over again because of their slow typing speed. Having repeated the same action many times, the elderly learners either lost interest or were too impatient and bored to carry on. Apparently, this hindrance dissuaded these elderly Taiwanese persons from using computers and the Internet. This is a frequent occurrence in Taiwan owing to the input method, that is, Microsoft New Phonetic IME.

Conclusions

The findings of this exploratory pilot study confirmed several factors about methods to be employed for the semi-structured interviews and classroom observation. Moreover, the issue of 'embodiment' emerged in the study; a male participant (P1), who is disabled, said that he would not lodge a complaint about the chair and the desk, which were designed for primary school pupils, even though he found them uncomfortable. It also became evident that, in line with the concept of 'embodiment,' regarding technology usage, mind and body are connected and inseparable. On the one hand, therefore, an elderly person's engagement with technology is not only mediated by the digital tools used, but also by her or his own body. To this extent, the human body and physicality may inhibit learning or constrain the level of digital engagement. On the other hand, depending on cultural difference, whereas physical constraints may have a negative impact on the learning process of elderly persons in the West, they would not have a significant, similar effect on elderly individuals from Asia. When carrying out studies of this sort with elderly learners, therefore, a socio-cultural perspective is required in order to anticipate and understand how and why similar behaviour patterns can be interpreted in different ways within different cultural contexts. Furthermore, the study also revealed that it is necessary to understand from the outset how elderly individuals are influenced by cultural context since this will condition their assimilation of new digital technologies and practices. This finding concluded the purpose of adopting a sociocultural perspective as the theoretical foundation in both pilot and in the main study to examine cultural difference.

Works Cited

Chen Hsueh-Hua, and Shu-Chuan Chang. "A Study of the Implementation of Information Usage Education for Graying Population – Case Study of Taipei Municipal Library." Taipei: Department of Library and Information Science. National Taiwan University, 1998.

Crook, Charles. "Theories of formal and informal learning in the world of web 2.0." Economic and Social Research Council (ESRC) *Theorising the benefits of new technology for youth: Controversies of learning and development*. ESRC Seminar series. *The educational and social impact of new technologies on young people in Britain*. Paper 3. Department of Education. University of Oxford, 2008.

Leander, Kevin M., Nathan C. Phillips, and Katherine Headrick Taylor. (2010) "The Changing Social Spaces of Learning: Mapping New Mobilities." *Review of Research in Education*. 34, 2010. 329-394. <www.sci.sdsu.edu/tlcm/all-data-files/leander-phillips-taylor-2010-the-changing-social-spaces-of-learning-mapping-new-mobilities.pdf>

Lin, Yi-Hsuan, and Shan-Ju Lin Chang. "Digital Divides Revisited: A Process View of the Acquisitions of Information and Communication Technology (ICT) Skills by the Elderly" *Journal of Library and Information Science Research*. 3. 2, 2009. 75-102. [Chinese] <journaldatabase.info/articles/digital_divides_revisiteda_process.html>

Livingstone, Sonia. "Seminar introduction. Setting the scene." Economic and Social Research Council (ESRC) *Theorising the benefits of new technology for youth: Controversies of learning and development*. ESRC Seminar series. *The educational and social impact of new technologies on young people in Britain*. Department of Education. University of Oxford, 2008.

Medel-Añonuevo, Carolyn, Toshio Ohsako, and Werner Mauch. *Revisiting Lifelong Learning for the 21st Century*. Hamburg: UNESCO Institute for Education, 2001.

Medel-Añonuevo, Carolyn. Ed. *Integrating Lifelong Learning Perspectives*. Hamburg: UNESCO Institute for Education, 2002.

Millward, Peter. The 'grey digital divide': Perception, exclusion and barriers of access to the Internet for older people. *First Monday*. 8. 7, 2003. <www.firstmonday.dk/ojs/index.php/fm/article/view/1066/986>

Selwyn, Neil. "The information aged: A qualitative study of older adults' use of information and communications technology." *Journal of Aging Studies*. 18, 2004. 369-384. <citeseerx.ist.psu.edu/viewdoc/download?doi=10.1.1.471.8718&rep=rep1&type=pdf>

Somtrakool, Kla. "Lifelong Learning for a Modern Learning Society." Carolyn Medel-Añonuevo. Ed. *Integrating Lifelong Learning Perspectives*. Hamburg: UNESCO Institute for Education, 2002. 29-36.

Sutherland, Peter, and Jim Crowther. Eds. *Lifelong Learning: Concepts and Contexts*. London and New York: Routledge, 2006.

UNESCO (1976) *Recommendation on the Development of Adult Education*. Nairobi: United Nations Educational, Scientific, and Cultural Organisation (UNESCO) General Conference. 19th Session. 26th November 1976.

UNESCO (2002) *Information and Communication. Technologies in Teacher Education: A Planning Guide*. Paris: United Nations Educational, Scientific, and Cultural Organisation (UNESCO), 2002.

UNESCO (2009) *Global Report on Adult Learning and Education*. Hamburg: United Nations Educational, Scientific, and Cultural Organisation (UNESCO) Institute for Lifelong Learning, 2009.

Vygotsky, Lev S. *Mind in Society. The Development of Higher Psychological Processes*. Revised edition. Eds. Michael Cole, Vera John-Steiner, Silvia Scribner, and Ellen Souberman. Cambridge, MA: Harvard University Press, 1978.

New Technology Systems

as

'Social Innovation'

'mobisaar' – a technology-based service providing mobility for everybody in public transport

Maurice Rekrut,[1] Jan Alexandersson,[1] Jochen Britz,[1] Johannes Tröger,[1] Daniel Bieber,[2] and Kathleen Schwarz.[2]

[1] DFKI GmbH, Saarbrücken;[2] iso-Institut e.V, Saarbrücken

Mobility is one of the keys for participation in social life. Especially in late-age, when people are dependent on regular visits to physicians and pharmacies, and mobility impairments cause them to face severe challenges, often resulting in social isolation. Regarding demographic change in Germany, these problems will soon have implications for a significant share of the German population and, by extension, elderly persons across Europe. Relying exclusively on the use of cars in daily life is impossible for most elderly people due to various impairments. Additionally, ecological reasons have to be taken into consideration.

Public transport offers an alternative but, in general, it is not really popular amongst elderly persons, as it comes along with additional barriers like big gaps between bus and bus stop, the use of complicated ticket machines, and cryptic timetables.[1] In an ageing society, projects that aim at improving mobility for the elderly gain in importance. In two recent German funding schemes by the Federal Ministry for Economic Affairs and Energy (BMWi) "Door to Door" (*Tür zu Tür*), and the Federal Ministry of Education and Research (BMBF) "Mobile till late-age" (*Mobil bis ins hohe Alter*), about twenty-five projects set out to address mobility issues within the scope of Ambient Assisted Living (AAL). Along similar lines, the Compagno Project[2] aimed at providing seamless mobility chains for the elderly by

---

[1] See Daniel Bieber, Jan Alexandersson, and Kathleen Schwarz. "Das Mobia-Projekt: Die Kombination von Dienstleistung und Technologie für den ÖPNV." *Lebensqualität im Wandel von Demografie und Technik*, 2013.

[2] See Tomas Hefter, Benno Kotterba, Daniela Peukert, Julia Hohl, Thomas Hauer, Joerg Muschiol, and Helga Schwall, and Klaus Wolf. "Assistenzsystem für eine barrierefreie Mobilität – Eine Disziplinen übergreifende Herausforderung." *Wohnen-Pflege-Teilhabe-Besser leben durch Technik*, 2014.

developing a companion application. This application offers help with planning a trip using public transport, and regional and supra-regional transportation providers, as well as offering information about the trip in such a way as to ensure a feeling of security on the road. Another travel-assistant tailored to public transport was developed in Project NAMO.[3] The application offers photos with directional arrows, railway station plans with marked paths, and contact to a service hotline to get direct support. The afore-mentioned projects, as with those of most competitors in this field, focus on plain technology development adapted to the needs of the elderly. Apart from a call-centre hotline, the service part of the assistance is carried out mainly by technology, but this cannot replace real social contact which is of great importance, especially for elderly people.

* * *

The research project 'Mobia'[4] aimed at reducing barriers within public transport systems in central Saarbrücken – capital of the German state Saarland – by developing and validating a technology-supported, human-based service system. The 'Mobia' Project augments public transport internal physical means[5] and internal digital means[6] with a public transport comprehensive, human-based means, namely, mobility-guides – *Mobilitäts-Lotsen* – who provide a service chain by helping passengers to travel from door-to-door, or to a specified point, or even along a sub-section of the journey during which the passenger, for whatever reason, may require assistance. This includes, for example, helping to get on a bus at a particular bus stop when bus and bus stop do not match up; assisting in the transfer from bus to tram over a long route; walking with the passenger from the tram to the surgery entrance whenever the elderly person is fearful of getting lost; and helping a young father with a child, push-chair, and shopping bags to enter the bus because he cannot handle that number of things at the same time. The technology consists of a software for the intelligent disposition and

---

[3] See Christian Bühler, Helmut Heck, Annika Nietzio, and Frank Reins. "The Mobile Travel Assistance System NAMO with Way-Finding Support in Public Transport Environments." *International Conference on Computers for Handicapped Persons.* (Springer, 2014). 54-57.

[4] See Jan Alexandersson, David Banz, Daniel Bieber, Jochen Britz, Maurice Rekrut, Kathleen Schwarz, Florin Spanachi, Martin Thoma, Johannes Tröger. "Oil in the Machine: Technical Support for a Human-Centred Service System for Public Transport." *Ambient Assisted Living.* (Springer, 2015). 157-167.

[5] For example, existing accessibility features in vehicles of transport like fold-out wheelchair ramps.

[6] For example, interfaces for accessing timetables.

coordination of the mobility-guides, and front-ends for mobility-guides and passengers. The coordination software directs the mobility-guides to the requested point of service.

The reason for choosing Saarland as the pilot region for the 'Mobia' Project is well-known in Germany. This part of Germany is experiencing the consequences of radical demographic alteration. With an area of 2,568.70 km² and a population of about one million inhabitants, population density is still quite high, with a total of 387 people per km². Nevertheless, population density in the region of Saarland is diminishing, and moreover, compared with neighbouring states – Luxemburg, Lothringen, and Rheinland-Pfalz – at a high rate.[7] The Federal Statistical Office of Germany forecasts a demographic decline in this region of 13·8% until 2030, and even 33·5% up to 2060.[8] During this process of reduction, the number of persons in work – 20-year-olds to 65-year-olds – will decrease by 27·2%, while the number of elderly people between 65 and 80 years old will increase by 16·2%, and the population aged 80 years old and over by 26·2%.[9]

* * *

Due to these distinctive geographical and economical characteristics of the region of Saarland, it was decided that the 'Mobia' follow-up project 'mobisaar' should spread the service from the capital Saarbrücken to the whole Federal State of Saarland. 'mobisaar' is a five-year research project, funded by the German Federal Ministry for Education and Research (BMBF), that addresses not only the ageing population in general, but also all those persons who suffer from mobility impairments. The goal is to provide a solution that ensures mobility for all.

Methodology
In order to accomplish this goal, 'mobisaar' uses the following architecture. Figure 1 gives an overview of the core components of the 'mobisaar' system that, in large part, have been adapted from the 'Mobia' Project. In the following paragraph, these components will be presented in detail and

---

[7] In the year 1970, the population density in Saarland was calculated to be 435 people per km². See Statistic Portal, S.L.L. <www.grande-region.lu/portal/de/>

[8] Comparative figures for the whole of Germany: 5·7% and 21·2%. See *Trendreport Demographie. Bevölkerungsentwicklung im Saarland.* (Statistisches Landesamt Saar, 2010). [Technical Report]

[9] *Bevölkerung im Saarland 2009, 2020 und 2030 im Regionalverband, der Landeshauptstadt Saarbrücken und den saarländischen Landkreisen nach Altersgruppen.* (Statistisches Amt Saarland, 2010). [Technical Report]

additional light will be shed on their adaptation for a roll-out covering the whole region.

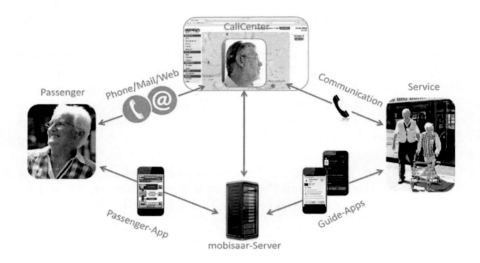

Fig. 1. Overview of the 'mobisaar' system. Passengers can request the service *via* phone, email, website, and app. The mobility-guides receive passenger requests *via* their app, and are instructed with further information, if needed, by the call-centre.

Service – mobility-guides

The mobility-guides are at the core of the 'Mobia'/'mobisaar' system, as they are the main touch-point of the system with the clients and the outer world. For those persons needing assistance with public transport, the mobility-guides provide seamless support on the spot. Whereas the 'Mobia' mobility-guide budget was financed through state-subsidised employment aimed at creating full-time jobs for long-term, unemployed people, 'mobisaar' will need to seek additional funding resources. Furthermore, although the public transport service in Saarbrücken kept running for one year following the end of the 'Mobia' Project current costs will be too high for most of the public transport providers in the region of Saarland, especially as many of them are in the red already and depend on subsidies from the government. For the entire period of 'mobisaar,' the mobility-guides will be paid out of project funds, but afterwards new business models need be developed in order to make the service self-sustainable. Therefore, 'mobisaar' plans to cooperate with voluntary organisations that could not only provide mobility-guides, but also "spontaneous mobility-guides," that is, people who feel comfortable with spontaneously helping persons who are in need nearby.

Existing mobility services that offer help, for example, with travelling by rail, and voluntary transport services will be included in the 'mobisaar' system in order to provide seamless service throughout the whole mobility chain. A particular challenge will be to establish the service in rural areas. Due to the migration of population from these areas to the city, the demand for public transport in the countryside is also in decline. In some regions, buses are still scheduled hourly, while in other regions they are scheduled only twice a day. This declining rate of public transportation opportunities in rural areas is due mainly to economic constraints, though supporting public transport companies with project funds in order to provide transportation on a more regular basis is not an option. A possible solution to this problem might be a ride-share service similar to that already in place in other regions. For instance, a person planning a trip from the countryside to the city would communicate his or her intention on the 'mobisaar' website or on one of the other 'mobisaar' interfaces so that other 'mobisaar' users can align their plans and drive together. Such a ride-share service depends on trust between the two parties that rely on each other; the elderly especially place strong emphasis on trust. Luckily, as people living in rural areas know each other well, social cohesion is still strong amongst neighbours in the countryside, and this makes a ride-share solution all the more feasible.

* * *

'mobisaar'-user interfaces
As with the 'Mobia' Project, 'mobisaar' developed three main 'mobisaar'-user interfaces: 1) Call-centre; 2) Passenger-app; and 3) Mobility-guide app. All three interfaces were designed following the User-Centred Design (UCD) methodology.[10] This design method puts the user's needs at the centre of development.[11] As the system itself is built up and established, the focus of 'mobisaar' lies, besides the roll-out of the service, on improving the existing user-interfaces.

---

[10] International Standardization Organization (ISO). DIS, I.: 9241-210: 2010. *Ergonomics of Human System Interaction-Part 210: Human-Centred Design for Interactive Systems.* Switzerland, 2009.

[11] See Johannes Tröger, Jan Alexandersson, Jochen Britz, Maurice Rekrut, Daniel Bieber, and Kathleen Schwarz. "Board Games and Regulars Tables – Extending User-Centred Design in the 'Mobia' Project." *International Conference on Human Aspects of IT for the Aged Population*, 2016. 129-140.

1. Call-centre

The establishment of a call-centre was demanded as a means of coordinating the service, while at the same time ensuring access for all age groups.[12] The job of the call-centre is to receive phoned-in requests from those users who either do not want, or who are unable to book the service using their smartphone, and to distribute the message to available mobility-guides on the road. During the roll-out of the system, installing multiple call-centres for each city was not considered a viable strategy. For this reason, the decision was taken to have one centralized call-centre to coordinate incoming requests and distribute them to those mobility-guides available in the corresponding region. A web interface connected to the 'mobisaar' backend supports the call-centre agents by finding available mobility-guides and assigning the passenger requests, contacting them through their smartphone apps.

2. Passenger-app

During the 'Mobia' Project, regular informal meetings with actual passengers were held each month to receive feedback about the user-interface, as well as the service as a whole, thereby enabling continuous improvement of the smartphone app and the identification of additional access channels requested by interface-users, such as website access. In 'mobisaar,' the monthly get-togethers are replaced by Co-Developer meetings every two months that are aimed primarily at even greater integration of the user-group in the development process. The activities in these meetings are planned to include a broad range of methodologies from usability tests and rapid prototyping – pen and paper, and computer mock-ups – to active testing sessions in the field where developers and users can identify possible stumbling blocks during joint usage of the technology. The meetings create empathy between both groups, between developers and users, and *vice versa*, and brings about an improvement in the quality of the user-interfaces developed, ensuring a perfect fit for everybody during interaction with the system.

3. Mobility-guide-app

The smartphone app for mobility-guides created during the 'Mobia' Project needs to be extended for use by all three types of mobility-guide, namely,

---

[12] During the 'Mobia' Project, this service was carried out by one of the mobility-guides who operated from the 'Mobia' head-office where the mobility-guides met every morning to start their working-day.

full-time, voluntary, and spontaneous voluntary. Apart from the smartphone app already developed, additional access channels through the web or over the phone can be used to best address the needs of the different types of mobility-guide and their proficiency with the technology.

'mobisaar' – backend

The 'mobisaar'-backend forms the technical backbone of the system. Requests from passengers are processed on this server. The call-centre can enter incoming requests received by phone in the front-end and the server distributes it to the next mobility-guide available or, alternatively, on special request from a customer, to a certain mobility-guide. A routing service, including timetable data for public transport, calculates the most suitable route from the passenger's starting-point to the desired end-point. As the 'Mobia' Project was limited to the city of Saarbrücken, this routing service excluded rail traffic. However, the fastest way between two locations within the region of the entire Federal State of Saarland demands the use of train connections. Hence, 'mobisaar' will include this information in the routing service.

Moreover, 'mobisaar' plans a holistic inquiry into bus stops and railway station information regarding their accessibility and possible mobility barriers. This information can be used to improve routing tailored to the special needs of the mobility-impaired. Gathering the data will be carried out within the runtime of the project, but the infrastructure of a federal state is a living system that changes frequently. Bus stops might be re-positioned, roadworks can block entire streets for several weeks, and substitute stops are seldom barrier-free. This requires user-app data to be updated and maintained regularly. Solutions might be found in crowdsourcing approaches which rely on passengers and mobility-guides. Users could share warnings of barriers they experience on their way *via* the 'mobisaar' smartphone app which would be verified in a second step by other users and mobility-guides. Depending on their mobility profile, the data can then be used to adapt route advice for users with similar profiles, thereby improving the routing service. Photos of bus stops and their surroundings can additionally help users to provide themselves with images of the stops, enabling them to decide on their own whether a route with these stops is convenient for them or not.

Results and Discussion

After one year, the next biggest city in the Federal State of Saarland, Homburg, has been integrated into the system, in addition to the district to which it belongs, Saarpfalz. Homburg has an important position in Saarland owing to its university hospital which has specialist units for certain diseases. Its geographical location, close to the eastern border of Saarland, makes it a crucial area in which to integrate the railway network into the system. Requested routes now include train connections, and mobility-guides accompany the passengers on board trains to their destination. The additional workload is covered by full-time mobility-guides who are located in the City of Homburg and its surrounding suburbs. Apart from the already-included district of Saarbrücken, the four remaining districts of Saarland will be integrated step-by-step until 2019 to provide a service that ensures mobility for all throughout the entire Federal State of Saarland.

The first Co-Developer workshops have been held, (see Figure 2) and a prototype of the website has been implemented. (see Figure 3)

Fig. 2. First Co-Developer workshop at DFKI.

Pen and paper mock-ups were used to create a proposal together with the users and the proposals were evaluated in the follow-up workshop employing a usability test. This website will lay the foundation for the development of user-interfaces that are tailored to the needs of those persons making up the user-groups. As the mobility-guides are users too and as they work with a smartphone app to get access to the system, the regulars' meetings held in the 'Mobia' Project will be pursued with them.

Fig. 3. First prototype of the 'mobisaar' web interface based on the outcomes of the Co-Developer workshops.

Volunteer mobility-guides went through their first training sessions to acquire the necessary skills, helping mobility-impaired people to use public transport. (See Figure 4)

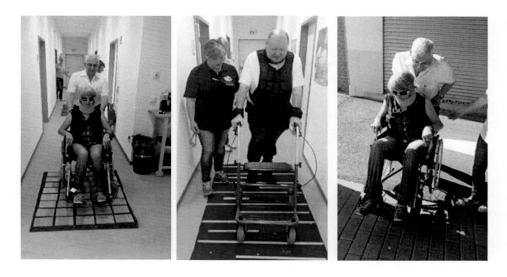

Fig. 4. Training for voluntary mobility-guides, including handling wheelchairs and walkers on uneven terrain.

Handling a wheelchair and a walker as well as a first-aid course are mandatory requirements for the job as 'mobisaar' mobility-guide, specialised work that is often underrated. Handling a wheelchair, especially on uneven ground, can be a challenge and should be practised in advance. After the successful completion of their training, the mobility-guides started work at the end of 2016.

Works Cited

Alexandersson, Jan, David Banz, Daniel Bieber, Jochen Britz, Maurice Rekrut, Kathleen Schwarz, Florin Spanachi, Martin Thoma, and Johannes Tröger. "Oil in the Machine: Technical Support for a Human-Centred Service System for Public Transport." *Ambient Assisted Living*. Springer, 2015. 157-167.

Bieber, Daniel, Jan Alexandersson, and Kathleen Schwarz. "Das Mobia-Projekt: Die Kombination von Dienstleistung und Technologie für den ÖPNV." *Lebensqualität im Wandel von Demografie und Technik*, 2013.

Bühler, Christian, Helmut Heck, Annika Nietzio, and Frank Reins. "The Mobile Travel Assistance System NAMO with Way-Finding Support in Public Transport Environments." *International Conference on Computers for Handicapped Persons*. Springer, 2014. 54-57.

Hefter, Tomas, Benno Kotterba, Daniela Peukert, Julia Hohl, Thomas Hauer, Joerg Muschiol, and Helga Schwall, and Klaus Wolf. "Assistenzsystem für eine barrierefreie Mobilität – Eine Disziplinen übergreifende Herausforderung." *Wohnen-Pflege-Teilhabe-Besser leben durch Technik*, 2014.

International Standardization Organization (ISO). DIS, I.: 9241-210: 2010. *Ergonomics of Human System Interaction-Part 210: Human-Centred Design for Interactive Systems*. Switzerland, 2009.

Statistic Portal. <www.grande-region.lu/portal/de/>

Saarland Region Office of Statistics. *Trendreport Demographie. Bevölkerungsentwicklung im Saarland*. Statistisches Landesamt Saar, 2010. [Technical Report]

Saarland Office of Statistics. *Bevölkerung im Saarland 2009, 2020 und 2030 im Regionalverband, der Landeshauptstadt Saarbrücken und den saarländischen Landkreisen nach Altersgruppen*. Statistisches Amt Saarland, 2010. [Technical Report]

Tröger, Johannes, Jan Alexandersson, Jochen Britz, Maurice Rekrut, Daniel Bieber, and Kathleen Schwarz. "Board Games and Regulars Tables – Extending User-Centred Design in the 'Mobia' Project."

International Conference on Human Aspects of IT for the Aged Population, 2016. 129-140.

Industrial Design

as

'Social Innovation'

Designing a Domestic Heating Product for Older People Within the Concept of 'Contained Living Spaces'

P.J. White

DesignCORE Research Centre

Institute of Technology Carlow, Ireland

Designing Independence for an Ageing Population

The world's population is ageing rapidly; by 2050 it is projected that two billion older people will be alive.[1] By this time, it is predicted that two in five persons will be aged 60 years old or over in some European countries.[2] The importance of maintaining independence as we age was first highlighted following the Vienna Plan of 1982. In this, the United Nations cite independence as one of the five principles for older persons.[3] The Irish population will have some unique challenges as it ages. It is forecasted that between 2010 and 2060, Ireland will have the largest overall population growth in Europe, equating to an increase of 46%.[4] With this growth, there will be a projected rise from 11% to 29% of the older adult population by the year 2041.[5] Maintaining independence by ageing at home or 'ageing-in-place' is not only a goal but a high preference for the older Irish population. Hannah McGee *et al.* have reported that up to 89% of Irish older adults would prefer to live at home rather than live in institutional care.[6] The environment

---

[1] See United Nations. *World Population Ageing 2013.* (New York: Department of Economic and Social Affairs. Population Division, 2013).

[2] See United Nations. *World Population Ageing: 1950-2050.* (New York: United Nations Department of Economic and Social Affairs. Population Division, 2001).

[3] See United Nations. *Vienna International Plan of Action on Ageing.* (New York: United Nations, 1983).

[4] See European Commission. *Europe in Figures. Eurostat Yearbook 2011.* (Luxembourg: Publications Office of the European Union, 2011).

[5] See Paul McGill. *Illustrating Ageing in Ireland North and South: Key Facts and Figures.* (Belfast: Centre for Ageing Research and Development in Ireland, 2010).

[6] See Hannah McGee, Ann O'Hanlon, Maja Barker, Anne Hickey, Rebecca. Garavan, Ronán Conroy, Richard Layte, Emer Shelley, Frances Horgan, Vivienne Crawford, Robert Stout, and

in which we age and live our daily lives has an immense bearing on our health and independence.

The products, and more precisely domestic products, that we use in our living environment greatly assist us in maintaining positive wellbeing. They provide for essential living conditions and, therefore, for health and independence. Independence provided by these products promotes positive ageing-in-place and an improved quality-of-life by assisting in everyday necessary tasks. Designers can do much to assist with daily requirements and, by doing so, increase the independence of ageing individuals. A study by Fisk *et al.* identified this, stating that more than 50% of the problems older adults have with daily living could be addressed through design efforts.[7]

In the future, health care will truly begin at home. Firstly, there will be a growing need to maintain a healthy, independent ageing population for social and economic purposes. Secondly, there will be a growing reliance on domestic products to help maintain this health and independence. Those domestic products that address fundamental health needs, enhance wellbeing, and improve qualities-of-life are of most importance. Products that provide better every-day basic health-care conditions require immediate attention. Central to this are products that provide for adequate environmental conditions.

Indoor Household Temperatures

Our physical environment and the conditions that we live in greatly influence our health and quality-of-life. There is increasing evidence that built-in environmental conditions have serious effects on physical, mental, and social health. For instance, poor environmental conditions are known to be influential in a range of illnesses, from cardiovascular diseases, obesity, and chronic depression.[8] Indoor and household temperatures have major effects on health and, more importantly, on mortality. A report by the World Health Organisation states that "Extreme high and low temperatures [are] an

---

Desmond O'Neill. *"One Island – Two Systems: A comparison of health status and health and social service use by community-dwelling older people in the Republic of Ireland and Northern Ireland.* (Dublin: Royal College of Surgeons in Ireland. Healthy Ageing Research Programme – HARP, 2005). <www.publichealth.ie/files/file/One_Island_2_System.pdf>

[7] See Arthur D. Fisk, Wendy A. Rodgers, Neil Charness, Sara J. Czaja, and Joseph Sharit. *Designing for Older Adults: Principles and Creative Human Factors Approaches.* 2nd ed. (Florida: CRC Press, 2009).

[8] See World Health Organisation. *Housing and health: Identifying priorities – Meeting Report.* (Bonn: Regional Office for Europe, European Centre for Environment and Health, 2003).

underestimated cause of ill health and premature death in many countries" (WHO 2001: 12). Factors such as poor mobility and health issues can confine elderly persons indoors for longer. Therefore, as we age, indoor temperatures have more serious implications for health and mortality. Temperature extremes, for example, from cold to hot indoor temperatures, are known to lead to more accidents and personal injuries in the home.[9] On a more serious level, in the United Kingdom, indoor temperatures were shown to cause an additional 40,000 deaths in winter months in comparison with other months of the year.[10] Furthermore, findings from this study show that colder indoor temperatures are the main cause of winter mortality, causing cardiovascular and respiratory diseases in elderly persons at greatest risk. A further study by Wilkinson *et al.* (2004), examining this rise in mortality, concluded that an upward adjustment in indoor temperatures lowers levels of vulnerability and mortality.[11] It should be noted that winter deaths do not directly correlate with colder climates. Spain, Portugal, and Ireland have the highest number of winter deaths amongst older people, while some countries with colder climates are ranked lower.[12]

Research Conducted – Fieldwork

To enquire into the domestic heating product requirements of older people, immersive and contextual field research was conducted. The research involved Design Ethnographic fieldwork over a twelve-month period within the homes of forty elderly participants. The participants were selected from various socio-economic groups across eight counties of the Republic of Ireland. Data was collected in interviews, through observation, and by appraising participation. Following fieldwork, the data was coded,

---

[9] See World Health Organisation. *Housing and Health in Europe.* (Copenhagen: WHO Regional Office for Europe, 2001).

[10] See Paul Wilkinson, Megan Landon, Ben Armstrong, Simon Stevenson, Sam Pattenden, Martin McKee, and Tony Fletcher. *Cold comfort-The social and environmental determinants of excess winter deaths in England 1986-1996.* (Bristol: The Policy Press and the Joseph Rowntree Foundation, 2001).

[11] Paul Wilkinson, Sam Pattenden, Ben Armstrong, Astrid Fletcher, R. Sari Kovats, Punam Mangtani, and Anthony J. McMichael. "Vulnerability to winter mortality in elderly people in Britain: population-based study." *British Medical Journal.* 329. 7467, 2004. 647. See also: Christine Liddell, and Chris Morris. "Fuel Poverty and Human Health: A Review of Recent Evidence." *Energy Policy.* 38. 6, 2010. 2987-2997; and Helen McAvoy. *All-Ireland Policy Paper on Fuel Poverty and Health.* (Dublin: Institute of Public Health in Ireland, 2007).

[12] Jonathan D. Healy. "Excess winter mortality in Europe: a cross country analysis identifying key risk factors." *Journal of Epidemiology & Community Health.* 57. 10th November 2003. 784-789.

visualised, and analysed through a grounded theory approach. The findings of this research supported the view that designed products should, in future, provide for the basic health needs essential to older adults within the domestic environment. The findings further showed that other factors should be considered on an equal basis if independence and ageing-in-place are to be addressed. It was demonstrated that heating products encompass a complex mix of factors of wellbeing, including emotional and social needs. Furthermore, it was also established that, in future, when designing heating products, cost factors, product safety, ergonomics, and the usage needs of elderly persons should be taken into account.

The Concept of 'Contained Living Spaces'

Findings from the research strongly indicated that the design of mobile heating products required immediate attention. To illustrate this, a specific pattern of usage by many elderly participants was recorded. It was found that limited mobility in older people leads to smaller and more confined living environments. Significantly, what was observed that older people create modular stations around themselves in order to have quick access to personal and important items. For the purposes of description, the researcher labelled these 'contained living spaces.' Figure 1. illustrates an example of this concept:

Fig. 1. Example of a 'contained living space,' constructed as a result of mobility issues and located near a heat source.

These spaces or 'stations' are constructed typically for functional use. Commonly, they are located around the elderly person and in close proximity to them. These are usually a configuration of moveable furniture, for example, tables and desks. These 'contained living spaces' are commonly located beside heat sources such as radiators and portable heating appliances, for example, small electric heaters. Within the 'contained living space,' it was observed that there is a need to make living spaces within the home more accessible through appropriate temperature control, thereby allowing the elderly person greater mobility and independence rather than causing her or him to remain in a contained space. This observation prompted the need for specific portable- and space-heating solutions for older people, supporting research by Hue-Chi Liao and Tsai Feng Chang who determined that the specific need for space-heating increases as we age.[13]

Further design requirements were also noted when researching the concept of 'contained living spaces.' Throughout the research, prominent links were established between heating-product usability and pain relief associated with arthritis and poor circulation (see Fig. 2).

Fig. 2. Portable pain relief: A research participant utilises his portable electric heater to alleviate arthritis pain in his sitting room.

---

[13] See Hue-Chi Liao, and Tsai Feng Chang. "Space-Heating and Water-Heating Energy Demands of the Aged in the US." *Energy Economics*. 24. 3, 2002. 267-284.

Placing affected areas such as fingers, hands, and feet on a warm surface – or a cool surface when the product is turned off – has been shown to offer gradual relief of pain. As the portability of mobile electric heaters allows more agility and provides flexibility of use, these are, commonly, a central source of comfort from physical pain when performing other activities such as watching television while relaxing in the evenings.

Design Process – Ideation Sessions

> One of the key purposes of sketching in the ideation phase of design is to provide a catalyst to stimulate new and different interpretations. Hence, sketching is fundamental to the cognitive process of design. (Buxton 2007: 115)

With the aim of creating heating-product solutions within 'contained living spaces,' design-ideation sessions were undertaken to explore ideas. During these sessions, a list of design requirements based on findings from the ethnographic field study was created. Using felt-tip ink pens on A3-size sheets of paper, the ideas were then sketched and surveyed comprehensively. Ideas were sketched until no more were forthcoming, and then sketching was switched iteratively to another idea. As a result of this, a large number of quick-succession sketches was created reflecting the momentum of ideas as they flowed.

Throughout the process, one sketch served as feedback for the next. Ideas emerged and developed in a free manner at times and, on other occasions, they adhered rigidly and strictly to the requirements. The ideas presented in the sketches varied from the conservative and practical to the chaotic and unconventional. The quality of the sketches varied in detail to allow interpretation of meaning when subjected to review later. To document the whole process of sketch ideation, a sketch book was compiled. The final sketchbook comprised of approximately five-hundred iterative and exploratory sketches. An extract of these sketches is featured in Figure 3.

Creating Concepts from Ideation
Completing the process of conceptualisation involved the convergence and synthesis of sketches. In traditional design processes, convergence involves synthesising conceptualised material – that is, ideas and sketches – into smaller groupings of concepts. First, the entire ideation sketchbook was fully reviewed using the afore-mentioned design-requirement-list created from the ethnographic field study. Second, to reduce the quantity of concepts, all

sketched items not relevant to the design requirements were filtered out and erased from the design-requirement-list. Third, to achieve a more in-depth convergence of ideas, the ideation sketchbook was reviewed for a second time, on this occasion to identify broad concept groupings that best represented all the remaining requirements. At this stage of the process, an external reviewer accompanied the researcher. During the review, the decision was taken to physically divide the contents of the sketchbook into three overarching concept groups for further advancement.

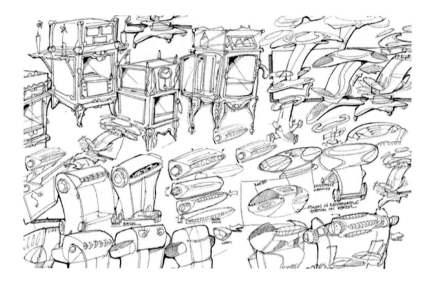

Fig. 3. A montage of images showing a series of evolving ideas from the ideation sketchbook.

The next step in the process of synthesising conceptualised material was to narrow down the three overlapping concepts into one in order to move forward. For the selection of concepts for design advancement, Karl Ulrich and Steven Eppinger recommend using a 'concept-screening matrix.' Based on the "Pugh concept selection process,"[14] a 'concept-screening matrix' that enables the rating and ranking of concepts for progression.

---

[14] See Karl T. Ulrich, and Steven D. Eppinger. *Product Design and Development.* 2nd edition. (New York: McGraw-Hill, 2000): 144.

Design Conclusions – The 'Hot Desk'

The product concept ranked highest for taking forward in the 'concept-screening matrix' was the "Hot Desk" (see Figures 4a and 4b). In its most basic form, this product is a portable desk or 'modular station' with a small heating device as a built-in feature. Within the 'contained living space,' the Hot Desk might well serve as a portable heating appliance for elderly users. Key features of this product are its flexibility of use and portability. The Hot Desk, with its 'ubiquitous' aesthetic that blends in with the furnishings of a conventional living-room, can in no way cause the stigmatisation of the elderly user. It has four caster wheels for easy mobility and, as it is based on a traditional desk format, it serves as a handy repository of personal items. The Hot Desk has a heating element built into the main structure that warms the user's hands, arms, and legs while sitting at the desk.

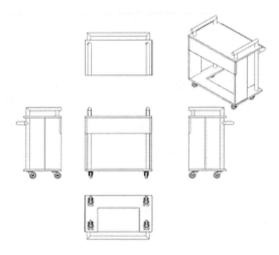

Fig. 4a. An early technical drawing.

This concept also has the potential to fulfil a further role for older people with limited mobility. The product has a long support handle and can be used on occasions as a mobility walker. The product is also equipped with a rechargeable electricity power source, thereby eliminating the need for electric cables which can cause elderly persons to trip and fall. A prototype of the Hot Desk has been constructed and will be used as a usability test rig.

In-field testing will take place in the selected homes of elderly people to analyse appropriateness of use.

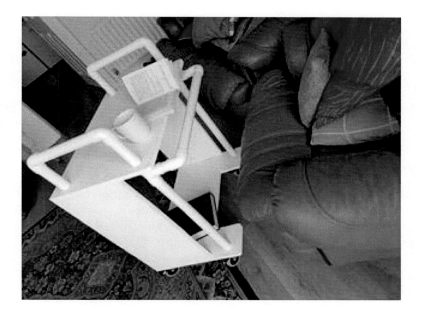

Fig. 4b. A prototype, for use in field usability testing.

Summary and further development

As the world's population ages, designers have an opportunity to create domestic products that provide for ageing-in-place. Domestic heating products that allow for the regulation of indoor temperatures are fundamental to this. This study identified that, for older people, heating products encompass a complex and diverse mix of wellbeing needs and usability/ergonomic factors. Within this, the concept of 'contained living space' was observed as an area that required immediate design intervention. Sketch ideation and prototyping were conducted to iteratively develop suitable concepts. From this, the "Hot Desk" concept – a mobile heater incorporated into a modular table – was selected for development. A prototype has been created for further improvement, and this prototype will undergo contextualised in-field testing to analyse appropriateness of use. The findings of this study will be further iterated through prototyping, and elderly users will be involved continually in the design process. The final product is intended to act as a means by which 'contained living spaces' can augment the use of spaces within the home, allowing for easiere mobility, improved comfort, and greater independence.

Works Cited

Buxton, Bill. *Sketching User Experiences: Getting the Design Right and the Right Design (Interactive Technologies)*. San Francisco: Morgan Kaufmann, 2007.

European Commission. *Europe in Figures. Eurostat Yearbook 2011*. Luxembourg: Publications Office of the European Union, 2011. <ec.europa.eu/eurostat/documents/3217494/5729317/KS-CD-11-001-EN.PDF/2b62ee78-6f91-4341-9098-1f815ff42536?version=1.0>

Fisk, Arthur D., Wendy A. Rodgers, Neil Charness, Sara J. Czaja, and Joseph Sharit. *Designing for Older Adults: Principles and Creative Human Factors Approaches*. 2nd ed. Florida: CRC Press, 2009.

Healy, Jonathan D. "Excess winter mortality in Europe: a cross country analysis identifying key risk factors." *Journal of Epidemiology & Community Health*. 57. 10. November 2003. 784-789.

Liao, Hue-Chi and Tsai Feng Chang. "Space-Heating and Water-Heating Energy Demands of the Aged in the US." *Energy Economics*. 24. 3, 2002. 267-284.

Liddell, Christine, and Chris Morris. "Fuel Poverty and Human Health: A Review of Recent Evidence." *Energy Policy*. 38. 6, 2010. 2987-2997.

McAvoy, Helen. *All-Ireland Policy Paper on Fuel Poverty and Health*. Dublin: Institute of Public Health in Ireland, 2007. <www.publichealth.ie/files/file/FuelPoverty_0.pdf>

McGee, Hannah, Ann O'Hanlon, Maja Barker, Anne Hickey, Rebecca. Garavan, Ronán Conroy, Richard Layte, Emer Shelley, Frances Horgan, Vivienne Crawford, Robert Stout, and Desmond O'Neill. *"One Island – Two Systems: A comparison of health status and health and social service use by community-dwelling older people in the Republic of Ireland and Northern Ireland*. (Dublin: Royal College of Surgeons in Ireland. Healthy Ageing Research Programme – HARP, 2005). <www.publichealth.ie/files/file/One_Island_2_System.pdf>

McGill, Paul. *Illustrating Ageing in Ireland North and South: Key Facts and Figures*. Belfast: Centre for Ageing Research and Development in Ireland, 2010.
<www.cardi.ie/userfiles/Master%20CARDI%20Statistical%20Paper_%28web%29.pdf>

Ulrich, Karl T., and Steven D. Eppinger. *Product Design and Development*. 2nd ed. New York: McGraw-Hill, 2000.

United Nations. *Vienna International Plan of Action on Ageing*. New York: United Nations, 1983.
<www.un.org/es/globalissues/ageing/docs/vipaa.pdf>

—. *World Population Ageing: 1950-2050*. New York: United Nations Department of Economic and Social Affairs. Population Division, 2001.
<www.un.org/esa/population/publications/worldageing19502050/>

—. *World Population Ageing 2013*. New York: Department of Economic and Social Affairs. Population Division, 2013.

Wilkinson, Paul, Megan Landon, Ben Armstrong, Simon Stevenson, Sam Pattenden, Martin McKee, and Tony Fletcher. *Cold comfort. The social and environmental determinants of excess winter deaths in England 1986-1996*. Bristol: The Policy Press and the Joseph Rowntree Foundation, 2001.
<www.jrf.org.uk/file/36717/download?token=eyTx87Lu>

Wilkinson, Paul, Sam Pattenden, Ben Armstrong, Astrid Fletcher, R. Sari Kovats, Punam Mangtani, and Anthony J. McMichael. "Vulnerability to winter mortality in elderly people in Britain: population-based study." *British Medical Journal*. 329. 7467, 2004. 647.
<www.jstor.org/stable/25469125>

World Health Organisation. *Housing and Health in Europe*. Copenhagen: WHO Regional Office for Europe, 2001.
<www.bvsde.paho.org/bvsacd/cd41/who5.pdf>

World Health Organisation. *Housing and health: Identifying priorities – Meeting Report*. Bonn: Regional Office for Europe, European Centre for Environment and Health, 2003.

Part Three

Services

Care Services
and
Caring

New Services for New Elders.
Welfare vs. Free Market: Technology, Cost Governance, and Human Caring

Dario Bracco and Ugo Marchisio

Centro Ricerche e Relazioni Cornaglia (Ce.R.R.Co), Turin[1]

We are living in a world *of* old people, but not *for* old people. The "Baby Boomers," getting old now, are a generation of wealthy, free, educated, and exigent people. But they are plenty ... too many for the much slenderer younger generations who look at them as an economic 'boomerang.'

In the pages of *The Independent,*[2] *The Telegraph, The Sun, The New York Post*, and many other newspapers and magazines, and on CBS News, it was announced that, "Scientists find key to longevity in an Italian village [Acciaroli] where one in ten people live beyond 100 years." In fact, official data for the year 2015 show that life-expectancy at birth in Italy is 80·1 years for men and 84·7 years for women. But time spent with a severe disability is 3·9 years for men and 6·3 years for women.

We – the Italian, Mediterranean, Latin Europeans – may not be number one in technology and management, but we do have the "human touch," a factor that is often neglected nowadays, whereas, in our opinion, it should be a key element in person-centred services. Only with a big injection of the so-called Medical Humanities[3] and Human Caring[4] will a real person-centred care service for the new generation of elderly persons be ensured. A

---

[1] The Centro Ricerche e Relazioni Cornaglia (Ce.R.R.Co), based in Turin (Italy), is an interprofessional 'think tank' involved in research leading towards the empowerment and defense of older people. This chapter shares research results about trends, problems, and experiences in the European Union and Italy over the past five years, as well as a vision about the future evolutions of services for the 'new older generation.'

[2] *The Independent*, 6th September 2016.

[3] See Enrico Larghero, Mariella Lombardi-Ricci, Rosaria Marchesi. *Medical Humanities e Bioetica clinica.* (Turin: Edizioni Camilliane, 2010).

[4] See Jean Watson. *Nursing: Human Science and Human Care.* (Sudbury, MA: Jones and Bartlett, 1999); 2nd edition. *Human Caring Science. A Theory of Nursing.* (Sudbury, MA: Jones and Bartlett Learning, 2012).

major breakthrough has been made by the United Nations by including the cause of elderly persons in long-term care in the list of human rights to be defended, promoted, and empowered. A direct operational development has been a European Union-funded project (2015-2017) that focused on this issue.[5] Zygmunt Bauman says: "Happiness is not independence, but interdependence."[6]

It is a matter of fact that, after 2007, during the financial-economic crisis, 7% of Italians needing a homecare worker relinquished the service due to a lack of money, and 40% took to the National Health Service (NHS) for services that, before, they had paid for out of their own pockets. Currently in Turin, the proportion of elderly people – persons aged 65 years old and over – is one of the highest in the world, reaching 25·2% in 2014 (see Figure 1).

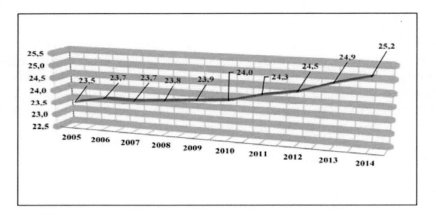

Fig. 1. Proportion (%) of elderly population – persons aged 65 years old and over – in Turin (2005-2014).

Due to the economic crisis with its accompanying disintegration of families and couples, in 2002 the possibility of staying in homecare service in Turin was implemented provisionally and with a low budget. Then, in 2005, since the National Health Service (NHS) took over the implementation of the new, extensive service, costs have increased dramatically. Moreover,

---

[5] See Francesca Ippolito, and Sara Iglesias-Sànchez. *Protecting Vulnerable Groups: The European Human Rights Framework*. (Oxford: Hart Publishing (Bloomsbury), 2015).
[6] Zygmunt Bauman, interview in the *The Swedish Theory of Love* (Dir. Erik Gandini, 2015).

after 2008, financial resources for the National Health Service (NHS) were cut and have continued to fall to this day (see Figure 2). For this reason, while hospitals are overcrowded, and long-term, transitional health services are under siege, the need for a solution based on residential care has increased. In 2014, those elderly people waiting for homecare or nursing home admission in Turin numbered 12,000, while in the whole Piedmont Region the number of elderly individuals waiting for assistance is 31,000. The waiting list grows longer every day. Tension over this issue grew to such a pitch that a fight broke out between the Turin Municipality and the Piedmont Region over social cost-sharing, and this even led to a court case. The argument is still going on! From 2014 onwards, the final figure for public spending is unavailable!

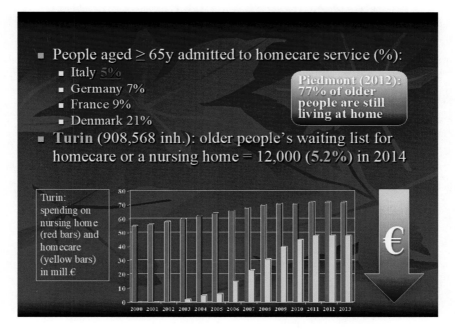

Fig. 2. Nursing home and homecare service coverage and cost trend in Turin (2000-2013)

On the other hand, elderly persons – aged 65 years old and over – who are still living at home, in Turin, account for an amazing 77% (CI 95% = 74·6-79·4), as has been shown in a recent survey of 1,339 cases.[7] The same study

---

[7] See "Passi d'Argento" Study, Piedmont Region (2012). <www.epicentro.iss.it/passi-argento/>

reveals high figures even for frail and disabled elderly people. The subgroups based on frailty and disability show the following percentage of elderly people living at home:

– Good health and low risk = 83%
– Good health but high risk = 75%
– Frail – concomitant chronic diseases = 71%
– With disability = 63%

The other side of the coin is, of course, loneliness. Figure 3 depicts the high proportion of elderly people living completely alone and shows how age and gender are the main risk factors for loneliness.[8]

Age	Men	Women	Total
65–74 years old	20%	33%	26%
75–84 years old	22%	47%	37%
≥ 85 years old	32%	66%	56%
Total Turin (≥ 65 years old)	22%	45%	35%
Total Piedmont	15%	31%	25%

Fig. 2. Elderly persons' loneliness in Turin (2012)
(CGIL/SPI Study "Older people in Turin" - 2014)

The huge social burden elderly persons are imposing nowadays in Italy, especially in the form of hospital admission costs, is well depicted in Figure 4.

---

[8] CGIL/SPI Study "Older people in Turin" (2014).

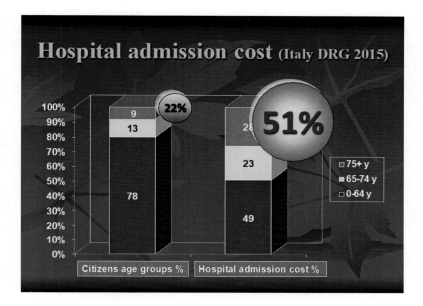

Fig. 4. In Italy, persons aged 65 years old and over make up 22% of the population, but they account for 51% of the hospital admission costs.

To avoid this huge economic burden of disease and disability, the economic temptation is to emulate the physicians of the Saint Ursula Hospital in the 17th century:

> We do not admit old people, of even 90 years old years or more, because if we put to bed such elderly persons and spoon-feed them, we would have our beds filled for ten years or more to the detriment of many a treatable person.[9]

"Locust" generation or "Crutch" generation?

With an "inverted" demographic pyramid, elderly people can be really seen as a "Locust Generation" that, unremittingly, eats up the national resources, at the expense of young people who fund their pensions.[10] And actually, 32% of public spending in Italy goes to pensions, the highest figure among OECD

---

[9] Decreto dell'Ospedale Sant'Orsola di Bologna (1670). [Ordinance]
[10] Emiliano Fittipaldi. *La Repubblica* (9/6/2015).

countries.[11] From a social point-of-view, elderly people hold onto their "acquired rights," have a good income from their pensions, and hold 35% of the domestic financial wealth,[12] let alone properties and other goods. Younger people, on the other hand, have low salaries, unstable job contracts, and endless years before being able to retire.

Fig. 5. Gian Lorenzo Bernini. *Aenea, Anchises and Ascanius* (1618) Borghese Gallery, Rome.

But in most Italian families, the elderly individual is not a 'locust,' but a member of the 'crutch generation,' supporting two, even three, members of the younger generation. Nowadays, Italian pensioners are providing "rescue welfare" for the greater working population, a humanist

---

[11] OECD report (2014) <www.oecd.org/pensions/oecd-pensions-outlook>
[12] Data from Banca d'Italia (2014) <www.bancaditalia.it/pubblicazioni/relazione-annuale/2014/>

characteristic of Italians who are still deeply attached to their families. The famous sculpture by Gian Lorenzo Bernini (see Figure 5), which depicts Aeneas fleeing from Troy with his father Anchises on his shoulders and his son Ascanius clinging to his knees, is a very good metaphor for the Baby Boomers' generation, the members of which are called on to look after their members from previous and subsequent generations.

Older persons' health as an investment
The new older generation should not be perceived as a useless burden or simply as an under-utilized resource, but rather as a true asset for younger people. But a healthy and active ageing for the elderly has to be guaranteed, and investments must be made in certain areas such as an early education and prevention. Investments in health, with a comprehensive, integrated plan, means prevention against chronic diseases, risk factors, and disability.

The way to go is, of course, 'active ageing,'[13] 'lifelong learning," and 'staying-in-place.' Governments are paying close attention to the promotion of these activities. For instance, "Healthy People 2020," a programme of the United States Department of Health and Human Services, a full comprehensive "road map" to health and well-being – social determinants of health, equity, correct lifestyles, and so on – includes specific chapters about older adults. But the spiritual, affective, artistic, ideal dimensions and the importance of resilience must not be forgotten.[14] In the Piedmont Region, the impact of 'active ageing' and 'lifelong learning' activities showed, in 2012, the following participation:[15]

– Courses: $6\cdot8\%$ (CI 95% = $5\cdot3$-$8\cdot2$)
– Social activities: $34\cdot2\%$ (CI 95% = $31\cdot6$-$36\cdot8$)
– Volunteering: $5\cdot4\%$ (CI 95% = $4\cdot1$-$6\cdot6$)
– Being a "resource." Caring and helping persons, living with them or not, and volunteering in the personal care field: $31\cdot0\%$ (CI95% = $28\cdot4$-$33\cdot6\%$)

To our mind, the numbers reflected in these statistics are too low and are insufficient. For this reason, promotion activities were intensified during the following years. The results of these activities will soon be available so that subsequent activities can be thought through again and re-planned.

---

[13] Colin Miller. <www.icaa.cc/activeagingandwellness/activeaging.htm>
[14] See Edmund Sherman. *Contemplative Aging: A Way of Being in Later Life.* (New York: Gordian Knot Books, 2010).
[15] Data from the "Passi d'argento" Study – 1,384 persons aged ≥65 years old.

What's up with Welfare, the National Health Service (NHS), and the free market?

In a free market, spending on health behaves as if it were a luxury item. This means it behaves with an exponential trend, not with a linear one as essential goods do (see Figure 6). For this reason, in Western Countries, policy-makers must be very wise when setting the cut-off point between "basic levels of care,"[16] with universal coverage by the Government – Welfare and the National Health Service (NHS) – and "optional services" that can be, and must be, up to the free market. The difference between "Need Medicine" and "Desire Medicine" can present difficulties both for politicians and public-service managers: citizens take their health very seriously, and the marketing by involved corporations is very aggressive.

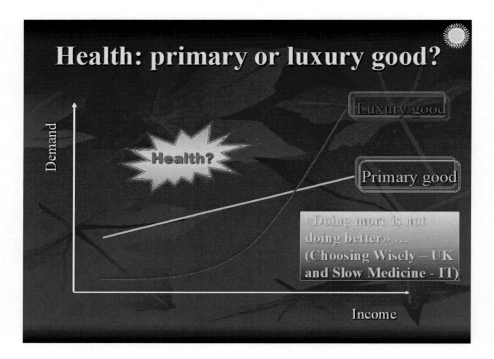

Fig. 6. Health in a completely free market behaves as a luxury item.

Actually, at least in Italy, basic levels of care for elderly people means a roof, full service to the person, even when severely disabled, good

---

[16] In Italy, Livelli Essenziali di Assistenza (LEA)

food, and free health coverage. All this is the remit of Welfare and the National Health Service (NHS); "Optional services" means everything else.

* * *

New 'silver industries' and 'ageing enterprises' promoting ageing-in-place are responding to a fast-growing market that is increasingly integrating public services, even in countries with a sound, inclusive welfare system, as is the case with the countries of the European Union. It is contended here that Public Private Partnership (PPP) is the winning formula, including franchising management, mixed – public and private – executive boards, with shared strategic planning, and so on. In this way, the 'new elderly,' with their new needs, even at a time of economic crisis and "liquid" cultures, will be able to find everything they like and need.

Moreover, some new trends, already well-known in the United States of America, are gaining purchase in the European Union, including Italy. Amongst such new trends are: 'thematic retirement homes' for healthy elderly persons with a shared interest, for example, former teachers, artists in general, culture adepts, and religious believers; community-based facilities, for healthy young persons and seniors, conveniently located close to a spa or a sports centre; custom-organized sea-cruises for the elderly, including frail and disabled persons, with prices similar to those of a good retirement home; co-housing and ageing-friendly communities; mixed kindergarten/retirement homes;[17] and a huge fan of optional activities implemented inside a multipurpose, elderly-person facility.

However, it could be argued that all these new opportunities will always be solely for healthy, independent, and well-off elderly people. But what about the disabled, the chronically-ill, and the not-so-well-heeled? To our mind, it is essential to rethink the 'nursing home' as a flexible but universal solution, a 'bridge' between homecare and hospital admission, offering all the solutions an elderly person might need when in good health, or when suffering from an illness or disability of any kind and severity. A complete and working unification of welfare and health services, professionals, and budgets must occur in order that 'active ageing' can be fostered, and in order to secure the best assistance when dependence comes up.

Examples are well known all around the world. For instance, near Turin, in Roero County – a land blessed with wine and truffles – the "Citadel

---

[17] See, for instance, "Preschool inside a living-care community, Providence Mount St. Vincent – Seattle." (The Mount's Intergenerational Learning Center – ILC).

of Health" is housed in Canale d'Alba, a restored 17th century villa, with new buildings in a single nursing facility, located in the land where people are used to living, with qualified professionals, including geriatricians, on duty every day (see Figure 7).

Fig. 7. The "Citadel of Health" in Canale d'Alba

The "Citadel of Health" complex includes mini-flats for independent elderly persons, both for single persons and for couples, and all manner of different healthcare settings, for individuals with mild dependence to those suffering from advanced Alzheimer's disease or severe disability. This nursing facility has one hundred and thirty-four beds in total, including those in the mini-flats, and the buildings are certified AAA, the highest level of energy-saving and environmental preservation. All rooms are furnished with two beds, with a surface area of $27m^2$, the present standard for three beds. Inside the "Citadel of Health," the Medical Emergency Service, the Operative Centre, an Out-Patients' Department, the Social Assistance Service, the Red Cross, and all the other volunteer organizations are also located.

The "human touch," and Personal Care Aids (PCA) training
"From care to take care" – this is our slogan for real person-centred care. Better than any definition, the core of "Human Caring" can be rendered by the inscription on the door of the ancient Hospital of St James in Rome, *viz.*:

> *Vieni per essere guarito* (You come here to be healed)
> *Se non guarito, almeno curato* (If not healed, at least treated)
> *Se non curato, almeno consolato* (If not treated, at least solaced)

The inscription implies not only 'health' as "life in the silence of organs,"[18] but also helping the ill person get back to a full human and social wellness and empowering her or his own self-sufficiency and freedom. Moreover, here "empowerment" means strengthening and expanding the psycho-biological resources, not only of the sick person, but also of the healer!

For this reason, Personal Care Aids (PCA) training is of paramount importance, not only from a technical point-of-view, but also from the perspective of motivation and empathy. A quick survey of informal professional caregivers – the current PCA situation in Italy – reveals that, today, due to the economic/financial crisis, they are just half what they were in 2010. More precisely, the "badanti" or "informal Personal Care Aids (PCA)" who look after more than 1,000,000 elderly persons, numbered 1,655,000 in 2010,[19] and 830,000 in 2015.[20] During 2015 alone, 500,000 informal Personal Care Aids (PCA) had their service hours reduced, while another 250,000 had their contracts cancelled.

Notwithstanding this reduction, the current, estimated, global cost of Personal Care Aids (PCA) in Italy exceeds €10,000 million per year.[21] More than 90% of the elderly in the care of Personal Care Aids (PCA) are immigrants. Among them, 26% have neither a residence permit nor a legal job contract; 30·5% have a residence permit but not a legal contract; and just 43·5% are in possession of both a residence permit and an employment contract. Only 14% are provided with qualified professional training, and co-operation with National Health Service (NHS) professionals is often far from the desired optimum. Despite the many, qualified courses the City of Turin and other private and public institutions have implemented, the need for

---

[18] Quotation from René Leriche (1879–1955). French surgeon. The Leriche syndrome is named after him.
[19] Data from *Censis*.
[20] Data from humanitarian agencies.
[21] *Istat* (2016).

Evidence-Based (EB) educational programmes and integration with professional health workers is still significant.

Conclusions

Elderly persons are not a burden – a "locust generation." Quite the opposite! They can be a valuable asset in today's society, performing as a "crutch generation" for the younger generations. But the "New Elders" – 'the Baby-Boomers' – differ in many aspects from the elderly of former generations, in that they have more extensive and sophisticated needs, aspirations, and, above all, potential.

The Welfare services and the National Health Service (NHS) cannot be responsible for, nor can they meet all these needs. However, in order for Welfare and the National Health Service (NHS) to satisfy some of the demands, the basic ones, Public Private Partnership (PPP) is, in our view, the best economic and management way to tackle the current "liquid" financial and cultural situation. New 'tailored life plans' and 'thematic nursing homes' for healthy retired persons, and 'bridge' nursing homes for disabled elderly people, are nowadays the best operational solutions.

Personal Care Aids (PCA) are a cornerstone, professional resource, but a more qualified, registered training is required, as well as better integration with National Health Service (NHS) professional workers. Above all, it is paramount that a 'human touch' culture be promoted, based on a personalised, individual-centred approach, medical humanities, and a fundamental "from care to take care" attitude.

Works Cited

Bauman, Zygmunt. "Interview." *The Swedish Theory of Love*. Dir. Erik Gandini, 2015. [Documentary film]
Decreto dell'Ospedale Sant'Orsola di Bologna (1670). [Ordinance]
Fittipaldi, Emiliano. *La Repubblica*. 9th June 2015.
Ippolito, Francesca, and Sara Iglesias-Sànchez. *Protecting Vulnerable Groups: The European Human Rights Framework*. Oxford: Hart Publishing (Bloomsbury), 2015.
Larghero, Enrico, Mariella Lombardi-Ricci, Rosaria Marchesi. *Medical Humanities e Bioetica clinica*. Turin: Edizioni Camilliane, 2010.
Miller, Colin. <www.icaa.cc/activeagingandwellness/activeaging.htm>
Mount's Intergenerational Learning Center (ILC) (The). "Preschool inside a living-care community. Providence Mount St. Vincent – Seattle."

<www.theatlantic.com/education/archive/2016/01/the-preschool-inside-a-nursing-home/424827/>

Sherman, Edmund. *Contemplative Aging: A Way of Being in Later Life*. New York: Gordian Knot Books, 2010.

Watson, Jean. *Nursing: Human Science and Human Care*. Sudbury, MA: Jones and Bartlett, 1999; 2nd edition. *Human Caring Science. A Theory of Nursing*. Sudbury, MA: Jones and Bartlett Learning, 2012.

Websites

<www.epicentro.iss.it/passi-argento/>

<www.oecd.org/pensions/oecd-pensions-outlook>

<www.bancaditalia.it/pubblicazioni/relazione-annuale/2014/>

<www.icaa.cc/activeagingandwellness/activeaging.htm>

Social Exclusion

(Female Elderly)

Older Women and Social Exclusion.
A Descriptive, Exploratory, Qualitative Study

Andrés Escarbajal-de Haro, Silvia Martínez de Miguel-López, and Juan Antonio Salmerón-Aroca

University of Murcia

The increase in life-age, together with the decrease in the number of births, has evolved into an inversion of the Spanish population pyramid, a demographic phenomenon that was becoming increasingly evident and impossible to ignore during the latter years of the twentieth century.[1] Faced with this situation, a concept of 'active ageing' has been established with the idea that ageing presupposes the need to accept the alterations and malfunctions associated with the evolution of life. But 'active ageing' also presupposes that, as they grow older, elderly individuals can increase their potential of personal development and growth.

On the other hand, the ageing process of the population has, at the same time, provoked an increasing gender imbalance: women live longer than men nearly all over the world. This is reflected in a bigger proportion of ageing women than of ageing men, a disproportion that has given rise to the term "female ageing."[2] In Spain, for example, elderly women represent 10% of the total population, they have a longer life than previous generations and, in terms of longevity, they really differ from men – 85·4 years is the average life span for women, while the average for men is 79·5 years, according to the latest available data.[3]

With this in mind and following the recommendations that the Institute for Elderly Persons and the Social Services (IMSERSO) – a Government agency that operates under the auspices of the Spanish Ministry of Health, Social Politics, and Equality – had collected in their White Paper

---

[1] See Julio Pérez-Díaz. "El envejecimiento de la población Española." *Investigación y Ciencia.* 410, 2010. 34-42.

[2] Instituto de Mayores y Servicios Sociales, El (IMSERSO). *Envejecimiento activo. Libro Blanco.* (Madrid: Ministerio de Sanidad, Política Social e Igualdad, 2011). 9.

[3] See Instituto Nacional de Estadística, El (INE). *Estimación de la población española actual.* 2014.

on 'active ageing,'[4] a research project was undertaken using a qualitative field and set up along two axes, namely, gender and the environment. The project focused on the danger for elderly women of social exclusion, and involved a search for inclusive alternatives, both in social centres and in the community environment.

Theoretical frame

The social exclusion of women, in general, is a contrasted fact,[5] a situation which is not new. History has shown that discrimination against women, referring that carried out by men, is as old as human existence.[6] Moreover, although social exclusion is just one amongst a number of different factors of risk which are interrelated, and which have ended up associated with certain social collectives, it can be stated that, in general, elderly women must face a double discrimination in society, namely, age-discrimination and gender-discrimination. As a result, and according to the European Parliament (2010), elderly women run a greater risk than elderly men of finishing their lives poor and, in their relative poverty, of being socially-excluded. This is due not only to the fact that they have a low-level retirement pension or widow's allowance – added to a lack of income from their non-compensated roles as carer or nursemaid – but they are also victims of their social and personal situations, and of administrations, which have taken control of the geographical area where they live. At the same time, this generation of elderly women is the last generation of carers-cum-nursemaids and, therefore, the first generation excluded from the direct family environment. This generation of elderly women can be seen as that generation of elderly persons who have lived for others,[7] and this portends a pessimistic future for this collective.

---

[4] Instituto de Mayores y Servicios Sociales, El (IMSERSO). *Envejecimiento activo. Libro Blanco.* (Madrid: Ministerio de Sanidad, Política Social e Igualdad, 2011).

[5] See Anna Freixas-Farré. *Tan frescas. Las nuevas mujeres mayores del siglo XXI.* (Barcelona: Paidós Ibérica, 2013).

[6] See Carol Gilligan. "In a Different Voice: Women's Conceptions of Self and of Morality." *Harvard Educational Review* (December 1977). 47. 4, 1977. 481-517; Magdalena Jiménez-Ramírez. "Aproximación teórica de la exclusión social: complejidad e imprecisión del término. Consecuencias para el ámbito educativo." Valdivia: *Estudios Pedagógicos.* 34. 1, 2008. 173-186; and Carmen Serdio-Sánchez. *Mujeres que envejecen, mujeres que aprenden.* (Salamanca: Universidad Pontificia de Salamanca, 2006).

[7] See Manuel Hernández-Pedreño. *Desigualdades según género en la vejez.* (Murcia: Secretaría Sectorial de la Mujer y de la Juventud, 2000).

The description of this situation reveals that elderly women are especially dependent on the public and private services, and on public health attention. This means that they can be seriously disadvantaged when those services either do not exist, or when the quality of the services and their administration is of insufficiently high standard, especially in the event that they reside far from the principal nucleus of population. In an attempt to tackle the discrimination and possible social exclusion that women suffer, above all elderly women in these circumstances, the Spanish Ministry of the Environment, and Rural and Coastal Areas introduced *The Strategic Plan for Equality of Sex in the Rural Environment (2011-2014).*[8]

Likewise, an analysis of statistics relating to the collective of illiterate elderly people reveals that it is elderly women who represent a high percentage – 75·4% – of the female cohort compared with 24% of the male cohort. The indicator of educational level is a clear example of the 'non-equality' which has been the marker for generations of women.[9] It seems evident, therefore, that there is a *cultural* rejection which gives rise to situations of social exclusion amongst elderly women.

* * *

The research involved reviewing the most important bibliography on this topic and carrying out a qualitative study with elderly women in those municipal areas which are located in the Valle de Ricote in the Region of Murcia, Spain. The principal reason for choosing this geographical environment is because the highest number of elderly people in the entire Region of Murcia are registered in the Valle de Ricote. For this reason, the following general objective was set up within the framework of the research project, namely:

– to identify those conditions in which social exclusion appears in elderly women, by analysing the possibilities and limits of their socio-educational and community participation as an alternative.

This general objective was further sub-divided into the following specific aims:

---

[8] Ministerio de Medio Ambiente y Medio Rural y Marino (MARM). *Plan estratégico para la igualdad de género en el desarrollo sostenible del medio rural (2011-2014).* (Madrid: Ministerio de Medio Ambiente y Medio Rural y Marino. Dirección General de Desarrollo Sostenible del Medio Rural. Subdirección General de Igualdad y Modernización, 2011).

[9] See Instituto de Mayores y Servicios Sociales, El (IMSERSO). *Envejecimiento activo. Libro Blanco.* (Madrid: Ministerio de Sanidad, Política Social e Igualdad, 2011).

– to describe the situation of elderly people who come to social centres in the Valle de Ricote;

– to ascertain, from the responses of the elderly people, whether or not it is their socio-cultural situation that gives rise to their social exclusion; and

– to analyse whether or not the process of socio-educational and community participation can be elements which favour their social inclusion.

Methodology

A special exploratory-descriptive type of investigation was applied to this field since the final objective was oriented towards studying the process of ageing using qualitative parameters such as personal assessments, perceptions, expectations, and feelings, and by looking for key factors which might make growing older different for women.

1. Participants

The number of elderly people in the Valle de Ricote is about 12,292, that is, 15·7% of the total population. Of these citizens, 56·9% are elderly women and 43·1% elderly men. Regarding the level of ageing, an indicator which measures the proportion of elderly people over 65 years old against those under 20 years old, this area shows a really high ratio, reaching 148·9%.[10] In human terms, this makes the Valle de Ricote the 'oldest' area in the Region of Murcia.

We proceeded to a selection of female informants by taking into account the following general criteria:

– the informants must be women over 65 years old;
– the women must reside in the municipal areas of the Valle de Ricote;
– the women must not live in residences or institutional centres;
– the women must not belong to any association or frequent any of the social centres in the area;
– the women must not be undertaking any socio-educational activities during the time the research is being carried out.

---

[10] See Consejería de Economía, Empresa e Innovación. *Territorialización. Plan estratégico de la Región de Murcia. Valle de Ricote.* (Murcia: Consejería de Economía, Empresa e Innovación, 2013).

In this way, eighty participants were selected, together with eight social centres which fulfilled the criteria.

2. Research tools

Regarding the research tools used, the 'semi-structured interview' and the 'discussion group' were chosen as the most suitable means by which to collect all the required information. These tools are in line with the objectives of this research since they allow for the collection and classification of all types of data provided by the elderly women. The information gathered is not merely descriptive; following the model proposed by Silvia Martínez de Miguel-López (2003),[11] these tools enable a physical, personal contact with the elderly female informants and an exchange of opinions, impressions, feelings, and personal meanings.

The categories chosen for the application of both the 'semi-structured interviews' and the 'discussion groups' were: a) Life trajectory; b) Health; c) Interpersonal relationships; d) Perception of Ageing; e) Socio-community Participation; f) Educational aspects; and g) Resources.

3. Procedure

To summarize, the procedure followed three phases:

a) Preparatory phase

This involved the in-depth tracing of printed and online documentation; the selection of texts and materials related to the topic; and the classification of the data compiled, followed by its subsequent allocation into operative files. The operative design of this research developed in loops. Several sections were subjected to scrutiny and discussion. Questions were raised about the study itself, the project topic, research methods, collection techniques, strategies for sample analysis and the treatment of data, and procedures for obtaining consent.

b) Collecting information

Everything started with the observation of the participants, and by taking down notes in the field. The written record of observed information, in an introspective register, helped to structure the data both theoretically and methodologically. Following this, eighty 'semi-structured interviews' with elderly women were carried out in different social centres, and ten

---

[11] Silvia Martínez de Miguel-López. *Reconstruyendo la educación de personas mayores.* (Granada: Grupo Editorial Universitario, 2003).

'discussion groups' took place in an attempt to add precision to the participants' information.

c) Data analysis

Data analysis is key to the project results. It is a problematic phase of the research process, requiring hard work, given the flexible and open-ended nature of the methodology used, as well as the diversity of the points-of-view which it involves. These factors condition the analysis of the data. In any event, basically analysis of the content was undertaken throughout the processes of theorization, that is, the exploration, description, and interpretation of data. In addition, general analytical procedures – for example, the management of data through categorisation – and strategies of sequential selection to generate categories, were carried out. These measures took into account the orientations of recognized experts, who are already widely-recognized for their contributions to qualitative methodology.[12] The process, which was developed regarding seven highlighted categories previously dealt with, allowed for the formulation of conclusions, following a corresponding discussion.

Results

In line with qualitative methodology, two traditional types of evidence are employed here for the presentation of the testimonies of the elderly people, that is, narrative text and stubs. Here follows a summary of the principal results of the research on the basis of selected categories:

a) Life trajectory

Most women in this sample married when they were young, and some of them state that they married when they were very young–

"Because I married very young and afterwards the children…"

---

[12] Margaret D. LeCompte, and Judith Preissle Goetz. "Problems of Reliability and Validity in Ethnographic Research." *Review of Educational Research*. 52. 1, Spring 1982. 31-60; Matthew B. Miles, and A. Michael Huberman. *Qualitative Data Analysis*. (Beverly Hills: Sage Publishing, 1984); Steven J. Taylor, and Robert Bogdan. *Introduction to Qualitative Research Methods. The Search for Meanings*. (New York: John Wiley and Sons, 1984). [Trans. Jorge Piatigorsky. 1984. *Introducción a los métodos cualitativos de investigación. La búsqueda de significados*. (Barcelona: Ediciones Paidós Ibérica, 1994)].

With reference to the type of education they received, the elderly women concurred with the fact that they were always focused on chores and housework–

> "I studied little, because my mother wanted me to sew; she ordered me to go to school in the morning and to sew in the afternoon."

The fact that the elderly women were not able to study had negative consequences throughout the lifetime of some of the participants–

> "When my children needed help, there was a moment when I could not afford more, and it was then when I regretted not having studied harder."

Many of the women gave up studying when they were very young. On the other hand, it is generally recognised that post-war societies offered limited possibilities for study–

> "There was no money for anything and less to study."

It should be emphasised that these women were very young when they had their first contact with extra-housework. In general, they used to start when they were very young, coinciding with the time they left school at the age of twelve–

> "I worked when I was a child; I started working when I was twelve."

Some of the women went on working, and they combined domestic tasks with breast-feeding and a paid job.

b) Health

In a meaningful way, it is necessary to recognise the emotional problems which the elderly women suffered over the years, and the reasons for which can be summarised as: a lack of social skills; of personal relationships; and of a project in their personal lives–

> "For a while, I could not find a future; I could not see well my life ahead."

as a personal shortcoming when solving daily problems–

"Since when I want to do something and I cannot do it, I feel nervous."

and, in the same way, an emotional overburden which relates to the attention and care of the family – grandchildren, children, husband. Furthermore, potential illnesses are one of the biggest problems the elderly women foresee, and the cause of great anxiety. The women are fearful of and worry about the possibility of being handicapped in some way, of loneliness, and of an inability to solve problems relating to family members, an emotion that is more intense in widows–

"What I am more afraid of are problems dealing with the mind."

c) Personal relationships
The relationships that the elderly women have with their families has been stated as satisfactory in general terms, and it is the area which is most important in their lives. Equally, the results which have been computed show that there are clear references to the satisfaction deriving from their social relationships, which are positive–

"I meet a group of women who are older than me; and then we go to the countryside to have lunch, and go out, and I have a great time."

d) Perceptions of growing old and ageing
With reference to the state of their self-esteem as they grow older, the elderly women displayed a positive self-evaluation, the result of a positive evaluation of their lives in general. Nevertheless, some comments in particular, though less frequently expressed, did reveal and reinforce a negative feeling–

"Over the years, we will miss something; you always miss something."

* * *

It was also of interest to this research to identify the deeply-held expectations and aspirations of the elderly women during the stages of their early-, mid-, and late-age. The results, in general, show clear tendencies towards a predisposition to enhance their personal growth, and to satisfy the need to fulfil their aims in life–

"As regards my personal life, I have a lot to do; I do not want to be static."

However, the elderly women themselves realise that these tendencies are not perceived by everybody. With reference to the image that people of other age groups have in mind about growing old, the opinions collected from the elderly women are usually negative–

"They think that old people are not useful for anything."

Moreover, the elderly women believe it to be important, too, that people of other age groups consider arguments with respect to the feeling of social discrimination–

"Elder people are usually kept apart."

e) Community participation
This important category involves information about elderly people relating to the assessment of their participative trajectory in different social centres. This area of enquiry has generated a wide diversity of answers which touch on leisure and entertainment, relationships with other women who are not family members, keeping up good physical and psychical standards and, of course, learning–

"To learn and to be active."

Oral expressions were elicited which show, in a clear way, the positive relation between the psycho-social dimension of health and socio-educational participation–

"A lot of women say that, if I go [to the social centre's fitness sessions], it is because I have no aches and it does not hurt, but I say that it is totally the opposite; I come here, and I forget my aches and pains."

f) Educational aspects
In terms of educational aspects, results are obtained which incline towards a positive evaluation. With these activities, evaluations centred on stimulation

objectives, personal appreciation, sharing experiences, and exchanging knowledge–

> "You learn more from elderly people as they have lived many more experiences."

It is important to emphasize the need to take into account the opinions of the elderly women when arranging these educational activities–

> "Let us be free to choose what we want to learn."

Regarding the format of the sessions, it has become clear that the elderly women participants prefer strategies which provide opportunities to ask and contribute–

> "When you contribute, you learn more. I like participating a lot, but I also like the participation of the others."

g) Resources

If we consider the present-day historical and socio-economical period, it is interesting to ask the participants for their opinion about the current situation and about the repercussions it might have on their late-life, in addition to involving them as referents and potential providers of solutions with which to tackle the problems.

With this in mind, the results show, in a clear way, that they are a group of survivors of these types of situation, above all as they have had to face economic problems earlier in life–

> "Since we were all very poor, I save money and I deal with it quite well."

> "If I receive my salary, six hundred euros, I have to spend four and save two for the time I need it in future."

Their main economic worry, totally independent from their personal situation, is the situation that their sons and daughters are having to face, as they consider themselves the family's nucleus and they, as the first person, assume the responsibility for maintenance–

"Life is dark due to the crisis, and for young people. While we can go onwards, we will help them."

It was also pointed out that their economic problems are not only rooted in the present-day situation; it is also an historical problem. Economic dependence has always existed for men and women, and it is one of the factors which cause social inequality and gender discrimination, especially for elderly women.

Lastly, one of the questions which the elderly women wanted to highlight is that, if the economic situation brought about by the crisis does not affect their domestic economy directly, they are aware that it is affecting their educational possibilities and the educational activities which their social centres are carrying out–

"We need more places, there are no places anywhere."

"There should be more services, and right now we are bad."

And what appears strongly, regarding these resources and the repercussions in the future, is a great concern and uncertainty about how they will be looked after and who will look after them when the need arises–

"We cannot expect young people to do what we have done for our sons and daughters."

Conclusions

In answer to the first aim of this research, it should be pointed out that it is predominantly married women and widows who live in their own houses. Most of them are between 65 and 75 years old. The processes of socialization they have been subjected to – due to the historical, generational, and socio-cultural frame of inequality – have dictated a clear path both in formal aspects of their education and in their dedication to technical activities. The training they received during childhood and adolescence amounted to indoctrination to be housewives, wives, and nannies. Moreover, they combined this 'education' with chores and housework in the countryside and in the orchard, as these were the places in which they spent most of their childhood. However, elderly women feel that they are at a stage in life of revindication and liberation in respect of previous epochs. They refuse to be involved only in housework, and they try to 'educate' their husbands to participate in domestic chores; they would like to bring into line this 'must,' which they regard as being "socially-imposed," with a higher level and degree of social participation.

Referring to their health, the elderly women generalized that they feel aches, that their joints hurt, and they admit to suffering from traditional illnesses such as diabetes, hypertension, psychological problems, and so on. Confronting these aches and pains, they generally show a positive attitude, adapting themselves to the circumstances with a varied range of behaviours, from taking medicines to participating in socio-educational activities and in community activities. Yet they also think and have doubts about how they will be cared for and, above all, by whom. This is a question that was not a cause for anxiety for previous generations; family tradition conferred this task to one's own family members – the youngest daughter or, alternatively, the single one, used to be entrusted with caring for elderly family members – so the elderly women have developed, in a singular way, capacities to look after others, despite difficulties for their own care.

The analysis of the data throws into relief the importance that the family environment has in the lives of the elderly women, with complex processes, relationships with the different family members, and their own dynamic processes. Everything seems to indicate that the degree of satisfaction with family relationships is key to the quality of early-, mid-, and late-life, acting as modulator of state-of-mind, if only at the same time, it provides the principal basis of human support, and reduces the feeling of loneliness and social exclusion.

* * *

Relating to the second proposed aim in this research, the perception that the elderly women have of themselves shows a high degree of satisfaction in the way they are living their lives nowadays, though several individual differences exist. Having said this, significantly several negative stereotypes have been found to exist when dealing with the image of elderly women. These views derive from ideas of physical damage, although they vary according to variable factors such as functionality and psychological state.

The elderly women who have participated in this study show a great concern about illnesses. They are preoccupied with keeping up an active physical and psychological state, and they consider this to be the principal problem of their ageing process, together with worries about family welfare and combining family life with their role as carer and nursemaid. Equally, they consider they have psychological problems – fears and worries which have to do with the anxiety they feel whenever they think of being handicapped somehow; with the sadness and distress of loneliness; and with a future inability to solve family problems, a feeling much more intense in elderly widows. By way of a conclusion, this study has revealed that elderly women do not feel socially-excluded, but that their personal circumstances, their situations, and their fears can contribute to varied degrees of exclusion.

* * *

As regards the third proposed objective – living and participation in social centres and in the community – it is necessary to acknowledge the exceptional capacity of improvement that social activities offer. It is clear from the study that the tradition of forming a partnership becomes really important, creating, as it does, a reference and an environment at this level for future generations. Furthermore, the elderly women offer themselves mutual support, encouraging each other to participate in activities in the centres and in the community environment. This participation, moreover, makes it compatible with their daily lives, their housework, and time spent supporting family members. The results of this research show the positive influence of socio-educational participation in that it produces within the elderly women a sense of satisfaction with their present-day existence. The women themselves refer to variables of a participative nature which justify their current welfare, together with that of the family nucleus. The fact of keeping in touch with a group of referents equal to them, to be able to communicate, to meet new people, to have a space of participation and independence, to carry out social projects, to manage their own leisure and free time – all this adds to their social-inclusion, although they are not necessarily aware of the concept itself.

Together with the family environment, participating actively in a socio-cultural environment – social centres and the community – forms part of a daily experience, and women feel strongly and positively satisfied about it. This process of association is recognised as one of the principal processes within the contexts of association; it is one of the most important and powerful tools for elderly women when dealing with social-inclusion.

* * *

To finish with, it should be insisted on here that, if elderly women are to avoid social-exclusion, it is not enough simply to participate in socio-cultural activities. Nevertheless, the results have shown that this kind of participation helps a lot. And it helps more when carried out by means of strategies of qualitative groups, a method that can lead to deep reflection about those activities offered to elderly people, both in social centres and in the community. But a word of warning! It has become evident that the actions of socio-educational intervention are in danger of reproducing stereotyped images of elderly people. On the other hand, these same actions of socio-educational intervention can help in a positive way to change minds and transform attitudes. So, it is necessary to think about ontological, methodological, and epistemological foundations, and to review the assumption of the heterogeneity of the process of ageing, imbuing the process with an individual variability and the characteristics of elderly people. The data obtained in this study can help with this reflection.

Works Cited

Consejería de Economía, Empresa e Innovación. *Territorialización. Plan estratégico de la Región de Murcia. Valle de Ricote*. Murcia: Consejería de Economía, Empresa e Innovación, 2013.

De-Juanas-Oliva, Ángel, María Rosario Limón-Mendizábal, and Enrique Navarro-Asencio. "Análisis del bienestar psicológico, estado de salud percibido y calidad de vida en personas adultas mayores." *Pedagogía Social. Revista Interuniversitaria*. 22, 2013. 153-168.

Freixas-Farré, Anna. *Tan frescas. Las nuevas mujeres mayores del siglo XXI*. Barcelona: Paidós Ibérica, 2013.

Gilligan, Carol (1977) "In a Different Voice: Women's Conceptions of Self and of Morality." *Harvard Educational Review*: December 1977. 47. 4, 1977. 481-517; [Translation] Carol Gilligan (1977) "Con otra voz. Las concepciones femeninas del yo y de la moralidad." María Teresa López-de la Vieja. Ed. *Bioética y feminismo: estudios multidisciplinares de género*. Salamanca: Ediciones Universidad de Salamanca, 2006. 15-55.

Hernández-Pedreño, Manuel. *Desigualdades según género en la vejez*. Murcia: Secretaría Sectorial de la Mujer y de la Juventud, 2000. <igualdadyviolenciadegenero.carm.es/documents/202699/216982/Desigualdades+seg%C3%BAn+g%C3%A9nero+en+la+vejez/fa74002d-0b2f-4abb-b215-1405ee8d4f35>

Instituto de Mayores y Servicios Sociales, El (IMSERSO). *Envejecimiento activo. Libro Blanco*. Madrid: Ministerio de Sanidad, Política Social e Igualdad, 2011.

Instituto Nacional de Estadística, El (INE). *Estimación de la población española actual*. 2014. <www.ine.es>

Jiménez-Ramírez, Magdalena. "Aproximación teórica de la exclusión social: complejidad e imprecisión del término. Consecuencias para el ámbito educativo." Valdivia: *Estudios Pedagógicos.* 34. 1, 2008. 173-186.
<www.scielo.cl/scielo.php?script=sci_arttext&pid=S0718-07052008000100010>

LeCompte, Margaret D., and Judith Preissle Goetz. "Problems of Reliability and Validity in Ethnographic Research." *Review of Educational Research.* 52. 1, Spring 1982. 31-60.
<pdfs.semanticscholar.org/7253/c6cd672281576a96db1037f135ce3e78fe41.pdf>

Ministerio de Medio Ambiente y Medio Rural y Marino (MARM). *Plan estratégico para la igualdad de género en el desarrollo sostenible del medio rural (2011-2014).* Madrid: Ministerio de Medio Ambiente y Medio Rural y Marino. Dirección General de Desarrollo Sostenible del Medio Rural. Subdirección General de Igualdad y Modernización, 2011.
<www.mapama.gob.es/es/desarrollo-rural/temas/igualdad_genero_y_des_sostenible/plan_estrategico_para_la_igualdad_de_g%C3%89nero_2011-2014_tcm7-171026.pdf>

Martínez de Miguel-López, Silvia. *Reconstruyendo la educación de personas mayores.* Granada: Grupo Editorial Universitario, 2003.

Martínez de Miguel-López, Silvia, and Andrés Escarbajal-de Haro. *Alternativas socioeducativas para las personas mayores.* Madrid: Dykinson, 2009.

Miles, Matthew B., and A. Michael Huberman. *Qualitative Data Analysis.* Beverly Hills: Sage Publishing, 1984.

Parlamento Europeo. "Sobre el papel de la mujer en una sociedad que envejece." Bruselas: Comisión de Derechos de la Mujer e Igualdad de Género, 2010. [European Parliament. "On the role of women in an ageing society. 2009/2205(INI)" Brussels: Committee on Women's Rights and Gender Equality. Rapporteur: Sirpa Pietikäinen.]

Pérez-Díaz, Julio. "El envejecimiento de la población Española." *Investigación y Ciencia.* 410, 2010. 34-42.

Sánchez-Palacios, Concepción. *Estereotipos negativos hacia la vejez y su relación con variables sociodemográficas, psicosociales y psicológicas.* University of Málaga, 2004. [PhD thesis]
<www.biblioteca.uma.es/bbldoc/tesisuma/16704046.pdf>

Serdio-Sánchez, Carmen. *Envejecimiento, mujer y educación. Estudio cualitativo sobre la participación educativa de la mujer mayor.* Granada: Grupo Editorial Universitario, 2004.

—. *Mujeres que envejecen, mujeres que aprenden.* Salamanca: Universidad Pontificia de Salamanca, 2006.

Taylor, Steven J., and Robert Bogdan. *Introduction to Qualitative Research Methods. The Search for Meanings.* New York: John Wiley and Sons, 1984. [Trans. Jorge Piatigorsky. 1984. Introducción a los métodos cualitativos de investigación. La búsqueda de significados. Barcelona: Ediciones Paidós Ibérica, 1994].
<mastor.cl/blog/wp-content/uploads/2011/12/Introduccion-a-metodos-cualitativos-de-investigaci%C3%B3n-Taylor-y-Bogdan.-344-pags-pdf.pdf>
<asodea.files.wordpress.com/2009/09/taylor-s-j-bogdan-r-metodologia-cualitativa.pdf>

Triadó-Tur, Carme, and Feliciano Villar-Posada. "Modelos de envejecimiento y percepción de cambios en una muestra de personas mayores." *Anuario de Psicología*, 73, 1997. 43-55.
<www.raco.cat/index.php/anuariopsicologia/article/viewFile/61352/88776&q=mujeres+de+78+anos+teniendo+sexo&sa=X&ei=zaHoT-6qG8SU-wbbzrWxAw&ved=0CDEQFjAH>

Concerning Dementia

(Alzheimer's)

We Are Not Ourselves: Matthew Thomas's Portrayal of Alzheimer's

Cristina Garrigós

UNED (National University of Distance Education, Spain)

One of the most important problems that the senior population faces nowadays in the world is Alzheimer's. Degenerative mental illnesses affect more and more elderly people every day. Alzheimer's is devastating for the person suffering from it, since it means the progressive disappearance of who one is in a mental, emotional, and physical deteriorating process. It is also devastating for the individual's family members on many levels – psychological, practical, financial, and so on. This disease has been the subject of important medical research, and it has also been at the centre of not a few films and books, which aim to acquaint the audience with what can be probably one of the most important epidemics of our age. Film adaptations of novels, such as *The Notebook* (Dir. Nick Cassavetes, 2004)[1] and *Still Alice* (Dir. Richard Glatzer and Wash Westmoreland, 2014),[2] address the issue, focusing on what it means to lose a beloved one when they are still alive. In both cases, the protagonists are women suffering from dementia. In the case of *Still Alice*, based on a novel written by the neuroscientist Lisa Genova in 2007, the author explores the 50-year-old Harvard professor Alice Howland's early-onset form of the disease. This text functions, according to Stefan Block, "both as an empathetic evocation of the internal experience of dementia and as a guidebook for those confronting a similar diagnosis."[3]

There are several ways in which novelists represent the disease in fiction: by focusing on sentimental relationships, practical issues, or even philosophical ones – the loss of one's identity, the sudden confusion of temporal frames, and so on. Moreover, since Alzheimer's is so frequent in our society, it is not strange to find authors who have, or have had, a parent with Alzheimer's, and who use their fiction to reflect on their personal

---

[1] *The Notebook* is a film adaptation of Nicholas Sparks' novel *The Notebook* (1996).

[2] *Still Alice* is a film adaptation of Lisa Genova's novel *Still Alice* (2007).

[3] Stefan Merrill Block. "A Place beyond Words: The Literature of Alzheimer's." *The New Yorker*. August 20, 2014.

experience. This chapter explores the handling of the subject of Alzheimer's by an author, Matthew Thomas, whose father suffered from Alzheimer's, and whose first novel, *We Are Not Ourselves* (2014), addresses this subject in what is, according to some reviewers, "The greatest Alzheimer's novel yet."[4]

Other authors, such as Jonathan Franzen, and Ruth L. Ozeki, have also faced the problem of having a parent with such disease, and have reflected in their novels on what it means to deal with it, and how it affects the lives of the person suffering it, as well of those around him or her.[5] For Stefan Merrill Block, who authored the novel *The Story of Forgetting* (2009),[6] fiction, as opposed to medical books, is useful to understand Alzheimer's because it provides answers to questions such as: "How do you locate the personhood in someone who, for neurobiological reasons, is no longer the person you knew? Is there a way to be true to medical fact and still find something that is transcendently human? What does it mean for the family to have a person with Alzheimer's? How do we cope with a situation where a person becomes different from whom we know?" These, and many other questions, are answered, or at least posed, in fictionalisations of personal experience.

Trying to understand Alzheimer's

Dementia is a distinctive feature of ageing societies. According to recent studies, "(o)f those who reach the age of eighty-five, nearly one in two will get it."[7] More than twenty-five million people in the world are currently affected by dementia, most suffering from Alzheimer's disease, with around five million new cases occurring every year, and the number of people affected is anticipated to double every twenty years up to 81·1 million by 2040.[8] According to the American Alzheimer's Association, "While

---

[4] Stefan Merrill Block. "A Place beyond Words: The Literature of Alzheimer's." *The New Yorker.* August 20, 2014.

[5] Jonathan Franzen discussed his father's disease in the essay "My Father's Brain: What Alzheimer Takes Away," published in *The New Yorker* 2011, and he also rendered it in fiction in the character of Alfred Lambert in *The Corrections* (2010). Ruth Ozeki, whose mother had Alzheimer's, depicted the disease in her novel *All Over Creation* (2003), which begins when Yumi, the protagonist, has to rush back home to Idaho to take care of her ageing parents – her father is very old, and her mother has Alzheimer's. In her last novel, *A Tale for the Time Being* (2013), Ruth Ozeki's mother, who lives with her, also suffers from dementia.

[6] Stefan Merrill Block. *The Story of Forgetting.* (London: Faber and Faber, 2009).

[7] Alzheimer's Association. "Generation Alzheimer's: The Defining Disease of the Baby Boomers." 2011.

[8] See World Health Organization and Alzheimer's Disease International. *Dementia: A Public Health Priority.* (Geneva: Publications of the World Health Organization, 2012).

Alzheimer's is not normal ageing, age is the greatest risk factor for the disease."[9] Right now, Alzheimer's disease is the most common cause of dementia in the elderly, accounting for sixty to seventy percent of all demented cases. The disease frequently starts with memory impairment but is invariably followed by a progressive global cognitive impairment. As such, it affects people in different ways, but the most common symptom pattern begins with a gradually worsening ability to remember new information. This occurs because the disruption of brain-cell function usually begins in regions of the brain that are involved in forming new memories. As the damage spreads, individuals experience other difficulties.

The following are warning signs of Alzheimer's disease: memory loss that disrupts daily life; challenges in planning or solving problems; difficulty completing familiar tasks at home, at work or at leisure; confusion with time or place; trouble understanding visual images and spatial relationships; new problems with words in speaking or writing; misplacing things and losing the ability to retrace steps; decreased or poor judgment; withdrawal from work or social activities; and changes in mood and personality.[10] As the disease progresses, the individual's cognitive and functional abilities decline. In advanced Alzheimer's disease, people need help with basic activities of daily living, such as bathing, dressing, eating, and using the bathroom. Those in the final stages of the disease lose their ability to communicate, fail to recognize loved ones, and become bed-bound and reliant on around-the-clock care.[11]

We Are Not Ourselves *(2014)*

In the novel *We Are Not Ourselves* (2014), Matthew Thomas conveys what is probably one of the most powerful literary portraits of Alzheimer's in the story of Edmund Leary, Ed. This family saga starts with the childhood of Eileen Tumulty, Ed's wife, the daughter of post-Second World War, Irish immigrants, and it closes with their son Connell's decision to have a child. The novel has powerful autobiographical resonances, since the author's father also suffered from early-onset Alzheimer's. In this debut novel, which took ten years to write, and which gave the author a millionaire contract, Thomas addresses the issue of what happens to a person and his family when

---

[9] Alzheimer's Association. "What We Know Today about Alzheimer's Disease: Age and Alzheimer's." <www.alz.org/research/science/alzheimers_disease_causes.asp#age>

[10] Alzheimer's Association. "10 Early Signs and Symptoms of Alzheimer's."
<www.alz.org/10-signs-symptoms-alzheimers-dementia.asp>

[11] See Alzheimer's Association Report 2013.

faced with the disease. Ed is only fifty-one when he is diagnosed. Although normally associated with elderly people, recent studies show that one-in-eight baby boomers will get Alzheimer's before they turn sixty-five.[12] The novel shows a detailed process of the consequences of Alzheimer's in a middle-class family, especially in the context of the United States of America as the promised land of opportunities.

However, even though the real protagonist of the novel is Ed, the novel focuses on the points-of-view of Eileen and Connell. We know everything about them – their childhood, education, background, thoughts, and desires – but the reader learns nothing about Ed. The reader never sees things from his perspective. The reason for this is that the author wants the readers to experience Ed's disease from a realistic perspective:

> In omitting such a focal character's point-of-view, I wanted to capture some of the essence of Ed's own isolating experience of dealing with the calamity that befalls him. There is a sense in which those on the other side of Alzheimer's, even the closest of family members, find the experience of the sufferer inscrutable, almost ineffable. And from a dramatic perspective, I was interested in telling the story of how each of the people closest to Ed, including extended family and friends, responds to Ed's disease in his or her own way. Ed became a fulcrum around which all the characters revolved, and his illness became a backdrop for a series of character studies and explorations into human nature. I tried to take my cues from the characters themselves in presenting a range of possible reactions that might capture the manifold ways people handle bad news.[13]

* * *

From the beginning, the narrative is focused on Eileen, the daughter of two alcoholic Irish immigrants from a poor neighbourhood of New York, who dreams of improving in life. We read about her marriage with Ed, her disappointment when he does not accept a position for a pharmaceutical company, or an offer to work at New York University (NYU), deciding instead to remain in the Bronx community college where he was teaching. We follow Eileen's dreams of having a big house, moving to the suburbs,

---

[12] See Alzheimer's Association. "Generation Alzheimer's: The Defining Disease of the Baby Boomers." 2011.
[13] K.J. Gormley. "Interview with Matthew Thomas." *The LibraryThing Blog*. July 25, 2014.

taking her son, Connell, to a good college, and so on. But, awkwardly, the voice of his father, Ed, who is the protagonist of the novel, is absent from the narrative. Again, as Thomas revealed in an interview:

> I made a very conscious decision to leave him out because I wanted to try to recreate for the reader the experience of the family dealing with Alzheimer's. Because there's an inscrutability to the consciousness of the sufferer, even for the people closest to that person. There is an unknowability of his thoughts, and I thought that if I left his thoughts out, I could help the reader to inhabit that mental space of these characters a little more. Because of the constant wondering of what it was that he was thinking.[14]

The only instance we have of Ed's thoughts is at the end of the novel. Before the disease is too advanced, he writes a letter for his son to read after his death. In it, he tells Connell how he wants him to remember him. Memory is central in the story. It is what configures a person. The preoccupation of the father about how his son will picture him in his mind is also an indication that he is aware that he has started a process of progressive deterioration, both mental and physical. As Matthew Thomas makes clear, when writing the novel, he wanted to focus on the effects of the disease on the family, and to show how little we know of what is going on inside the patient's brain.

* * *

The economic situation is also central to the novel, as it will determine an important perspective in the novel, which is how a family's economic situation is affected by such a disease which implies that a person is no longer able to work and needs important caring. *We Are Not Ourselves* (2014) is a realistic novel. There are, in the text, many references to paying bills, budgets, and loans. For the author, money is the stuff of real life, what everybody cares about, but talking about it is…

> the last taboo in American life, so frank discussions of money, as long as they don't delve into the most obscure minutiae and leave the reader behind, can create a frisson in the reader perhaps even

---

[14] Becky Anderson. "Matthew Thomas. We Are Not Ourselves." Authors Revealed, with Becky Anderson.

more potent than the one created when a writer trains the lens on a character's bedroom and intimate life."[15]

When Eileen goes to seek professional advice, she is told that the only way her husband can get Medicaid[16] is to impoverish themselves. After that, she visits a lawyer, and she is told that she should divorce her husband to keep her assets, because she is at risk of losing everything if she has to pay for her husband's expensive treatment. Kerry Peck and Rick L. Law, authors of *Alzheimer's and the Law*, explain how difficult it is for families alone to face this dire situation when their State does not offer support for middle-class families with this problem.[17] Thus, *We Are Not Ourselves* (2014) constitutes an implicit critique of the American health system, when a lecturer at a college, who has worked there for almost thirty years, cannot get his full pension, since he has to quit working when students complain of his erratic behaviour – he forgets things, is not able to post the grades correctly, and so on – and his wife, a senior nurse, has to struggle to pay the bills. According to Matthew Thomas:

> I tried, through telling the story of this one family, to tell some of the story of the middle-class in America – their hopes and fears, dreams and disappointments, and quiet achievements over the course of the twentieth century. I wanted to explore the enduring appeal of the American Dream and examine its viability in an environment that is squeezing out the middle-class. In the end, I wanted to see what residual deposits might be left in the spirit when a person achieves that elusive dream at any cost.[18]

In terms of the financial burden on society, Alzheimer's is the third most costly disease in the United States of America, after cancer and coronary heart disease.[19] Average annual costs of caring for patients with

---

[15] K.J. Gormley. "Interview with Matthew Thomas." *The LibraryThing Blog*. July 25, 2014.

[16] Medicaid is a programme administered at a federal and a state level in the United States of America that assists persons who have insufficient funds to pay for their medical, nursing-home care, and personal care services.

[17] See Kerry Peck, and Rick L. Law. *Alzheimer's and the Law: Counseling Clients with Dementia and Their Families*. American Bar Association, 2014.

[18] K.J. Gormley. "Interview with Matthew Thomas." *The LibraryThing Blog*. July 25, 2014.

[19] See P.D. Meek, E. Kristin McKeithan, and Glen T. Schumock. "Economic considerations in Alzheimer's disease." *Pharmacotherapy*. 18. 2. 2, 1998. 68–73, as quoted in Carolyn W.

Alzheimer's in the United States of America have been estimated at between 80- and 100-thousand million dollars (US$).[20] Total costs include direct, indirect, and intangible costs. Direct costs include multiple dimensions of medical care costs – for example, nursing-home care, medication, doctors' visits, hospitalizations, and so on – and non-medical care costs – for example, home health aides, respite care, adult day-care, and so on. Indirect costs are imputed values of resources lost due to illness, including premature deaths, patient and caregiver lost productivity, and unpaid caregiving time. Intangible costs are those related to pain and suffering endured by patients and families, and those related to the deterioration of patient and caregiver quality-of-life.[21]

* * *

Besides the added economic strain of suffering from this disease in the United States of America, patients with Alzheimer's demand constant attention, and that is always a cause of stress for the family. Such a demand is considered an indirect cost by clinical studies. *We Are Not Ourselves* (2014) portrays this by addressing uncomfortable issues such as what it means for the wife and the son, on a personal level, to relate to a beloved one when this person loses her or his independence, memory, and judgement. The very title of the novel, *We Are Not Ourselves,* calls attention to this fact, the fact, that is, that Alzheimer's does not only imply the loss of identity of the sufferer, but also the loss of identity of the whole family, since the effects of the disease change the lives of all its members. Thus, while it may be difficult for the reader to understand why Matthew Thomas should focus so extensively on Eileen's childhood in the first part of the novel, the authorial intention is to help the reader empathise with the persona she would become later, with her dreams and disappointments, her obsession with money, and her preoccupation with the family. The fact that she is a nurse also makes it that much more difficult for her. Since she needs the health insurance, she

---

Zhu, and Mary Sano. "Economic considerations in the management of Alzheimer's disease." *Clinical Interventions in Aging*. 1. 2, June 2006.

[20] Centers for Disease Control (CDC), and National Center for Chronic Disease Prevention and Health Promotion (NCCDPHP). "Unrealized prevention opportunities: reducing the health and economic burden of chronic illness." (Atlanta, GA: US Department of Health and Human Services, Centers for Disease Control and Prevention, 2000), as quoted in Carolyn W. Zhu, and Mary Sano. "Economic considerations in the management of Alzheimer's disease." *Clinical Interventions in Aging*. 1. 2, June 2006.

[21] See Carolyn W. Zhu, and Mary Sano. "Economic considerations in the management of Alzheimer's disease." *Clinical Interventions in Aging*. 1. 2, June 2006.

must remain in employment to continue her contributions to the health care system. Yet she knows she cannot both work *and* take care of her husband at the same time. She is left with no alternative but to hire a nurse at home first and, later, pay a nursing-home.

* * *

Connell Leary, as argued earlier, is the *alter ego* of the author. Like his mother Eileen, he is also unable to take care of his father. For instance, one day, when left alone at home for an hour while Connell is out with his friends, Ed has an accident; he falls to the kitchen floor and loses a tooth. In his mind, for Connell it is easier to get a job and contribute financially to the family's many expenses, than to stay at home and take care of his father. This creates tension between Connell and his mother, a conflict which is not resolved until later on in his life. "Keep your money. You're going to need it for therapy later" (*We Are Not Ourselves* 2014: 466), says Eileen. Connell will have to come to terms with his sense of guilt for what he considers his neglect of his own father, since he decides to go to Chicago to study instead of remaining in New York to help. He does not want to accept that the situation that his father is living demands real solutions. By putting distance between them, he is trying to negate that he can do anything to make things easier for all of them.

Taking care of Ed is physically and psychologically exhausting. Eileen searches for help in a spiritual seer who takes advantage of her and her money, until her son makes her realize that she is also losing her mind, though in a different way. In the end, Eileen convinces herself that the best solution for all of them is to have Ed in a nursing home. The fact is that life is easier for both Eileen and Connell when Ed is not with them. As a matter of fact, when Connell takes Ed out of the nursing home one evening to attend a family dinner, the result is a disaster, both for the man suffering from a psychological and physical disconnection with his reality, and for the family members who want to act as "normal" as possible.

* * *

The portrayal of the nursing home as a place of loneliness, and the sense of guilt that the characters have for leaving Ed there, mark Matthew Thomas's narrative as a reflection on individualism in modern society, and the failure of those values cherished by 'the American dream' – the family, the house, the importance of a well-paid job. *We Are Not Ourselves* (2014) is, thus, a critique of the lack of state-funded resources and, more specifically, of the United States of America's health system, in particular the lack of coverage for workers, especially for middle-class workers. It is also a critique of the lack of community support. Part of the novel deals with Eileen's desire to move to a better area of town, because she is afraid that her neighbourhood is becoming a place occupied by foreigners – mostly Asiatic people – who represent a menace for her 'White-American dream.' But when she moves to a bigger house in the suburbs, she becomes increasingly isolated. Eileen and Connell's friends disappear when they hear about Ed's disease, and Eileen is left alone, with only the help of Sergei, a Russian engineer who works as a nurse for Ed, and eventually, when Ed is taken to the residence, who remains in the house, becoming Eileen's lover for a short period.

As said before, loneliness is one of the central issues in *We Are Not Ourselves* (2014). The novel closes with Eileen's going back to the house where she had been living when she got married. She visits the Indian family who bought her house, and is warmly received, sharing an Indian dinner with them, which she enjoys despite her initial prejudices. In this way, the novel is not only about Alzheimer's; the disease becomes an allegory for contemporary society in the United States of America. The narrative sheds some light on the difficulties of having a parent with Alzheimer's in the United States of America, given that this disease affects not only the patient, but family members as well. Yet it is not only something emotional and physical for the people around the patient; it can become economically devastating. The society portrayed by Matthew Thomas is a highly-individualistic and aggressively-capitalistic world, ruled by economic empires, insurance and pharmaceutical companies while, at the same time, citizens struggle with their own ambitions to attain 'the American dream.' This 'dream,' which is fundamentally economic, is shattered when a disease such as Alzheimer's comes into the picture.

Works Cited

Alzheimer's Association. "Generation Alzheimer's: The Defining Disease of the Baby Boomers." 2011.
<www.alz.org/boomers/overview.asp>

—. "2015 Alzheimer's Disease Facts and Figures." *Alzheimer's and Dementia*. 11, 2015. 332-384.
<www.alzheimersanddementia.com/article/S1552-5260(15)00058-8/pdf>

—. "2015 Alzheimer's Disease Facts and Figures." *Alzheimer's and Dementia*. 11, 2015. 332-384.

<www.alzheimersanddementia.com/article/S1552-5260(15)00058-8/pdf>

Anderson, Becky. "Matthew Thomas. We Are Not Ourselves." Authors Revealed, with Becky Anderson.
<www.youtube.com/watch?v=R7GmPtZLXm4>

Block, Stefan Merrill. "A Place beyond Words: The Literature of Alzheimer's." *The New Yorker*. August 20, 2014.
<www.newyorker.com/books/page-turner/place-beyond-words-literature-alzheimers>

—. *The Story of Forgetting*. London: Faber and Faber, 2009.

Centers for Disease Control (CDC), and National Center for Chronic Disease Prevention and Health Promotion (NCCDPHP). "Unrealized prevention opportunities: reducing the health and economic burden of chronic illness." Atlanta, GA: US Department of Health and Human Services, Centers for Disease Control and Prevention, 2000.

Franzen, Jonathan. "My Father's Brain. What Alzheimer's Takes Away." *The New Yorker*. September 10, 2001.
<frederickwm.weebly.com/uploads/1/1/6/8/11687708/my_fathers_brainwhat_alzheimers_takes_awa.pdf>

—. *The Corrections*. New York: Farrar, Straus and Giroux, 2001.

Gormley, K.J. "Interview with Matthew Thomas." *The LibraryThing Blog*. July 25, 2014.
<www.librarything.com/author/thomasmatthew-1/interview>

Meek, P.D., E. Kristin McKeithan, and Glen T. Schumock. "Economic considerations in Alzheimer's disease." *Pharmacotherapy*. 18. 2. 2, 1998. 68–73.
<www.ncbi.nlm.nih.gov/pubmed/9543467>

Ozeki, Ruth L. (2003) *All Over Creation*. London: Penguin, 2004.

—. *A Tale for the Time Being*. Edinburgh: Canongate Books, 2013.

Peck, Kerry, and Rick L. Law. *Alzheimer's and the Law: Counseling Clients with Dementia and Their Families*. American Bar Association, 2014.

Thomas, Matthew. (2014) *We Are Not Ourselves*. London: Fourth Estate, 2015.

World Health Organization (WHO), and Alzheimer's Disease International. *Dementia: A Public Health Priority*. Geneva: Publications of the World Health Organization, 2012.
<apps.who.int/iris/bitstream/10665/75263/1/9789241564458_eng.pdf?ua=1>

Zhu, Carolyn W., and Mary Sano. "Economic considerations in the management of Alzheimer's disease." *Clinical Interventions in Aging*. 1. 2, June 2006. 143–154. <www.ncbi.nlm.nih.gov/pmc/articles/PMC2695165/>

Preventing dementia as a defence against ageing: A pilot study at the Primary Care Services

Glòria Mateu-Vives

Sant Pere Claver – Fundació Sanitària, Barcelona

The risk of suffering dementia grows with age, rising to a one-in-five chance over the age of eighty. There are four identified types of dementia, the most common being Alzheimer's Disease, characterized by short-term memory loss and difficulties with language in the early stages, gradually becoming more severe over time. Vascular dementia is the consequence of strokes and insufficient blood supply to the brain. Dementia with Lewy bodies is associated with symptoms similar to those of Parkinson's disease, such as slowness, muscle stiffness, and trembling of the limbs. In addition, people may experience hallucinations and a tendency to fail or fall. However, our interest here lies with another type of early, precocious dementia, a type characterised by non-organic causes that, when emotional impact during ageing generates anxiety, activates more disorganizing defences. The target group in this study is made up of individuals, who are 65 years old and over, whose General Practitioner (GP)[1] considers the patient to be presenting the first symptoms of dementia, but that it is not yet installed. The major goal is to attend to the anxieties that these people suffer related to the process of ageing.

General Practitioners can listen to their elderly patients on the subjects of bodily impairment, and of mental and emotional pains and worries. Attentive listening can discriminate between 'physical pain' and 'emotional pain' during the process of ageing. Owing to loneliness, elderly people look out for attentive attention, and they quite often drop in at their General Practitioner's (GP's) consultancy with no evident organic pathology, but with the need to be with someone who can listen to their fears about imminent memory-loss and physical impairment. 'Family doctors' realize that this hyper-frequentation in their surgeries is due to anxiety

---

[1] General Practitioner (GP) is also known more popularly as "Family doctor."

promoted by loss, and the difficulties elderly patients face on contemplating the fact of their 'getting older,' reflections that sometimes give rise to 'narcissistic injuries' of ageing.

Elderly people must cope with several lifelong losses and griefs that are uniquely and intimately related to them: the young body, working life, cognitive function, the loss of family members and friends, independence, anxiety about the future, and so on. They come to experience their ageing as a process imbued with sadness, loneliness, and despair. A loss of vigour and youthful body functions brings about a decline into dependence on others, and the recognition that new achievements can be complicated or impossible. This dependence and feeling of impotency often adds to the feeling of having failed as a parent, to the feeling of the loss of a partner and privacy, and to the feeling of the proximity to death, experienced sometimes as persecutory anxieties, depressive feelings, and even denied catastrophic anxieties.[2]

The grief and the anxieties associated with this quality of ageing demand more attention. In fact, such factors give rise to the idea or mental representation of "to stop *being*." We know what this means when a close loved-one dies, when the final stage in the life cycle – the 'end' – begins, but we have no idea about what it means "to stop *being* oneself." Depending on the culture and religion, 'growing old' and 'ageing towards death' may have different connotations and interpretations and, therefore, be experienced differently.

Perceived success or failure on reaching old age depends on how the elderly person has experienced early-life separations and losses, grief, and the lack of future prospects, experiences that in late-life induce feelings of guilt, envy, and ambivalence. The way an elderly individual manages these perceptions will depend on his or her emotional experience to cope with that emotional pain, and the degree of integration that has already been established between the different parts of the 'self,' as well as the ability to solve conflicts with others. If the degree of anxiety is high, there may be an unconscious tendency to minimize it through defence mechanisms, from denial to emotional disengagement. This form of minimization can lead to an instrumental usage of dementia as a way of disconnection when faced with emotional pain. When the involution of loss acquires traumatic signification, anxieties become overwhelming, and destructive defences are activated. At this point, it is time for action in the form of psychotherapy.

---

[2] Josep Oriol Esteve, Pere Folch, and Lluís Isern. "Problemàtica i psicopatologia de la senectut (i II)." *Revista Catalana de Psicoanàlisi*. 30. 1, 2013. 9-29.

Psychodynamic psychotherapy groups targeted at elderly persons can bring about the tuning of body and mind, and the resuscitation and revival of old, dormant parts. Group therapy helps to avoid isolation, to stimulate an interest in being with others, to open up and join new groups, and to prevent an over-use of medication. More accurate analysis is needed in order to assist General Practitioners (GPs) in helping elderly people to listen to their own bodies and minds as integrated elements, and to assess and identify the cause whenever emotional pain promotes mental dissociation. One of the aims of these targeted psychotherapy groups is to help elderly people to integrate these elements, and to work through unsolved, lively, emotional conflicts and, in return, to promote socializing activities and avoid isolation.[3]

Sigmund Freud said that psychoanalytical psychotherapy could fail with people who were too old – that is, aged 50 years old and over, in his time – on the understanding that an excessive amount of time would need to pass before the treatment ended, to allow for the patient's emotional pain to work through and the patient's mental health to improve.[4] This view was in contrast to the opinions of other psychoanalysts of his time, as well as those of the current generation of psychoanalysts.[5] We can also add that psychotherapists treating elderly persons experience great difficulties in engaging with their patients owing to the transference and counter-transference quality; the reason why group psychotherapy for elderly people is not given is due to a tendency towards gerontophobia and adverse emotional feelings within the therapists themselves.

Methodology

a) Objective

The aim of this research is to determine whether group psychotherapy helps elderly persons to improve their capacity to cope with the fact of 'growing

---

[3] See Víctor Hernández-Espinosa. "Comprensión y abordaje psicodinámico de las patologías de la tercera edad." (Martorell: V Simpòsium Internacional, Centro Neuropsiquiátrico "Sagrado Corazón," 1994).

[4] See Sigmund Freud. (1898) *La sexualidad en la etología de las neurosis.* (NoBooks Editorial, 2015).

[5] See Georges Abraham, Philippe Kocher, and Georges Goda. "Psychoanalysis and aging." *International Review of Psychoanalysis.* 7, 1980. 147-155; Lillien Jane Martin, and Clare de Gruchy. *Salvaging Old Age.* (New York, Macmillan, 1930); Joost Abraham Maurits Meerloo. "Transference and resistance in geriatric psychotherapy." *The Psychoanalytic Review.* 42. 1, January 1955. 72-82; Stanley H. Cath. "Aging or Aged: Development or Pathology." George H. Pollock, and Stanley I. Greenspan. Eds. *The Course of Life / Vol. VII: Completing the Journey.* (Madison, CT: International Universities Press, 1997). 41-86.

old' and, thereby, to use more structured defences that may avoid mental disconnection and dementia. From October 2010 to July 2016, hyper-frequentation, primary-care, outpatients suffering from depression and anxiety symptomatology were invited to participate in a psychoanalytic group-psychotherapy, delivered by a trained therapist. Four therapists employed at Primary Mental Health Services run a group each year – twelve patients for thirty-five sessions. A final assessment was completed at the end of each group session, and the compiled data analysed.

b) Setting

This trial was conducted in collaboration with four National Health Service (NHS) Primary Care Services (PCS) in Barcelona, and a private, non-profit organization that provides eight Primary Care Services (PCSs) with a mental health service. The recruitment of elderly persons starts in May and ends in July each year, and the thirty-five Primary Group Psychotherapy (PGP) sessions are delivered from September to June the following year. Using grounded theory methodology, the first three years were dedicated to observing the dynamics of these groups, and to thinking about the differences between Primary Group Psychotherapy (PGP) for young and adult persons in contrast to Primary Group Psychotherapy (PGP) for elderly people. This helped to identify the more frequent anxieties elderly people experience, and the use of defences against these anxieties inspired applying psychoanalytic theory. The findings showed that the more unstructured the defences, the more disconnection from reality and, consequently, the greater the activation of impairment of cognitive capacities.

c) Participants

Patients were recruited from those seeking the services of their General Practitioner (GP) with hyper-frequentation, with no organic cause, and with a symptomatology related to anxiety, depression, and somatization. The *Older Adult Self-Report* (OASR)[6] was administered.

d) Clinicians

Senior, experienced psychotherapists ran the Primary Group Psychotherapy (PGP) sessions, with co-therapists. The average age of the clinicians was 53·5 years old.

---

[6] See Thomas M. Achenbach, Paul A. Newhouse, and Leslie A. Rescorla. *ASEBA®Older Adult Self-Report & Behavior Checklist*. <www.parinc.com/Products/Pkey/282>

n=49		%
Age (mean)		74·57
Gender	Male	8·2
	Female	91·8
Civil status	Single	6·20
	Partner	40·80
	Widowed	49·00
	Divorced	4·00
	Lives alone	
Schooling	Illiterate	2·00
	Primary school	61·20
	Secondary school	20·04
	Technician	12·20
	University	4·20
Previous job	Home	69·40
	Sales	6·10
	Education	4·10
	Administrative Assistant	4·10
	Industry	2·00
	Health	4·10
	Arts	10·20
Symptomatology	Anxiety	34·70
	Depression	63·30
	Somatization	2·00

Table 1. Baseline social demographic and clinical characteristics

Treatment – Group psychoanalytic psychotherapy

The psychoanalytic psychotherapy assessment format was a weekly, one-hour session over a 30-week period. The group psychotherapy technique was focused on psychoanalytic psychotherapy, supervised once a month by experienced senior psychoanalysts to review the transference, countertransference, resistances, and defences in those elderly persons present during treatment.[7]

---

[7] More details can be read in Marta Lleonart i Camps, and Glòria Mateu-Vives. "Un diari d'hivern: psicoteràpia psicoanalítica grupal a la vellesa." *Intercambios, papeles de psicoanálisis / Intercanvis, papers de psicoanàlisi.* 31, 2013. 35-42; Glòria Mateu-Vives, and Marta Lleonart i Camps. "De les sabatilles a les sabates. El treball psicoterapèutic amb gent

Variable	Pre-intervention N; Mean (SD)	Post-intervention N; Mean (SD)	Z	p
Friends	47; 40·77 (10·81)	25; 41·48 (9·29)	-·131	·896
Spouse/Partner	19; 43·63 (10·81)	8; 44·38 (11·66)	-·535	·593
Personal strength	49; 46·47 (8·22)	25; 45·48 (7·10)	-·192	·848
Anxious / Depressed	49; 67·49 (9·02)	25; 65·44 (7·51)	-1·368	·171
Worries	48; 63·08 (7·75)	25; 63·12 (6·53)	-·378	·706
Somatic complaints	49; 62·57 (7·70)	25; 6·04 (8·66)	-·774	·439
Functional impairment	48; 58·58 (8·28)	25; 58·92 (6·20)	-·245	·806
Memory / Cognition problems	48; 60·73 (8·14)	25; 59·40 (7·59)	-1·306	·192
Thought problems	48; 62·24 (8·25)	25; 64·12 (8·22)	-·767	·443
Irritable / Disinhibited	48; 63·00 (7·76)	25; 64·40 (6·95)	-·468	·640
Total problems	49; 67·71 (10·86)	25; 68·28 (8·69)	-1·068	·285
Depressive problems	49; 65·31 (9·73)	25; 65·08 (7·57)	-·114	·909
Anxiety problems	49; 68·92 (8·45)	25; 66·56 (9·23)	-1·142	·253
Somatic problems	49; 62·57 (7·70)	25; 66·40 (8·83)	-1·707	·088
Dementia problems	48; 60·27 (8·14)	25; 58·88 (7·47)	-·767	·443
Psychotic problems	48; 59·46 (7·95)	25; 63·48 (8·73)	-·992	·321
Antisocial Personality problems	49; 61·37 (7·26)	25; 63·52 (7·04)	-1·288	·198

Table 2. Pre- and post-test Achenbach's *Older Adult Self-Report* score differences

gran a les Àrees Bàsiques de Salut." *Revista Catalana de Psicoanàlisi*. 30. 1. 2013. 79-96; and Glòria Mateu-Vives, and Marta Lleonart i Camps. "La psicoterapia de grupo en la vejez. Un proyecto de investigación." *Temas de Psicoanálisis / Revista de la Sociedad Española de psicoanálisis*. 11, January 2016. 1-15.

Measures and Outcomes

Patients were evaluated before and after participating in the above-mentioned group psychotherapy sessions using the following assessment tool: *Older Adult Self-Report* (OASR) (Achenbach, *et al.* 2004).[8] This is a reliable and valid tool for measuring diverse aspects of adaptive functioning in elderly people. It assesses adaptive functioning on three scales: a) adaptive functioning scales; b) syndrome scales; and c) DSM-oriented scales.[9] Textual analysis from the session transcriptions' grounded theory focused content in order to identify the quality of anxieties and defences observed during the sessions. The Statistical Package for Social Sciences (SPSS) was used to analyse the outcome measure for Achenbach data. The Wilcoxon signed-rank test was run, and approximate values $- \leq 0.05 -$ were set.[10]

Results

Any significant changes were observed using Thomas M. Achenbach *et al. Older Adult Self-Report* (OASR) data analysis. Only slight differences in anxiety, depression, and somatization symptomatology were observed.

Theoretical findings – pilot study experience session analysis

The major findings after the five-year research programme enable us to understand the quality of anxieties and defences on 'growing old.' The results from that research are displayed in Table 3.[11]

Adverse Events

Those patients with pathologies and functional impairment had more difficulties in committing to group psychotherapy, and work is being carried out to help practitioners improve, and identify better, referrals so that all participants are able to attend sessions for the entire duration of the treatment, thereby avoiding abandonment. Whenever the referral is not accurate, there is an increase in the number of drop-outs; thus, the practitioners' assessment

---

[8] See Thomas M. Achenbach, Paul A. Newhouse, and Leslie A. Rescorla. *ASEBA®Older Adult Self-Report & Behavior Checklist.* <www.parinc.com/Products/Pkey/282>

[9] Previous studies suggest that the *Older Adult Self-Report* (OASR) test shows excellent correlation in the diagnosis of dementia and memory.

[10] The Wilcoxon signed-rank test is employed to find out whether any two samples have been selected from populations having identical distribution.

[11] See Josep Oriol Esteve, Pere Folch, and Lluís Isern. "Problemàtica i psicopatologia de la senectut (I)." *Revista Catalana de Psicoanàlisi.* 29. 2, 2012. 9-26; and Josep Oriol Esteve, Pere Folch, and Lluís Isern. "Problemàtica i psicopatologia de la senectut (i II)." *Revista Catalana de Psicoanàlisi.* 30. 1, 2013. 9-29.

Mourning shortcomings	Traumatic significance	Anxieties	Impairing defences	Creative defences
Body's features Locomotive Cognitive Sexual functions	**Mourning shortcomings**	**Pursuing (resentment)** Castration anxieties variants Depressive (Wasted possibilities)	**Underestimation of possibilities** Sarcastic Scepticism Autoerotic regressions Hippomaniac denials Addictions	**Body care (anti-ageing)** Integration of erotica to objects relationship Re-significance of links Re-encouragement of cognitive activities
Professional Cognitive functions	**Social Handicap**	**Narcissistic dispossession**	**Retraction-Underestimation** Resentment-Despotism	**Assumption of new state** Reconciliation with new generations
Deficits and dependency - Body's pathology	**Unsteadiness-Desertion**	**Catastrophic Detachment**	**Symbiosis with caregiver object** Sadomasochistic links Hypomaniac evasion	**Elaboration of dependency**
Loss of family and friends	**Isolation-Emptiness** Disappointment	**Death anxieties** Guilty feelings by under-estimation of possibilities	**Retraction vs. Evasion** Pursuing guilt Hypocondriacal fears	**Re-socialization-kernels of co-existence**
Independence and Hierarchy - Mourning	**Shamefulness-posture in/with family**	**Loss of love and self-esteem feeling**	**Disregard and underestimation** Grievances	**Couple or family group** Therapy
Future Mourning-meaning	**Catastrophic loss of hereafter**	**Uncertainty-Perplexity**	**Denial-Compulsive Evasions** **Denial-Compulsive Fun**	**Re-search of life lived** **Re-search of life's meaning**

Table 3. Identification of anxieties and the quality of used defences

is crucial in order to make the selected elderly participants aware of the importance and relevance of these groups.

Discussion

The hypotheses explored in this study provide the necessary foundation to predict some aspects against dementia as mental disconnection from emotional pain. Increasingly, elderly-person autonomy improves quality-of-life, not only for themselves but also for the people around them. Psychodynamic work has shown the meaning of the symptomatology, allowing participants to understand and cope better with the difficulties of their 'growing older.' The first ten sessions focused on worries related to body impairment, the difficulties associated with it, and the loss of vitality. Up to the tenth session, the elderly persons were able to talk about their worries regarding parenthood, the difficulties of their relationships with other persons, and their loneliness. In the eighth session, for instance, one elderly person said: "We have not come here just to complain ..." In the following session, another elderly woman said: "I see the group different. Today we can speak more deeply not only about our worries, but even about our feelings."

While in these first group sessions complaints about body impairment, fragility, and so on, were elicited, in the following sessions the elderly persons were able to speak freely about their fears and anxieties associated with disease, about their offspring, about their fears of losing dependency payments, and so on. It was then that they understood that in the group they can talk in a more profound way and, thereby, work through their anxieties.

The first sessions have a cathartic quality – "at least here we can talk about our past and feel relieved" – and later on, groups were able to experience a place in which to share and elaborate the process of their ageing. In subsequent sessions, the elderly individuals were able to speak about their deep worries – "I'm afraid to stay alone." By listening and empathizing with the elderly persons, and by giving meaning to their experiences using their personal and emotional responses as a source of understanding, their anxiety and despair are contained, their hostility and criticism softened, without a desire for revenge, and the distorted perceptions of their relationships identified. It may be easier to see changes in young people, and even in middle-aged people, because changes in the external reality happen in parallel with changes in the internal life. In fact, Alison Culverwell and C.

Martin (1999) suggest that working with older people requires rethinking the idea of changes in therapy.[12]

Precisely because expectations are low, there is a greater desire to go on with these age groups. If group psychotherapy provides an opportunity for elderly individuals to open up, to take the first steps on the path towards socialization, and to enable better connections with the people they come into contact with – in short, to live an improved quality-of-life, allowing for better emotional connections – then the primary goal has already been attained.

Conclusion

Successful psychotherapeutic treatment improves quality-of-life, not only for today's elderly persons, but also for those of subsequent generations. The most relevant outcomes from this intervention at the Primary Care Services (PCS) are those that confirm that elderly individuals do not need to retreat into isolation, and that they can participate actively in social life. In order for this to take place, in some elderly individuals it is necessary to awake the need to be with others, to belong to a group. As Jan van de Sande aptly writes, the motto can be: "[add] life to years; not just more years to life."[13]

Works Cited

Abraham, Georges, Philippe Kocher, and Georges Goda. "Psychoanalysis and Ageing." *The International Review of Psycho-Analysis*. 7, 1980. 147-155.

Achenbach, Thomas M., Paul A. Newhouse, and Leslie A. Rescorla. *ASEBA®Older Adult Self-Report & Behavior Checklist*. <www.parinc.com/Products/Pkey/282>

Cath, Stanley H. "Aging or Aged: Development or Pathology." George H. Pollock, and Stanley I. Greenspan. Eds. *The Course of Life / Vol. VII: Completing the Journey*. Madison, CT: International Universities Press, 1997. 41-86.

Corley, Gianetta. Ed. *Older People and Their Needs: A Multi-Disciplinary Perspective*. London: John Wiley, 1999.

---

[12] See Alison Culverwell, and C. Martin. "Psychotherapy with older adults." Gianetta Corley. Ed. *Older People and Their Needs: A Multi-Disciplinary Perspective*. (London: John Wiley, 1999).

[13] Jan A.A.M. van de Sande. "Adventures of the Old Narcissus. On Psychoanalytic Psychotherapy for Seniors." *EFPP Psychoanalytic Psychotherapy Review*. 06/2013.

Culverwell, Alison, and C. Martin. "Psychotherapy with older adults." Gianetta Corley. Ed. *Older People and Their Needs: A Multi-Disciplinary Perspective*. London: John Wiley, 1999.

Esteve, Josep Oriol, Pere Folch, and Lluís Isern. "Problemàtica i psicopatologia de la senectut (I)." *Revista Catalana de Psicoanàlisi*. 29. 2, 2012. 9-26.
<www.raco.cat/index.php/RCP/article/view/307327>

—. "Problemàtica i psicopatologia de la senectut (i II)." *Revista Catalana de Psicoanàlisi*. 30. 1, 2013. 9-29.
<www.raco.cat/index.php/RCP/article/view/303118>

Freud, Sigmund. (1898) *La sexualidad en la etología de las neurosis*. NoBooks Editorial, 2015.

Hernández-Espinosa, Víctor. "Comprensión y abordaje psicodinámico de las patologías de la tercera edad." Martorell: V Simpòsium Internacional. Centro Neuropsiquiátrico "Sagrado Corazón," 1994. [Lecture]

Lleonart-Camps, Marta., and Glòria Mateu-Vives. "Un diari d'hivern: psicoteràpia psicoanalítica grupal a la vellesa." *Intercambios, papeles de psicoanálisis / Intercanvis, papers de psicoanàlisi*. 31, 2013. 35-42.

Martin, Lillien Jane, and Clare de Gruchy. *Salvaging Old Age*. New York: The Macmillan Company, 1930.

Mateu-Vives, Glòria, and Marta Lleonart-Camps. "De les sabatilles a les sabates. El treball psicoterapèutic amb gent gran a les Àrees Bàsiques de Salut." *Revista Catalana de Psicoanàlisi*. 30. 1. 2013. 79-96.
<www.raco.cat/index.php/RCP/article/view/303363>

—. "La psicoterapia de grupo en la vejez. Un proyecto de investigación." *Temas de Psicoanálisis / Revista de la Sociedad Española de psicoanálisis*. 11, January 2016. 1-15.
<www.temasdepsicoanalisis.org/la-psicoterapia-de-grupo-en-la-vejez-un-proyecto-de-investigacion/>

Meerloo, Joost Abraham Maurits. "Transference and resistance in geriatric psychotherapy. *The Psychoanalytic Review*. 42. 1. January 1955. 72-82.

Pollock, George H., and Stanley I. Greenspan. Eds. *The Course of Life / Vol. VII: Completing the Journey*. Madison, CT: International Universities Press, 1997.

Sande, Jan A.A.M. van de. "Adventures of the Old Narcissus. On Psychoanalytic Psychotherapy for Seniors." *EFPP Psychoanalytic Psychotherapy Review*. 06/2013.
<www.efpp.org/review/EFPP_review_06_2013.pdf>

The Need

for

'Social Innovation'

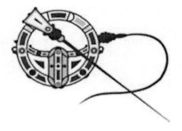

The Need for 'Social Innovation' for Active and Healthy Ageing (AHA): Lessons from Turkey Active and Healthy Ageing Research[1]

Emine Özmete

University of Ankara

Ageing is not only dependent on chronological criteria, but it is also a process that needs to be holistically evaluated, with its physiological, biological, psychological, socio-cultural, economic, and social dimensions. The process of ageing varies from individual to individual, according to genetic factors and environmental effects as well as lifestyle.[2] Lifestyle constitutes differences in the protection of an individual's functional capacity and health. It has been reported that diseases could be rapidly treated by adopting an active and healthy lifestyle on the one hand, and by developing medical technologies on the other, while the number of years that individuals have been living as patients and dependent on others could be reduced during an individual's later years.[3] As life expectancy increases in the world, decreasing the number of years in which individuals may experience health issues, social-inclusion policies for the elderly and increasing the number of years in which individuals can live healthily have become the targets of societies.[4]

Although Active and Healthy Ageing (AHA) focuses on the lifestyle of an individual at a micro level, it also covers the quality of opportunities and services offered at a macro level. The World Health Organization (WHO) defines 'active ageing' as "the process of optimizing opportunities for health, participation and security in order to enhance quality of life as

---

[1] The project is supported by TR Ministry of Health.

[2] See Charles Zastrow. *Introduction to Social Work and Social Welfare: Empowering People.* (Belmont, CA: Thomson-Brooks/Cole, 2008).

[3] See WHO (2015) *World Report on Ageing and Health.* (Geneva: World Health Organization, 2015).

[4] See WHO (2014) *Core Health Indicators in the WHO European Region 2014: Special focus: Health 2020 targets indicators.* (Copenhagen: World Health Organization Regional Office for Europe, 2015).

people age."[5] As the definition suggests, 'active ageing' comprises three main factors: health, participation, and security. Health is one of the most significant determinants of the 'active ageing' process. The 'active ageing' model generally includes some comprehensive determinants. These determinants are demonstrated in Figure 1 below.

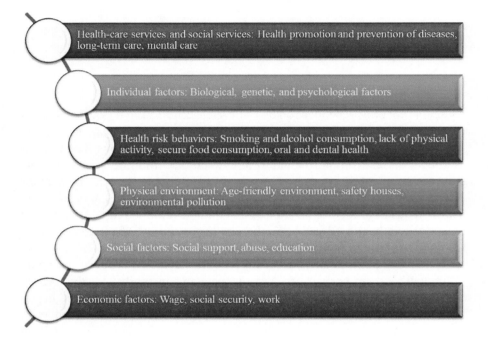

Fig. 1. Determinants of Active Ageing (Paúl, Ribeiro, and Teixeira 2012)

The concept 'active' not only refers to being physically active and participation in the workforce, but it also refers to continuous participation in social, economic, cultural life, and non-governmental works.[6] Therefore, 'active life' and 'active ageing' refer to processes which begin at a youthful age and extend through a period of preparation for old age, prior to the onset

---

[5] See WHO (2002) *Active Ageing: A Policy Framework*. (Geneva: World Health Organization, 2002).

[6] See Asghar Zaidi. *Active Aging Indicators*. Presentation at 6th Session of Open-ended Working Group (OEWG). *Active Ageing Index Project*. United Nations Economic Commission for Europe and European Commission. University of Southampton, 16th July 2015.

of 'growing old.' Forming supportive environments and strong healthy options for individuals are significant for all periods of life.[7]

One of the determinants that designate both the adoption of healthy lifestyles and the scope of opportunities presented by societies for individuals during the process of 'active ageing' is culture. Culture offers a frame for the understanding of 'active ageing.' Culture affects and shapes all the other determinants of 'active ageing,' while framing all individuals in a society. Cultural values and traditions determine the view of a society of older individuals, and of the ageing process.[8] For instance, culture is the key factor that determines a preference for living with a member of the younger generation in the same house, and *vice versa*. Likewise, protective and preventive healthcare services, early diagnosis, and appropriate therapeutic measures are given less importance if disease symptoms are considered to be the natural results of ageing in a society.

* * *

The current study was conducted in order to analyse the perceptions, attitudes, and behaviours of individuals in Turkey, who are now in the process of ageing, regarding Active and Healthy Ageing (AHA). The increasing number of elderly persons and meeting the needs of the elderly population are novel issues for Turkey. Europe has the most-elderly population in the world. Therefore, it has had to confront the social, cultural, and economic issues brought about by ageing and the ageing process. The European population has grown older following completion of its economic developmental process. For its part, Turkey, though still a rapidly-developing country in economic and social terms, has quickly joined in the advanced-ageing process.

Meeting social needs structurally for 'active ageing,' helping individuals maintain their functional capacities throughout their old age and meeting elderly persons' needs for care in a way that is compatible with human dignity – all this requires innovative solutions![9] Novel and creative

---

[7] See United Nations Population Fund (UNFPA) and HelpAge International. 2012. *Ageing in the 21st Century: A Celebration and A Challenge*. (New York and London: United Nations Population Fund and HelpAge International, 2012).

[8] See WHO (2015) *World Report on Ageing and Health*. (Geneva: World Health Organization, 2015).

[9] See UNECE/European Commission (2015) "Active Ageing Index 2014: Analytical Report." Report prepared by Asghar Zaidi of Centre for Research on Ageing, University of Southampton and David Stanton, under contract with United Nations Economic Commission

ideas that render the meeting of unmet needs possible constitute 'social innovation.' The results of 'social innovation' are not only the concern of members of a specific generational group, but of society as a whole, that is, of each one of us. For this reason, questions about 'ageing' and 'the ageing process in the world' such as: "Why are 'the concept of 'active ageing,' and the need for 'social innovation' being discussed?" and "How can this be put into practice?" should be answered.

* * *

In Turkey, the proportion of the elderly population started to grow more rapidly than other population groups, accounting for the fact that the population growth rate started to decline, especially at the end of the 1990s, and that this process kept up this pace through to the end of the first decade of the 21st century. In Turkey, in 2015, the median age was 31 years old. The 15–64 age group – the population at working age in Turkey – constitutes 67·8% of the total population of the country.[10] While the annual population growth rate in Turkey was 2·64% in 1985, this rate declined to 1·34% in 2015. On the other hand, while the elderly population in Turkey was 4·2% in 1985, the growth rate of this population almost doubled in 2015, rising to 8·2%. According to population projections, the number of elderly people in Turkey, expressed as a percentage of the total population, is estimated to be 10·2% in 2023, 20·8% in 2050, and 27·7% in 2075.

Turkey occupies 66th place among one hundred ad sixty-seven countries in the world in ageing ranking. The 'elderly dependency rate,' which refers to the number of elderly individuals per one hundred working-age persons, is 12·2% in Turkey. There are 5,293 individuals in Turkey who are 100-years-old or older. While the number of 80-year-old and older individuals in Turkey was 1,261,273 in 2013, the same figure rose to 1,315,845 in 2014, and to 1,328,924 in 2015. Likewise, there has been an increase in the number of 90-year-old and older individuals. While the number of 90-year-old and older individuals was 89,709 in 2012 and 99,005 in 2013, the fact that this figure rose to 115,277 in 2014 and to 127,986 in 2015 proves to be noteworthy in respect of the increase in the elderly

---

for Europe (UNECE/Geneva), co-funded by the European Commission. Directorate General for Employment, Social Affairs and Inclusion, Brussels, April 2015.

[10] See Turkish Statistical Institute (TurkStat). 2016a. *The Results of Address Based Population Registration System, 2015*. Ankara: Turkish Statistical Institute Press Release. Nº 21507. 28th January 2016.

population growth.[11] The average life-expectancy at birth in Turkey is seventy-eight years. This figure was determined to be 75·3 years for men and 80·7 years for women.[12]

* * *

A long life is, on the one hand, one of the most significant achievements of humankind, and is a cause for celebration. On the other hand, it represents an important challenge. The fact that the elderly population has been increasing gained attention for the first time in the world in the 1990s. Strategies for 'active ageing' and 'intergenerational solidarity' were devised, especially in Europe. From 2010 onwards, the European Union (EU) began coming to terms with the challenges presented by its rapidly-ageing communities. 2012 was declared European year of 'active ageing' and 'intergenerational solidarity.' During this process, the World Health Organization (WHO) has focused on the concept of 'healthy ageing,' which has proved to be one of the most important dimensions of 'active ageing' that it had defined at the beginning of the 2000s, the noughties.

All these concepts draw attention to the fact that the increase in the elderly population cannot be stopped while approaches to successful ways of managing the challenges are in the process of development. One of the most recently discussed concepts to meet the needs of the ageing population by proposing novel ideas and creative solutions is 'social innovation' because, as the number of issues requiring solutions increases, novelty becomes a necessity. On the one hand, 'innovation' is based on an awareness of the difference between the current state of the situation, and what it needs to be. On the other hand, 'innovation' is rooted in an understanding that it is the difference between the needs of the elderly and the services offered to meet these needs that prescribes what should be the novel information, technologies, and creative solutions in this field.[13]

The "Turkey Active and Healthy Ageing Study" was conducted in Turkey, with its rapidly-growing elderly population, in order to determine the need for 'social innovation.' The study focused specifically on the difference between the current situation regarding Active and Healthy Ageing (AHA), and what it should be.

---

[11] See Turkish Statistical Institute (TurkStat). 2016b. *Elderly Statistics, 2015*. Ankara: Turkish Statistical Institute Press Release. N° 21520. 17th March 2016.

[12] See Turkish Statistical Institute (TurkStat). 2015b. *Life Tables, 2013-2014*. Ankara: Turkish Statistical Institute Press Release. N° 18618. 7th October 2015.

[13] See Robin Murray, Julie Caulier-Grice, and Geoff Mulgan. *The Open Book of Social Innovation*. (London: The Young Foundation, 2010).

Method

This study was conducted in Turkey in order to analyse the behaviour and attitudes of 40-year-old and older individuals, and their perceptions of Active and Healthy Ageing (AHA). The Turkish Statistical Institute (TurkStat) has been carrying out the "Turkey Health Survey" regularly since 2008.[14] The "Turkey Active and Healthy Ageing Study," which was conducted alongside the "Turkey Health Survey," proves to be the first of its kind in Turkey in respect of its content and scope of sampling.

The "Turkey Active and Healthy Ageing Study" utilizes a quantitative research method. This is a descriptive study. The research population is made up of 40-year-old and older women and men. The research sample population comprises a total of 3,082 individuals and is made up of two subgroups: a) women and men in the 40–64 age group;[15] and b) women and men in the 65+ age group.[16] When the study sampling was designated, it had a 95% confidence level, with a 2·2% confidence interval throughout Turkey. At the time, Turkey was considered to have twelve regions, and one city from each region was included in the study. Those persons in the 40–64 age group were covered by sampling individuals in a representative population percentage for each city included in the study. (see Table 1)

The sampling unit of the study is 'the individual.' Following a random selection process, those individuals included in the study were met on visits to their households. A questionnaire-based survey was carried out by means of face-to-face interviews with women and men in the 65+ age group. Furthermore, from each household, one person from the 65+ age group and one person from the 40–64 age group from among those individuals appropriate for purposeful sampling, were included in the study on a voluntary basis. Ethical consent was obtained from the participants after informing them of the fact that this study was being conducted for scientific purposes, that their identity and address information would not be revealed that the results of the study would be utilized only for scientific purposes, and that they could leave the study whenever they wished to do so.

---

[14] See Turkish Statistical Institute (TurkStat) 2015a. *Turkey Health Survey, 2014*. Ankara: Turkish Statistical Institute Press Release. Nº 18854. 1st October 2015.

[15] The sample population in the 40–64 age group numbers 1,546 individuals, 51·2% of whom are women, and 48·8% of whom are men.

[16] The sample population in the 65+ age group numbers 1,536 individuals, 52·56% of whom are men, and 47·44% of whom are women.

Socio-demographic characteristics	Participant profiles	40–64 age group n:1546	65+ age group n:1536	Total n:3082
Gender	Women	51·20	52·56	49·4
	Men	48·80	47·44	50·6
Education	Illiterate	1·64	12·02	6·7
	Literate, but no school certificate	2·36	15·18	8·7
	Primary-school	16·41	25·23	20·6
	Secondary-school,	18·32	16·95	17·5
	High-school	35·46	21·48	28·2
	University	25·81	9·08	17·5
Occupation	Housewife	27·02	30·73	26·2
	Blue collar	16·82	19·03	16·3
	White collar	21·40	20·88	20·8
	Technician	2·51	2·53	2·4
	Artisan	11·67	11·16	11·3
	Professional	6·47	4·24	6·3
	Other (farmer, cook etc.)	14·11	11·43	13·7
Marital status	Married	75·52	57·07	66·0
	Never married	7·06	4·2	5·7
	Widowed	4·62	32·68	18·4
	Divorced	12·70	6·04	9·4
Family structure	Nuclear family, with kids	72·84	51·91	61·4
	Nuclear family, without kids	8·64	15·74	12·0
	Extended family	8·44	14·94	11·5
	Lives alone	10·08	17·41	13·5
Number of children	No children	13·91	8·09	11·1
	1 child	18·97	8·61	13·8
	2 children	32·49	23·87	28·1
	3 children	22·48	26·43	24·3
	4+ children	12·15	33·00	22·4
Satisfaction with income	Very satisfied	6·09	6·84	6·3
	Satisfied	31·11	32·47	31·2
	Making ends meet	36·93	35·19	35·4
	Dissatisfied	18·40	18·26	18·0
	Very dissatisfied	7·48	7·24	7·3

Socio-demographic characteristics cont'd	Participant profiles cont'd	40–64 age group n:1546 cont'd	65+ age group n:1536 cont'd	Total n:3082 cont'd
Usage of social benefits	Yes	**18·16**	**27·31**	**21·3**
	No	**81:84**	**72·69**	**72·6**
Presence of patients, children, and elderly needing home care	None	89·17	88·46	82·6
	Children	4·85	5·58	5·2
	Elderly	4·33	10·97	7·5
	Patients	1·64	4·98	3·3
Use of home care services	I use home care services	3·47	12·82	8·0
	I do not need services.	63·11	49·57	55·7
	I do not use services, although I need them.	3·99	11·70	7·7
	I do not know about services	29·43	25·91	27·5
Knowledge of emergency call number (ambulance)	Knows	94·64	84·95	89·8
	Does not know	5·36	15·05	10·2

Table 1. Socio-demographic characteristics of participants (%)

* * *

A questionnaire form was devised to collect data to analyse the current situation regarding Active and Healthy Ageing (AHA) in Turkey. The questionnaire form was predicated upon 'active ageing' reports written by Asghar Zaidi (2015) for the European Commission (EC), the United Nations Economic Commission for Europe (UNECE), and the World Health Organization (WHO), together with Canadian and Australian Health

Surveys.[17] Moreover, other domestic and international studies were also taken into consideration. This study takes into account primarily current Turkish Statistical Institute (TurkStat) data, official reports, and other studies on the subject. Questions that would achieve data on subdimensions of the subject were created, based on the 'active ageing' approach within the scope of this study. These dimensions are:

a) Independent, healthy, and safe life
      1. Physical exercise
      2. Access to health care services
      3. Arrangements for independent life
      4. Level of income
      5. Absence of poverty risk
      6. Level of material wealth
      7. Physical safety
      8. Life-long learning
b) Participation in society
      1. Participation in voluntary activities
      2. Children and grandchildren care
      3. Elder family member care
      4. Political participation
c) 'Active ageing' capacity
      1. Success in life expectancy and healthy years
      2. Mental welfare
      3. Internet and PC use
      4. Social ties
      5. Participation into education by the elderly
d) Work
      1. Participation in working life, 40–64 and 65+ age groups

This study takes the above-mentioned main points on 'active ageing,' as determined by the United Nations (UN), into consideration, in addition to the presence of chronic diseases, the level of accomplishment in everyday life activities, smoking and alcohol consumption, factors that pose a risk to health and accelerate secondary ageing like obesity, the condition of

---

[17] See Asghar Zaidi. "Active Aging Indicators." Presentation at 6th Session of Open-ended Working Group (OEWG). *Active Ageing Index Project.* (United Nations Economic Commission for Europe – UNECE, and European Commission – EC. University of Southampton, 16th July 2015).

physical and mental functions, and evaluations on 'ageing' and 'healthy ageing.'

  A pilot study for the questionnaire form was also conducted. Following a final revision of the questionnaire form, pollsters who had been trained in the subject of the project and the content of the survey carried out fieldwork using face-to-face interviews, in twelve cities in Turkey, between June and October 2015. The integrity of the surveys was checked by calling 46% of the participants on the telephone. Following the content check of the questionnaires, a decision was passed not to include two hundred and fifteen questionnaires in the study. This figure constitutes about 7% of the total number of samples. For this reason, two hundred and fifteen surveys were re-conducted in order to reach the targeted number of samples. In this way, the target number of 3,082 surveys was reached. SPSS 23 was used for data-entry and analyses.

Results

This part of the study offers an explanation on Active and Healthy Ageing (AHA) in Turkey under four main headings: 1. Independent, Healthy, and Safe Life; 2. Social Participation; 3. 'Active Ageing' Capacity; and 4. Conditions of Work.

1. Independent, Healthy, and Safe Life

Under the heading "Independent, Healthy, and Safe Life," questions were asked on the following topics: 1. Diseases and disabilities; 2. Dependency in primary and secondary life-activities; 3. Risk factors for healthy living; 4. Maintenance of physical and mental functions; 5. Exercise; 6. Access to and satisfaction with health care services; 7. Issues considered to be significant in order to be healthier; 8. Level of stress; 9. Healthy and safe food intake; and 10. Feeling safe in the environment within which one lives.

1.1. Diseases and disabilities
In respect of diseases and disability, the study listed diabetes, arthritis/joint diseases, cancer, asthma, chest diseases, stroke, hearing loss, vision loss, cardiac diseases, hepatic diseases, and renal diseases. Participants were asked whether they had been diagnosed with one of these diseases. "Yes" responses were scored 1, while "No" responses were scored 2 points. The minimum score that could be attained from this section of the study was 11, while the maximum score was 22. An increase in score signified a decrease

in the presence of diseases. The mean score of female and male participants in the 40+ age group was 20·28 in this section. The most frequent diseases diagnosed in participating individuals were diabetes (33%) and arthritis/joint diseases (32%), while about one fifth had problems with vision loss (20·4%).

The results of the study revealed that male participants were in better health conditions within the framework of these diseases (p<0·01) than female participants. It was also discovered that those individuals in the 40–64 age group were healthier than those in the 65+ age group with regard to diagnosed diseases (p<0·001).

It was observed that, as individuals aged, the health conditions of those in the 40–64 age group deteriorated, causing an increase in risk of disease, and furthermore, that the health conditions of those in the 56–64 age group were shown to be worse than those in the 40–55 age group (p<0·001).

The presence of diseases varied according to the level of education (p<0·001),[18] with an increase in the number of diagnosed diseases as the level of education increased. As the level of education declined, the number of diagnosed diseases decreased. This result suggests that, as the level of education declines, so individual awareness on health literacy, that informs about and facilitates access to health care services, doctors' visits, and types of diseases, also decreases.

About half of the female and male participants in the 65+ age group covered by the study had diabetes (47·1%). This was followed by arthritis and joint diseases (43·0%). About a third of the participants in this age group had visual (29·0%) and auditory (28·8%) loss. It was also observed that about a quarter (24·8%) of the female and male participants in the 65+ age group had chest diseases. While the proportion of those who had asthma was 19·0%, the proportion of those who had cardiac diseases was 18·8%, and the proportion of those who had cancer was 8%. The number of diagnosed diseases in female participants of the 65+ age group was higher than that of the male participants (p<0·001).

---

[18] The educational level of elderly women in Turkey is lower than that of men. While the proportion of elderly widowers with little or no education is 12·9%, the proportion of elderly widows with little or no education is 50·5%. Those elderly persons who live as members of a single household constitute 45·8% of the elderly population. While women account for 76·5% of the elderly living alone, this figure is 23·5% for men. Moreover, the poverty rate for the elderly is 18·3%. It is also seen that 74·1% of the working elderly population is engaged in the agricultural sector. See Turkish Statistical Institute (TurkStat). 2016b. *Elderly Statistics, 2015*. Ankara: Turkish Statistical Institute Press Release. N° 21520. 17th March 2016.

1.2. Dependency in primary and secondary life-activities

In terms of dependency in primary and secondary life-activities, the level of dependency of individuals covered by the study to accomplish their daily primary and secondary activities was divided into three groups: a) completely dependent on others; b) dependent/partially dependent on others; and c) independent/not dependent on others.

Primary (or main) life-activities included such activities as dressing, lying down on and getting up from the bed, sitting on and getting up from a chair, carrying out personal grooming – nail, teeth, eyes, skin cleaning, and washing the face – taking a bath, going to the toilet, nutrition, doing household chores, and going shopping. While the minimum score that could be attained from these activities was 9, the maximum score was 27. Higher scores referred to the lower level of dependency in main life-activities. The mean score of female and male participants covered by the study in the 40+ age group in main life-activities was $25 \cdot 12$ out of a possible 27. While the score of individuals in the 40–64 age group was $25 \cdot 89$, the score of those in the 65+ age group dropped to $24 \cdot 31$.

The results of the study revealed that the level of dependency and the need to depend on others of the female participants in the 40–64 age group were higher than those of the male participants ($p<0 \cdot 05$). The level of dependency in main life-activities of the individuals in the 40–64 age group did not differ with regards to marital status ($p>0 \cdot 05$). It was also observed that the level of dependency in main life-activities of illiterate participants was higher than that of those who were literate and who were primary school, secondary school, and high-school graduates ($p<0 \cdot 05$).

The one-way ANOVA analysis was utilized to reveal whether there were differences in the dependency levels in main life-activities among the 65–75, 76–85, and 86+ age groups that is, within the 65+ age group. While the mean score was $24 \cdot 68$ for the 65–75 age group, this score dropped to $23 \cdot 52$ in the 75–85 age group, and to $19 \cdot 00$ in the 86+ age group. In other words, the level of dependency in main life-activities increased significantly as individual participants aged ($p<0 \cdot 001$).

No differences were found between the levels of dependency in main life-activities of the female and male participants in the 65+ age group ($p>0 \cdot 05$). The dependency levels in main life-activities of elderly persons who had never married, who were single, who were widows/widowers, or who had divorced, were found to be higher than those of married individuals ($p<0 \cdot 01$). While the dependency levels of illiterate participants were higher, those of literate persons – primary school, secondary school, and high-school graduates – were found to be lower ($p<0 \cdot 001$).

1.3. Risk factors for healthy living

With regard to risk factors for healthy living – smoking, alcohol consumption, obesity, and hypertension – the results of the study revealed that 38·6% of the individuals in the 40+ age group covered by the study were smokers, while 13·9% consumed alcohol, and about a quarter of the individuals (25·8%) had hypertension. The obesity rate was found to be 5·2%.[19]

When the risk factors affecting Active and Healthy Ageing (AHA) were evaluated for the individuals in the 40–64 age group, it was observed that just over half (50·3%) of the participants in this age group were smokers, while 17·8% consumed alcohol. Moreover, the proportion of those individuals who had been diagnosed with hypertension in this age group was 16·5%. It was noteworthy to see that the figure for smoking, one of the most significant risk factors accelerating secondary ageing in the 40–64 age group, was high, while the risk of hypertension started at earlier ages. The male participants in the 40–64 age group smoked more in comparison to the female participants ($p < 0.001$).

The female and male secondary school and high-school graduate participants in the 40–64 age group smoked less than other school graduates and illiterate participants ($p < 0.001$). It was also observed that widows, widowers, and married participants smoked more than participants who were single ($p < 0.05$). Furthermore, it was found that those persons in the 56–64 age group smoked more than those in the 40–55 age group ($p < 0.001$).

In the 40–64 age group, more male participants consumed alcohol than did the female participants ($p < 0.001$). It was observed, too, that married participants, widows, and widowers consumed more alcohol than single participants ($p < 0.001$). Moreover, with regard to alcohol consumption, no differences were found between the 40–55 age group and the 56–64 age group ($p > 0.05$). Again, in the 40–64 age group, as the level of education declined, so the level of alcohol consumption increased. Alcohol consumption was at its highest level amongst illiterate participants and primary school graduates ($p < 0.001$).

It was seen that the participants in the 56–64 age group were diagnosed with hypertension at a greater rate than those in the 40–55 age group ($p < 0.001$). No differences were found between the female and male participants regarding the risk of hypertension ($p > 0.05$). The risk of

---

[19] What 'obesity' refers to here depended solely on the responses of individual participants when asked they considered themselves to be obese or not.

hypertension increased, however, as the level of education declined (p<0·05).

When the risk factors affecting Active and Healthy Ageing (AHA) were evaluated for those individuals in the 65+ age group, it was observed that more than a quarter (26·5%) of the participants in this age group were smokers, while 9·9% consumed alcohol. The proportion of those persons in this age group who were diagnosed with hypertension was 35·1%.

In order to establish whether there was a difference between female and male participants in the 65+ age group in terms of the total risk score – including the presence of smoking, alcohol consumption, obesity, and hypertension – evaluation of the results revealed that the female participants were exposed to fewer risk factors in comparison to the male participants (p<0·001). The male participants smoked more than the female ones (p<0·001). Furthermore, those in the 65–75 age group smoked more than those in the 76–85 and 86+ age groups (p<0·001).

Amongst the male participants in the 65+ age group (p<0·001), those who had never married, those who had remained single, and those who had divorced (p<0·001) consumed more alcohol. As the level of education increased in individuals in the 65+ age group, the level of alcohol consumption rose as well (p<0·001).

Individuals in the 86+ age group were diagnosed with hypertension in greater proportion than those in the 76–85 and 65–75 age groups (p<0·001). The risk of hypertension was greater for female participants in the 65+ age group in comparison to male participants (p<0·001). As the level of education declined, the risk for hypertension increased (p<0·001).

The presence of obesity in individuals covered by the study was evaluated initially on the basis of statements by the participants themselves. This proportion was found to be 6·8%. When the Body Mass Index (BMI) was calculated according to height and weight statements, it was found that almost half (47·4%) of the individuals in the 40+ age group were overweight, in other words, slightly fat. While the proportion of those with normal weight was 38·7%, the proportion of those with Stage 1 obesity was 10·7%. The female participants in the 40–64 age group were more overweight than the male participants (p<0·01). Marital status in the 40–64 age group had no effects on obesity. Individuals in the 56–64 age group were more overweight than those in the 40–55 age group (p<0·01).

It was seen that 45·2% of the individuals in the 65+ age group covered by the study were overweight, in other words, were slightly fat, while 39% of them had normal weight, and the proportion of those with Stage 1 obesity was 11·2%. It was also revealed that the proportion of those with

Stage 2 obesity was 2·2%, and that the proportion of those with Stage 3 obesity was 1·1%.

The presence of obesity in participants of the 65+ age group was evaluated according to different variables. The female participants were found to be more overweight than the male participants (p<0·001). It was also observed that, as the level of education increased, the likelihood of being overweight increased as well (p<0·01). The results of the study revealed that the individuals in the 65–75 age group were more overweight than those in other age groups, and that weight decreased as individuals aged (p<0·01).

1.4. Maintenance of physical and mental functions

As for the capacity to sustain physical functions, ten activities were included within the scope of the part exploring the capacity to sustain physical functions covered by the section on Active and Healthy Ageing (AHA). The participants were asked to respond either "Yes" or "No" to statements. "Yes" had a score of 1, while "No" was scored as 2. According to the scoring, the minimum score that the participants could get was 10, while the maximum score was designated to be 20. Lower scores referred to a higher capacity to sustain physical functions. The mean score of the participants in the 40+ age group within the framework of this study was found to be 10·64. This score was 10·30 for the individuals in the 40–64 age group. The capacity to sustain physical functions in this age group was lower for female participants in comparison to male participants (p<0·05). The capacity to sustain physical functions in the 55–64 age group was lower than that of the 40–54 age group (p<0·01). The capacity to sustain physical functions declined in the 65+ age group as the individuals aged, and it reached its lowest level in the 86+ age group (p<0·01).

1.5. Exercise

In respect of the frequency of physical exercise and sportive activities, about a third (29·75%) of the participants covered by the study stated that they engaged in sportive activities less often, and about a third (29·16%) of them declared that they never engaged in such activities. While the proportion of those in the 40–64 age group who stated that they generally exercised on a daily basis was 12·44%, the proportion of those who exercised at least once weekly was 12·44%, and of those who exercised less often was 32·77%. It was observed that about one fifth (19·87%) of the participants in the 40–64 group never exercised. The female participants in the 40-64 group exercised less than the male participants (p<0·01). As the level of education increased, so did the frequency of exercise (p<0·01).

The proportion of individuals in the 65+ age group who generally exercised daily was 8·7%. While the proportion of those who exercised at least once weekly was 7·51%, that of those who never exercised was 38·67%. The proportion of those who stated that they exercised less often was 26·68%, while that of those who declared they were unable to exercise because they were sick was 10·41%. When the individuals in the 65+ age group were evaluated, it was observed that individuals who never exercised or who did not exercise regularly constituted the majority of the group. The male participants in the 65+ age group (p<0·01), those in the 65–75 age group, and those with a higher level of education, exercised more (p<0·01).

1.6. Access to and satisfaction with health care services

The individuals covered by the study were asked whether they had easy access to health care services when they needed to see a doctor, to receive medical care and dental care. 79·6% of the participants responded positively to this question, while 20·4% responded negatively. It was observed that access to health care services got harder as individuals aged, and the easy access to health care services in the 55–64 age group got harder in comparison to those in the 40–55 age group (p<0·05). It was also found that those who had graduate degrees had easier access to health care services in comparison to those with lower educational levels (p<0·01).

The male participants in the 65+ age group had easier access to health care services when compared to the female participants (p<0·05). It was also observed that access to health care services got harder as individuals aged, and that easy access to health care services was harder for those in the 76–85 and 86+ age groups in comparison to those in the 65–75 age group (p<0·05). It was pointed out that those with primary school and secondary school qualifications had easier access to health care services when compared to others with different levels of education. Those who had the hardest time in accessing health care services were the illiterate individuals (p<0·01).

The degree of satisfaction with health care services, one of the determinants of healthy, independent, and safe life, was found to be 2·14 out of a possible 4. 63·71% of the participants stated that they were satisfied with health care services, while 14·72% declared that they were very satisfied. While the proportion of those who were dissatisfied with health care services was 13·8%, the proportion of those who were very dissatisfied was 7·77%.

The degree of satisfaction with health care services increased in the 40–64 age group as the level of education of the individuals increased (p<0·01). The degrees of satisfaction of individuals in the 40–55 age group (p<0·01) and of the married participants (p<0·01) were found to be high.

The level of education in the 65+ age group did not affect satisfaction with health care services (p>0·05). It was found that married individuals in the 65+ age group were more satisfied with health care services in comparison to the widows, widowers, and divorcees in the same age group (p<0·05). The satisfaction with health care services in the 65–75 age group was higher than that of those who were 76 years old or older (p<0·05).

1.7. Issues considered to be significant to be healthier

The individuals covered by the study were asked what they thought was the most significant activity to carry out in order to be healthier. 23·8% of the participants in the 40+ age group stated that the activities they considered significant were regular visits to the doctor, while 21·6% said starting exercises, or doing more exercises. Of those actions deemed most significant by the individuals, 15·6% of the participants considered quitting smoking, 14·9% considered losing weight, and 14% considered changing their nutritional habits. Moreover, when asked about the obstacles preventing the things they wanted to do in order to be healthier, 15·2% responded that they were not able to accomplish what they saw as necessary to being healthier because of family responsibilities, 12·9% admitted poor self-discipline, 11·4% laid blame on a heavy workload, and 10·9% cited economic shortcomings and a high level of expenses. There were also participants who said they could not live more healthily, citing extreme stress (6·9%), inability to quit smoking and drinking (6·4%), and having many health issues (9·9%).

1.8. Level of stress

About half (49·2%) of the participants in the 40+ age group covered by the study were slightly stressed. One out of four participants (24·7%) responded "I am slightly more stressed" (15·8%) and "I am very stressed" (8·9%). The proportion of those who stated that they were not stressed out was found to be 24·9%. While the female and male participants in the 40–64 age group had similar levels of stress, the female participants in the 65+ age group were more stressed out than the male participants (p<0·01).

1.9. Healthy and safe food intake

The participants were asked whether they had been eating healthy and safe foods. 68·3% of the participants stated that they were eating healthy and safe foods, while 31·7% said they were not eating healthy and safe foods.

1.10. Feeling safe in the environment within which one lives

With regard to their sense of security outside their homes, the individuals covered by the study were asked whether they felt safe while walking outside, especially after dark. Their responses were divided into four groups: a) very safe; b) safe; c) unsafe; and d) very unsafe. Having been scored between 1 and 4, the mean score of the responses was found to be 2·15. This result referred to a medium level of confidence. About three quarters of the participants (56·1% + 18·1% = 74·2%) considered the environment they lived in to be safe. The proportion of those who did not consider their environment safe was 25·8% (18·3% + 7·5%). When the responses of the female and male participants in the 40+ age group were compared, it was observed that women felt less safe in their environments when they went out (p<0·01).

2. Social Participation

Under the heading "Social Participation," questions were asked on the following topics: 1. Participation in voluntary activities; 2. Children and grandchildren care; 3. Disabled and elderly family member care. These issues were evaluated as determinants of Active and Healthy Ageing (AHA).

2.1. Participation in voluntary activities

As a determinant of 'social participation,' the individuals covered by the study were asked whether they participated in associations, social movements, political parties, and other voluntary organizations, and whether they engaged in philanthropic and charitable activities. The minimum score that could be attained from the "Voluntary Activities" section was 6, while the maximum score was 24. Higher scores refer to the high level of participation in voluntary activities. The mean score of individuals in the 40+ age group covered by the study was 8·91 out of a possible 24. This showed that participation in voluntary activities was very low.

The proportion of male individuals participating in voluntary activities was higher than that of female participants (p<0·001). Moreover, those in the 40–64 age group participated in voluntary activities more than those in the 60+ age group (p<0·001). It was also observed that the illiterate and primary school graduates participated in voluntary activities less frequently than those individuals with higher educational levels. In other words, those individuals who participated in voluntary activities the least were the illiterate, while the ones who participated in voluntary activities the most were persons with university degrees (p<0·001).

2.2. Children and grandchildren care

27·93% of the individuals covered by the study stated that they took care of children or grandchildren every day, while 9·52% declared that they took care of children or grandchildren two days a week, and 9·71% said once or twice a week. It was seen that 12·39% of the participants had no children or grandchildren to take care of. It was also observed that those individuals in the 40–64 age group took care of children or grandchildren more in comparison to those in the 65+ age group (p<0·001). 23·83% of those in the 65+ age group took care of children and grandchildren on a daily basis. The proportion of the elderly persons taking care of children and grandchildren two days a week was found to be 22·05%.

2.3. Disabled and elderly family-member care

It was determined that 7·43% of the individuals covered by the study took care of an elderly or disabled family member on a daily basis. When the options two days a week (7·85%), once or twice a week (11·13%), and less frequently (29·32%) were taken into consideration, it was observed that about half of the individuals covered by the study had a family member who needed attention, care, and support. Only 21·17% of the participants stated that they had no disabled or elderly family-members who needed care. It was also seen that more individuals in the 40–64 age group took care of and supported their elderly and disabled family members compared to those in the 65+ age group (p<0·001).

3. The Capacity for 'Active Ageing'

The capacity for 'active ageing' was also evaluated as a determinant of 'active ageing' within the scope of this study, focusing on active and healthy ageing. The subgroups designated under this heading were: 1. The age at which ageing begins; 2. 'Satisfaction with life,' with its different aspects; 3. 'Mental well-being'; 4. 'Life-long learning'; 5. Participation in training sessions, seminars and conferences; 6. Going to the movies and plays; 7. Internet use; 8. Participation in religious activities and worship.

3.1. The age at which ageing begins

The individuals in the 65+ age group thought that being elderly started at the age of 59·6. The individuals in the 40–64 age group, on the other hand, believed that old age started at an average figure of 59·01. These results supported the results of a study conducted by Eurobarometer for the European Commission (EC). The results of this study on 'active ageing' in

European Union (EU) countries and Turkey revealed that the perception 'old age' started at the age of fifty-eight was an overwhelming view in Turkey. The perception prevalent in the European Union (EU), however, was that 'old age' started at sixty-four years of age.[20]

3.2. 'Satisfaction with life'

Five items constituted 'satisfaction with life': 1. general condition of health; 2. the level of accomplishment in everyday life activities; 3. work life (for workers); 4. life and living conditions in general, and 5. personal relationships. Satisfaction items were scored as very dissatisfied – 1, and very satisfied. – 10. While the minimum score that could be attained on the 'satisfaction with life' scale was 6, the maximum score was 60. The mean score of the 40+ age group in terms of 'satisfaction with life' was 41·80 out of a possible 60. It was observed that individuals were most satisfied with personal relationships (7·16), followed by general condition of health (6·33), the level of accomplishment in everyday life activities (6·33), their lives in general (6·56), and living conditions (6·56). The score of 'satisfaction with working life' for workers was found to be 6·63 out of 10.

Male participants were more satisfied with their lives in comparison to female participants ($p < 0.05$). The 'satisfaction with life' for those individuals in the 65+ age group was lower than that of the ones in the 40–64 age group ($p < 0.001$). It was observed that 'satisfaction with life' declined as individuals aged, and that the 'satisfaction with life' in the 56–64 age group was lower than that of the individuals in the 40–55 age group ($p < 0.001$). Moreover, those in the 86+ age group had a very low level of 'satisfaction with life' ($p < 0.001$). In other words, it was seen that each year added to the age of participants as they grew older negatively affected their 'satisfaction with life.'

Another factor that affected 'satisfaction with life' was the level of education. As the level of education increased, so did 'satisfaction with life' ($p < 0.001$).

3.3. 'Mental well-being'

The aspects evaluated in this sub-group were an individual's conditions for: 1. feeling joyful and good; 2. remaining calm and comfortable; 3. being active and spry; 4. being rested; and 5. being able to allocate time to subjects they were interested in. There were five statements within the 'mental well-

---

[20] See European Commission. *Commission Staff Working Document. Turkey 2012 Progress Report.* (Brussels: European Commission, 10th October 2012).

being' part. Evaluation options between never – 1, and always – 4 were scored between 1 and 4. The minimum score that could be obtained from this part was 5, while the maximum score was 20. Higher scores referred to a better, that is, higher capacity for 'mental well-being' as well.

The results of the study revealed that the mean score of the participants was 13·71. This result demonstrated that the individuals covered by the study had a medium level of capacity for 'mental well-being.'

Moreover, the study explored the capacity for 'mental well-being' of the individuals in the 40–64 and 65+ age groups who made up the two main age groups. The results showed that the individuals in the 40–64 age group had a higher capacity for 'mental well-being' than those in the 65+ age group (p<0·01).

Male participants had a better capacity than did female participants for 'mental well-being' (p<0·05). As the level of education increased, so did the capacity for 'mental well-being' (p<0·001). The capacity for 'mental well-being' of widows, widowers, divorcees, and single individuals was lower than that of married couples (p<0·001). The capacity for 'mental well-being' of those who had stated that their income was 'very insufficient' and 'insufficient' was lower than those who found that their income was 'sufficient' and 'very sufficient' (p<0·001).

3.4. 'Life-long learning'

Individuals in the 40+ age group were asked whether they attended any courses, training and tutoring sessions, seminars, or conferences. Only about a quarter of the participants responded positively to this question (24·9%). It was seen that 75·1% responded negatively. Those who responded negatively were asked "why?" According to the results of this question, 44·6% of these individuals responded: "I was never interested," while 48·82% said "I have no idea."

3.5. Participation in training sessions, seminars, and conferences

The proportion of elderly individuals who participate in educational activities such as training sessions, seminars, courses, and conferences in the 40–64 age group was found to be only 34·31%. This proportion drops down to 15·24% for individuals in the 65+ age group. When the reasons why individuals in the 40–64 age group, whom we considered to be active and healthy, did not participate in such educational and cultural activities were scrutinized, it was observed that 44·44% did not have any interest in such subjects, while 51·25% did not have any ideas on these subjects. 4·51% of the individuals in the 40–64 age group stated that they did not attend such educational and cultural activities, citing their illnesses. The proportion of those individuals who were unable to attend such activities in the 65+ age group was double (8·58%) that of the 40–64 age group. The individuals in the 65+ age group said they did not attend training sessions, seminars, courses, and conferences, either because they were never interested in such activities (44·62%), or because they had no idea about any of these activities (46·79%).

3.6. Going to the movies and plays

The results of the study showed that 41·1% of the individuals in the 40+ age group had never been to a movie or a play. While 22·8% of the individuals stated that they went to the movies or theatre less frequently, 10·4% of them said they went once every six months, and 9·4% said they went once a month, showing a low rate of cultural participation. The proportion of those in the 40–64 age group who stated that they had never been to the movies or theatre was 23·28%, while this figure went up to 59·03% for individuals in the 65+ age group.

3.7. Internet use

42·2% of the individuals in the 40+ age group stated that they had never used the Internet, and it was seen that those who used the Internet (26·6%) mostly did so on a daily basis. While 21·1% of those in the 40–64 age group had never used the Internet, this proportion goes up to 63·72% for individuals in the 65+ age group. The proportion of those who used the Internet on a daily basis rises up to 42·74% for individuals in the 40–64 age group.

3.8. Participation in religious activities and worship

It was observed that 57·1% of the individuals in the 40+ age group stated that they participated in religious activities and worshipped, while 28·6% said they were sometimes engaged in religious activities, and 14·3% responded negatively to this subject. While the proportion of those in the 40–64 age group engaging in religious activities was 50·30%, this figure went up to 64·23% for persons in the 65+ age group. The proportion of those individuals in the 40–64 age group who stated that they did not attend religious activities and did not worship was found to be 17·01%, while the same rate was 11·52% for persons in the 65+ age group.

4. Conditions of Work

The results of the study revealed that, in the 40+ age group, 36·83% of the individuals were working, while 39·64% were retired. It was also observed that about a quarter (25·53%) of the individuals were not working, although they were of working age. When the subject of work was explored according to gender distribution, it was seen that 63·3% of those who were working were male, while 36·7% were female. 63·6% of those persons who were retired were male, while 36·3% of them were female.

In the 40–64 age group, 25·53% of the individuals were not working, while 39·64% of them were retired. The proportion of those persons who were working in this age group was 36·83%. While the proportion of working women in the 40–64 age group was 36·7%, the figure for working men was almost double that of women (63·3%). In other words, those who were not working in this age group were women in a proportion of 89·8% compared to men.

One of the most significant factors affecting work in the 40–64 age group was the level of education. As the level of education increased, so did the proportion of those individuals in work. While the proportion of those persons in work for the literate was 12·3%, it was 17·6% for primary school graduates, and this proportion went up to 29·5% for secondary school graduates, 47·9% for high-school graduates, and 69·1% for university graduates.

Conclusion

This study explored the results of the "Turkey Active and Healthy Ageing Survey." The conditions and evaluations of the individuals in the 40+ age group regarding Active and Healthy Ageing (AHA) were analysed by means of a descriptive approach within the framework of the study. This study revealed the Active and Healthy Ageing (AHA) conditions not only of the currently 'old' 65+ age group, but also of those in the 40+ age group who would also be 'old' in the future.

The results of the study revealed that only a quarter of the individuals in the 40–64 age group, who would be 'old' in the short and medium terms, were university graduates. About a third of the women in this age group had no income and were housewives. It was observed that 36·93% of the individuals in the 40–64 age group were making do with their income, while a quarter of them were not satisfied with their level of income. 5·3% of those in the 40–64 age group did not know the ambulance telephone number in case of emergencies. It was seen that the next generation of elderly persons in Turkey were disadvantaged with regard to these issues, issues that would contribute to their active and healthy ageing.

Thus, it was stipulated that the need for 'social innovation' should be evaluated as a protective and preventive approach with regards to Active and Healthy Ageing (AHA). However, the results of the study showed that the individuals in the 40+ age group covered by the study were diagnosed with various diseases, among these hypertension, diabetes, and joint diseases. They also had disadvantageous behaviour patterns and negative features, among which a very low level of physical exercise, a high rate of obesity, and smoking. Furthermore, one fifth of them did not have easy access to health care services and were dissatisfied with health care services; a high proportion had a very low level of social and voluntary activity participation; some did not have a very high level of capacity for 'active ageing' and 'mental well-being'; some had a very low rate of participation in 'life-long learning' activities and were not generally interested in such activities; some retired early and did not wish to work after retiring; and some women, mostly housewives, did not have any income. Moreover, it was determined that, as a significant issue pertaining to functional solidarity within the family, about half of the elderly individuals took care of their grandchildren on a daily basis or a couple of days a week.

As the results of the study revealed, the individuals in the 40+ age group in Turkey had a rather low capacity for Active and Healthy Ageing (AHA). According to the *Global AgeWatch Index: Insight Report* (2015),[21] Turkey occupies the 75th place among ninety-six countries. Moreover, Turkey ranks 35th in respect of Income Safety, 40th with regard to having an active environment, 52nd concerning health status, and 93rd with respect to the level of capacity for Active and Healthy Ageing (AHA). Although there has been an increase in life expectancy at birth in Turkey, it is clear that an increase in the number of years lived healthily should be rendered a significant target because what is important is to enable an increase in the number of years lived healthily and actively, with a focus on long life.

According to the *Turkey Health Statistics Year Book (2016)*,[22] 28·6% of the individuals in the 65–74 age group had good or very good

---

[21] See Jane Scobie, *et al. Global AgeWatch Index: Insight Report.* (London: HelpAge International, 2015).

[22] See Republic of Turkey. Ministry of Health. *Health Statistics Yearbook, 2015.* Ministry of Health Publication N° 1055 [N° 1054]. (Ankara: General Directorate of Health Research, 2016).

health conditions, while 31·9% had poor or very poor conditions. The proportion of individuals in the 75+ age group whose health was evaluated as being good dropped (17·5%), while the proportion of those who thought their health was poor increased (44·3%). While the proportion of those who considered their health to be poor in the 45–54 age group was 10%, this figure almost doubled in the 55–64 age group (19·9%).[23] According to the results of the *Research on Family Structure in Türkiye (TAYA, 2011)* survey, 88·7% of 65-year-old and older individuals had never exercised, while 85·2% passed time frequently watching television.[24]

The study entitled *Expectations Regarding Old Age in Turkey (2011)* put forward significant results regarding healthy ageing.[25] 95% of the individuals in the 65+ age group had functional inabilities at different levels. Moreover, the results of the study revealed that hypertension, rheumatism, back problems, cholesterol disorders, and diabetes were widespread in the 40+ age group, and 21·9% of 65-year-old and older individuals had vision loss, while 7·6% of them had hearing loss.

According to the 2013 study of the Turkish Healthy Cities Association entitled *Urban Health Indicators for Turkey*, the mortality rate of circulatory system diseases in Turkey was 37·9%, and ranked the first in mortality causes.[26] Circulatory system diseases and malign tumours were seen most frequently in individuals of the 65+ age group. The number of physicians per one hundred thousand individuals was one hundred and sixty-seven in Turkey.

* * *

The results of the "Turkey Active and Healthy Ageing Survey" supported the results of previous studies. These pieces of evidence revealed that creative solutions and 'social innovation' practices were needed in order to meet the needs for Active and Healthy Ageing (AHA), beginning at very

---

[23] See Republic of Turkey. Ministry of Health. *Health Statistics Yearbook, 2015*. Ministry of Health Publication Nº 1055 [Nº 1054]. (Ankara: General Directorate of Health Research, 2016).

[24] See Republic of Turkey. Ministry of Family and Social Policies. *Research on Family Structure in Türkiye. TAYA 2011*. (Ankara: General Directorate of Family and Community Services, 2011).

[25] Republic of Turkey. Ministry of Family and Social Policies. *Expectations Regarding Old Age in Turkey*. (Ankara: General Directorate of Family and Community Services, 2011).

[26] See Emel Irgil, Kayıhan Pala, Nalan Akis, Alpaslan Turkkan. Eds. *Urban Health Indicators for Turkey, 2013*. (Bursa: Turkish Healthy Cities Association, 2013).

early ages in Turkey. What proved to be important was to answer the following questions:

1. What is the definition of 'social innovation' for Active and Healthy Ageing (AHA)?
2. Who carries out 'social innovation' for Active and Healthy Ageing (AHA)?
3. How can 'social innovation' for Active and Healthy Ageing (AHA) be carried out?

1. What is the definition of 'social innovation'?

'Social innovation' is related to increasing societies' capacity for problem-solving. Therefore, issues that need to be dealt with in the most urgent manner have priority. The difference between the resulting problems and the solutions to these problems refers to the need for 'social innovation.' Meeting needs and the resulting creative solutions to deal with these problems refer to 'social innovation.' 'Social innovation' incorporates novel ideas to meet social ends.[27] According to the life-cycle approach for Active and Healthy Ageing (AHA) beginning with very early ages, regulations should be carried out at the individual, family, and society levels. For instance, on the one hand, children need to be directed in order to gain sports and exercise habits. On the other hand, local administrations or governments should build sports arenas, like basketball and tennis courts, football fields, and swimming pools, where everyone can exercise. Such amenities should be made widespread and accessible.

2. Who carries out 'social innovation'?

'Social innovation' is considered to be a perspective within the industrialization, modernization, and social transformation process. There are three foci regarding the ways in which such transformation can be achieved by means of 'social innovation.' These foci are: 1. individuals; 2. movements; and 3. organizations. Individuals are the ones who are seen as leaders by the society and spearhead social transformation with their behaviour and ideas.[28] Moreover, civil-society movements such as women's rights, disability rights, consumer rights, and patient rights set examples for

---

[27] See Geoff Mulgan, *et al. Social Innovation: what it is, why it matters and how it can be accelerated.* (Oxford University Working Paper. London: The Young Foundation, 2007).

[28] See Robin Murray, Julie Caulier-Grice, and Geoff Mulgan. *The Open Book of Social Innovation.* (London: The Young Foundation, 2010).

Active and Healthy Ageing (AHA) policy creation. For example, the Ministry of Health in Turkey has recently prepared public service announcements on subjects such as reducing salt, encouraging movement and exercise, and discouraging obesity, while introducing people who had successfully lost weight as community leaders. The Ministry of National Education enabled the replacement of 'junk food,' like chips and coke, with 'snack food,' like ayran, yoghurt, and fruit, thanks to the efforts of non-governmental organizations (NGOs).

3. How can 'social innovation' be carried out?

With the increase in life expectancy and the increase in the rate of growth of the elderly population, the retirement system was revised, and the retirement age was gradually raised to sixty-five in Turkey. There is a growing need for creating alternatives for care and support services for Active and Healthy Ageing (AHA), and for 'social innovation' that enables accessibility in the environment. Self-help health groups and self-built housing, telephone help-lines, neighbourhood nurseries, and neighbourhood wardens, easy access to Wikipedia and the Open University, complementary medicine, holistic health and hospices, charity shops, and the fair-trade movements provide examples for 'social innovation.' Innovations in medicine have resulted in developments in the field of health. Science and technology have had a profound impact on the capacity of human beings to live longer and to stay healthier. Individuals, however, need to develop attitudes and behaviour patterns, like exercising regularly, visiting their doctors regularly for early diagnosis, shunning away from health risk factors like smoking and alcohol consumption, having sufficient and balanced diets, being useful for society by participating in voluntary activities, being interested in life-long educational activities, continuing working for as long as possible, and being willing to work for an active and healthy ageing.

Many obstacles need to be overcome in order for 'social innovation' to be effective. These can be listed as: to strive for good design and productivity; to trigger the interests of people; to create changes in people's values, norms, and ideas; and to establish successful relationships between those who start social innovation movements and other people.[29] 'Social innovation' for Active and Healthy Ageing (AHA) centres on the individual on a micro level ecologically, and contains individuals' ideas, attitudes, and behaviour patterns regarding active and healthy ageing at every stage of life.

---

[29] Geoff Mulgan, *et al. Social Innovation: what it is, why it matters and how it can be accelerated.* (Oxford University Working Paper. London: The Young Foundation, 2007).

For instance, it refers to the development of the understanding that being active for individuals is not only about participation in voluntary and other non-governmental activities, but also about meaningful participation in family, social, cultural, and spiritual lives. 'Social innovation' is related to health care and social services at the meso level, to equal opportunity in having access to such services, and to social awareness to achieve these. On the macro level, however, 'social innovation' entails the formation of social policies and structural regulations for the popularization of novel and creative practices in order to solve problems and meet the needs for an Active and Healthy Ageing (AHA).

Works Cited

European Commission. *Commission Staff Working Document. Turkey 2012 Progress Report*. Brussels: European Commission, 10th October 2012.
    <ec.europa.eu/neighbourhood-enlargement/sites/near/files/pdf/key_documents/2012/package/tr_rapport_2012_en.pdf>

European Commission. *The 2015 Ageing Report: Underlying Assumptions and Projection Methodologies*. European Economy 8/2014. Brussels: European Commission Directorate-General for Economic and Financial Affairs Unit Communication and interinstitutional relations, 2014.
    <ec.europa.eu/economy_finance/publications/european_economy/2014/pdf/ee8_en.pdf>

He, Wan, Daniel Goodkind, and Paul Kowal. *An Aging World: 2015. U.S. Census Bureau, International Population Reports*. P95/16-1. Washington, DC: U.S. Government Publishing Office, 2016.
    <www.census.gov/content/dam/Census/library/publications/2016/demo/p95-16-1.pdf>

Irgil, Emel., Kayıhan Pala, Nalan Akis, Alpaslan Turkkan. Eds. *Urban Health Indicators for Turkey, 2013*. Bursa: Turkish Healthy Cities Association, 2013.

Mulgan, Geoff, Simon Tucker, Rushanara Ali, and Ben Sanders. *Social Innovation: what it is, why it matters and how it can be accelerated*. Oxford University Working Paper. London: The Young Foundation, 2007.

<youngfoundation.org/wp-content/uploads/2012/10/Social-Innovation-what-it-is-why-it-matters-how-it-can-be-accelerated-March-2007.pdf>

Murray, Robin, Julie Caulier-Grice, and Geoff Mulgan. *The Open Book of Social Innovation*. London: The Young Foundation, 2010. <www.nesta.org.uk/sites/default/files/the_open_book_of_social_in novation.pdf>

Organisation for Economic Co-operation and Development (OECD), and European Commission (2013). *A Good Life in Old Age? Monitoring and Improving Quality in Long-term Care*. OECD Health Policy Studies. OECD Publishing. [16th June 2016] <www.keepeek.com/Digital-Asset-Management/oecd/social-issues-migration-health/a-good-life-in-old-age_9789264194564-en#.V5Uq29KLTIU#page4>

Organisation for Economic Co-operation and Development (OECD). *Ageing and Employment Policies*. 2016. [25th December 2016] <www.oecd.org/employment/ageingandemploymentpolicies.htm>

Paúl, Constança, Oscar Ribeiro, Laetitia Teixeira. "Active Ageing: An Empirical Approach to the WHO Model." *Current Gerontology and Geriatrics Research*. 2012. Article ID 382972. 10 pages. <dx.doi.org/10.1155/2012/382972>

Republic of Turkey. Ministry of Health. *Health Statistics Yearbook, 2015*. Ministry of Health Publication N° 1055 [N° 1054]. Ankara: General Directorate of Health Research, 2016. <www.saglikistatistikleri.gov.tr/dosyalar/SIY_EN_2015.pdf> <www.saglikistatistikleri.gov.tr/dosyalar/SIY_2015.pdf>

Republic of Turkey. Ministry of Family and Social Policies. *Research on Family Structure in Türkiye. TAYA 2011*. Ankara: General Directorate of Family and Community Services, 2011. <ailetoplum.aile.gov.tr/data/54292ce0369dc32358ee2a46/taya2011-eng.pdf>

Republic of Turkey. Ministry of Family and Social Policies. *Expectations Regarding Old Age in Turkey*. Ankara: General Directorate of Family and Community Services, 2011.

Scobie, Jane, Lauren Asfour, Sylvia Beales, Peter McGeachie, Sarah Gillam, Aleksandr Mihnovits, Eppu Mikkonen-Jeanneret, Caitlin Nisos, Flynne Rushton, and Asghar Zaidi. *Global AgeWatch Index: Insight Report*. Eds. Amy Barry, Scarlett McGwire, and Karen Porter. London: HelpAge International, 2015. <www.helpage.de/material/Weltalten-Index2015.pdf>

Turkish Statistical Institute (TurkStat) 2015a. *Turkey Health Survey, 2014.* Ankara: Turkish Statistical Institute Press Release. N° 18854. 1st October 2015.
<www.turkstat.gov.tr/PreHaberBultenleri.do?id=18854>

Turkish Statistical Institute (TurkStat). 2015b. *Life Tables, 2013-2014.* Ankara: Turkish Statistical Institute Press Release. N° 18618. 7th October 2015.
<www.turkstat.gov.tr/PreHaberBultenleri.do?id=18618>

Turkish Statistical Institute (TurkStat). 2016a. *The Results of Address Based Population Registration System, 2015.* Ankara: Turkish Statistical Institute Press Release. N° 21507. 28th January 2016.
<www.turkstat.gov.tr/PreHaberBultenleri.do?id=21507>

Turkish Statistical Institute (TurkStat). 2016b. *Elderly Statistics, 2015.* Ankara: Turkish Statistical Institute Press Release. N° 21520. 17th March 2016.
<www.turkstat.gov.tr/PreHaberBultenleri.do?id=21520>

United Nations (UN) (2013) *World Population Aging 2013.* New York: United Nations Department of Economic and Social Affairs. Population Division, 2013. [ST/ESA/SER.A/348]
<www.un.org/en/development/desa/population/publications/pdf/ageing/WorldPopulationAgeing2013.pdf>

United Nations (UN) 2015 *World Population Prospects: Key Findings and Advance Tables. 2015 Revision.* New York: United Nations Department of Economic and Social Affairs Population Division, 2015.
<esa.un.org/unpd/wpp/publications/files/key_findings_wpp_2015.pdf>

United Nations Economic Commission for Europe (UNECE) / European Commission (2015) "Active Ageing Index 2014: Analytical Report." Report prepared by Asghar Zaidi of Centre for Research on Ageing, University of Southampton and David Stanton, under contract with United Nations Economic Commission for Europe (Geneva), co-funded by European Commission's Directorate General for Employment, Social Affairs and Inclusion (Brussels), April 2015.
<www.age-platform.eu/images/stories/Publications/AAI_2014_Report.pdf>

United Nations Population Fund (UNFPA) and HelpAge International (2012) *Ageing in the 21st Century: A Celebration and A Challenge.*

New York and London: United Nations Population Fund and HelpAge International, 2012.

WHO (2002) *Active Ageing: A Policy Framework*. Geneva: World Health Organization, 2002.

WHO (2014) *Core Health Indicators in the WHO European Region 2014: Special focus: Health 2020 targets indicators*. Copenhagen: World Health Organization Regional Office for Europe, 2015.

WHO (2015) *World Report on Ageing and Health*. Geneva: World Health Organization, 2015.

Zaidi, Asghar. "Active Aging Indicators." Presentation at 6th Session of Open-ended Working Group (OEWG). *Active Ageing Index Project*. United Nations Economic Commission for Europe (UNECE) and European Commission. University of Southampton, 16th July 2015. <social.un.org/ageing-working-group/documents/sixth/Presentation_Asghar%20Zaidi.pdf>

Zastrow, Charles. *Introduction to Social Work and Social Welfare: Empowering People*. Belmont, CA: Thomson-Brooks/Cole, 2008.

Socially-Dynamic Environments
for
'Active Ageing'

Social innovative projects for seniors in Poland – ways to constructive attitudes towards ageing

Katarzyna Ziomek-Michalak

The Maria Grzegorzewska Pedagogical University, Warsaw

'Old age' is not homogenous. Depending on the biological factors of the body, mental, and environmental aspects, 'old age' can vary significantly. The internal division of 'old age,' according to the concept as defined by the World Health Organization (WHO), distinguishes three phases of 'old age': "young old," that is, 60–74-year-olds (also called 'the third age'); "old old," that is, 75–89-year-olds (also called 'mature old age – the fourth age'); and the "oldest old," that is, long life exceeding 90 years old.[1] In connection with the dynamics of the ageing process taking place between these three periods, there is the environment which includes people in need of both care benefits at different levels, from aid in simple daily-life activities to continuous nursing care. However, with the trend for increased life-expectancy, numerous seniors are presenting a potential for an active attitude in their late-age more and more frequently. Actions initiated in the environment to promote the stimulation of elderly persons to take up activities induce a positive attitude towards ageing, lessen the fear of solitude, and strengthen social skills necessary in difficult situations during late-age.

The goal of this chapter is to present innovative social projects initiated in Poland that help model a constructive attitude towards growing old. For the purposes of this analysis, an innovative project is understood to be a project aimed at searching for new, better, and more effective ways to solve problems within support areas. Innovative projects are designed to work through, disseminate, and include new solutions in mainstream policy.

---

[1] See Zofia Szarota, and Remigiusz J. Kijak. *Starość. Między diagnozą a działaniem.* (Warsaw: CRZL, 2013): 14.

The socio-demographic situation of Polish seniors

In Poland, the number of elderly people increased by nearly 1·9 million between 1989-2013 (see Table 1), and their share in the total population increased by 4·7 percentage points, that is, from 10% in 1989 up to 14·7% in 2013. For the sake of comparison, the proportion of children and young people decreased by more than 10 percentage points during that time, that is, from nearly 30% to slightly more than 18%.[2]

Economic age groups	1989			2013		
	Total	**Men**	**Women**	**Total**	**Men**	**Women**
Total (000)	38,038,4	18,540,5	19,497,9	38,495,7	18,629,5	19,866,1
	% of total					
Pre-productive age	29·8	31·3	28·4	18·2	19·3	17·1
Productive age	57·5	61·0	54·2	63·4	69·0	58·2
Post-productive age	12·6	7·7	17·3	18·4	11·7	24·6

Table 1. Population according to economic age groups in 1989 and 2013 [3]

At the end of 2014, the population of Poland numbered 38·5 million, including more than 8·5 million people (more than 22% of the total population) aged 60 years old and over.[4]

As a result of increasing longevity, the share of elderly people in the resident population of Poland will increase from 21·5% in 2013 (8·3 million) to 40·4% (13·7 million) in 2050.[5] This fact indicates a potentially greater demand for various forms of help and support from the oldest inhabitants of the cities. Characteristics of Polish late-age are: 1. feminization of late-age –

---

[2] <stat.gov.pl/download/gfx/.../pl/.../18/.../ludnosc_w_starszym_wieku.pdf>

[3] Pre-productive age: 0–17 years old; productive age for women: 18–59 years old; productive age for men: 18–64 years old; post-productive age for women: 60 years old and over; post-productive age for men: 65 years old and over. Source: *Sytuacja demograficzna osób starszych i konsekwencje starzenia się ludności Polski w świetle prognozy na lata 2014-2050.* (Warsaw: Central Statistical Office: 2014): 3.

[4] *Ludność w wieku 60 lat i więcej. Struktura demograficzna i zdrowie.* (Warsaw: Central Statistical Office, 2016): 3.

[5] *Ludność w wieku 60 lat i więcej. Struktura demograficzna i zdrowie.* (Warsaw: Central Statistical Office, 2016): 9.

the number of elderly women is greater than the number of elderly men; 2. singularization of late-age, whereby nearly 50% of individuals aged 65 years old and over manage one-person households;[6] 3. double-ageing, whereby the proportion of people aged 80 years old and over increases at a faster rate than that of persons of the other age groups in the rest of the population; 4. internal differentiation of 'old age,' that is, in terms of health, activity level, educational attainment, family situation, material situation, and place of living.[7]

In the light of research carried out by the Central Statistical Office, 43% of elderly people evaluate their health condition as fair, neither good nor bad, 29% as bad or very bad, and only 28% as good or very good. Self-evaluations of own health deteriorate with the passage of years. Only the inhabitants aged 65 years old and over of Croatia, Estonia, Hungary, Portugal, Latvia, and Lithuania evaluated their health as worse than that of Polish citizens. According to the generalized information obtained from the research, every third person aged 65 years old and over has difficulties carrying out daily, self-care activities.

Polish seniors taking advantage of pension benefits remain professionally inactive for a long period, with one free-time resource. Deviation from the model of multi-generational families, widowhood, children's decisions to start a family late, children's studies and, more and more frequently, flexible working hours, offer the possibility of carrying out activities in areas other than family matters.

The policy for seniors in Poland

Responding to demographic changes, the government has taken action to determine the direction of policy in respect of elderly persons. Assumptions laid down in the *Long-term Senior Policy in Poland for the years 2014–2020* (ASOS 2014-2020 Programme)[8] fulfil the undertakings provided for in the *Governmental Programme for Social Activity of the Elderly for the years*

---

[6] According to data of the Central Statistical Office, Warsaw. See *Ludność w wieku 60 lat i więcej. Struktura demograficzna i zdrowie*. (Warsaw: Central Statistical Office, 2016).

[7] Piotr Błędowski, *et al. Raport na temat osób starszych w Polsce*. (Warsaw: Institute of Labour and Social Studies, 2012): 5-6. <senior.gov.pl/source/raport_osoby%20starsze.pdf>

[8]<www.mpips.gov.pl/seniorzyaktywne-starzenie/zalozenia-dlugofalowej-polityki-senioralnej-w-polsce-na-lata-20142020/>

<das.mpips.gov.pl/source/Long-term%20Senior%20Policy.pdf>

2012–2013 (ASOS from 2012).[9] Main challenges determining the direction of actions taken were identified, being the requirements of the policy for elderly persons currently implemented by the Ministry of Family, Labour, and Social Policy. The challenges included: 1. an increasing share of the elderly in the population and the preparation for many social and economic consequences of that phenomenon; 2. prolongation of the professional activity period; 3. inclusion of the potential of the elderly in the area of social and civic activity; and 4. the demand for solutions enabling working persons aged 50 years old and over to achieve a balance between work and family-life, including the need to care for parents and other dependents.

The objective of state policy for elderly persons in Poland is to support and ensure the possibility of experiencing 'active ageing' in good health, and of having an autonomous, independent, and satisfactory life, even with certain functional limitations. Areas of government policy include: health and autonomy; safety; professional activity for persons aged 50 years old and over; educational, social, and cultural activity of the elderly; the 'silver economy'; and intergenerational relations. For its part, the programme *Social Activation for the Elderly* relates to the possibilities of funding, by way of a tender, of public welfare organizations matching the following priorities: education of the elderly; social activity promoting intra- and inter-generational integration; social participation of the elderly; and social services for the elderly.[10]

Lifestyles of seniors

In the changing reality of the demographic prolongation of life expectancy, an elderly person participates in transformations taking place in her or his environment. In this regard, an elderly person can adopt either a passive attitude to life which, according to Elaine Cumming and William Earl Henry, is one that can lead to exclusion and withdrawal,[11] or, alternatively, an active one which, according to Robert C. Atchley's 'theory of continuity,' can lead to the maintenance of previous activities.[12]

---

[9] *Governmental Programme for the Social Activity of the Elderly* (ASOS from 2012). [Rządowy Program na rzecz Aktywności Społecznej Osób Starszych na lata 2012- 2013. Załącznik do Uchwały nr 137 Rady Ministrów z dn.24 sierpnia 2012 r] <mopact.group.shef.ac.uk/wp-content/uploads/2013/10/Country-report-Poland.pdf>

[10] <www.mpips.gov.pl/seniorzyaktywne-starzenie/rzadowy-program-asos>

[11] See Elaine Cumming, and William Earl Henry. *Growing old: The process of disengagement.* (New York: Basic Books, 1961): 13.

[12] See Robert C. Atchley. *The social forces in later life: An introduction to social gerontology.* (Belmont, CA: Wadsworth, 1972).

The Polish gerontologist Olga Czerniawska[13] distinguishes the following lifestyles of the elderly, accurately reflecting the functioning of a Polish senior: 1. an entirely passive lifestyle; 2. family style, whereby elderly persons devote all their time to the family, and to their grandchildren; 3. a style resulting from the cultivation of an allotment garden when work on a plot of land becomes a way of living for the elderly person; 4. a style based on work in associations; 5. home-centred lifestyle; and 6. religious lifestyle. To this list of classification of lifestyles, Zofia Szarota adds one more style, namely, the institutional style, that is, an imposed lifestyle that relates to the model of life of the institution in which the senior is staying.[14]

An analysis of Robert C. Atchley's 'theory of continuity'[15] shows how important preparation for late-age is, together with the organization of a local community that encourages elderly people to be active. Human life-expectancy elongation generates new challenges for the environment. Seniors more and more frequently engage in learning at universities of 'the Third Age,' meet in Seniors' Clubs or activation centres, participate in meetings organized by libraries, and commit themselves to volunteering and project work. When participating in lectures and seminars addressed to them, elderly persons acquire and deepen their knowledge, as well as gain various skills. They develop a sense of their own effectiveness in overcoming difficulties, and an internal locus of control, which empowers them to manage their own lives and take care of their personal health rather than transfer the responsibility to other service providers or to leave it to chance. Moreover, active people receive greater social support from the community.

Internal research
The goal of the research conducted in the years 2009 and 2010 was to identify dependencies between health expectations and personal resources of the Polish seniors. Participants in the study made up a sample of purposefully-selected elderly individuals, in two parallel groups. A snowball sampling technique was employed. In the first stage of the research, the first basic group comprised students from the University of the Third Age (U3A) in Lublin, Poland. The second stage was made up of elderly persons who were

---

[13] See Olga Czerniawska. *Drogi i bezdroża andragogiki*. (Łódź: Wydawnictwo Wyższej Szkoły Humanistyczno-Ekonomicznej w Łodzi, 2000): 170-176.
[14] Such institutions might be day-centres, and round-the-clock care institutions that determine the rhythm and style of the lives of their elderly users. See Zofia Szarota, and Remigiusz J. Kijak. *Starość. Między diagnozą a działaniem*. (Warszawa: CRZL, 2013): 95.
[15] See Robert C. Atchley. *The social forces in later life: An introduction to social gerontology*. (Belmont, CA: Wadsworth, 1972).

not students of the University of the Third Age (U3A). A total of two hundred elderly people made up the sample. It was revealed during the research that the support obtained by students of the University of the Third Age (U3A) is significantly greater than that obtained by those elderly persons who are not students of the University of the Third Age (U3A). Furthermore, the elderly students of the University of the Third Age (U3A) feel happier, more admired, and more respected. This is the reason why sample participants who were students of the University of the Third Age (U3A) acknowledged the higher level of support given them, a recognition expressed in the form of positive emotions. The elderly students of the University of the Third Age (U3A) also reported a higher level of affirmative support, support expressed in the form of a sense of being accepted by family and friends.

The fact that the elderly persons who are students of the University of the Third Age (U3A) are trusted to a large degree helps facilitate their adaptation to late-age, strengthening their sense of security, and sustaining their health. When compared to those elderly persons who are not students of the University of the Third Age (U3A), the elderly University of the Third Age (U3A) students can count on aid in the form of practical support, material provision, and functional help to a greater degree. It can be assumed that, as participants in the University of the Third Age (U3A) culture, the elderly students are more aware of their needs, communicate them more openly and, therefore, obtain social support adequate to their requirements.

Participation in University of the Third Age (U3A) classes promotes the building of a social-support network. In general, university students have more-developed interpersonal skills. For this reason, they tend to be pro-active in respect of interactions with others, rather than adopting attitudes of withdrawal and passivity. Elderly students are motivated also by a strong desire to live their lives. For this reason, too, their level of self-control over their health is higher than among those elderly persons who are not so active. Consequently, most elderly persons who study at university retain some control over their own destinies, avoiding disease and, thanks to their strengthened active attitude towards personal health, remaining healthy. That is why activity is very important for those persons who are 'growing old.'[16]

---

[16] Katarzyna Ziomek-Michalak. "Uczenie się przez całe życie na przykładzie uniwersytetu trzeciego wieku." Żłobicki Wiktor, and Beata Maj. Eds. *Nierówność szans edukacyjnych – przyczyny, skutki, koncepcje zmian.* (Krakow: Oficyna Wydawnicza Impuls, 2012): 357-375.

Activation of seniors as a path to constructive attitudes towards 'growing older'

It is not so much the ageing process itself, but rather isolation from society and the lack of mental and physical activity that determines quality-of-life. In order to make people more active during the last phase of life, it became a popular idea to organize their free time, including educational activities for seniors. Learning during 'old age' entails neither changes nor new orientations, but rather a new cognitive consumption. Late-age learning is a support for elderly persons in their ageing process; it fulfils the postulate of educational help for elderly persons.[17] The education of seniors and their participation in lectures on current issues, on knowledge of health, and on nature, can contribute to improved self-awareness, and encourage the taking up of activities aimed at the care of personal health. Additionally, such people do not feel socially isolated because of their systematic contact with a peer group. This gives elderly persons a greater sense of social support.

An appropriate arrangement of the social environment and taking advantage of its potential to work with the elderly can help activate seniors and change their attitudes towards their own late-age and 'growing old' in general. The creation of space for an activity adapted to the abilities of elderly persons on the one hand and showing the elderly person in action to society on the other hand, can help change the perception of the last phase of life that many people do not look forward to.[18] An important thing is to carry out a reliable analysis of the local environment to manage the potential of the elderly individuals living there. Animators of local communities should cooperate with social workers who carry out field community interviews and know the needs of the environment they work in.

'Growing older' is inevitable. Notwithstanding, the process of ageing can be slowed down. Zofia Szarota shows desirable factors with regard to the preparation for the ageing process. [19] These factors are instrumental in serving as a prophylaxis for 'growing older' on the biological, mental, intellectual, social, and economic levels. Moreover, what is supposed to prevent 'growing older' is the prerequisite of an active late-

---

[17] See Jerzy Halicki. *Obrazy starości rysowane przeżyciami seniorów*. (Bialystok: Trans Humana, 2003): 30.

[18] See Katarzyna Ziomek-Michalak. "Wykorzystanie potencjału środowiska lokalnego do pracy na rzecz seniorów." Marta Mikołajczyk. Ed. *Praca socjalna i pomoc społeczna*. (Warsaw: Wydawnictwo Akademii Pedagogiki Specjalnej, 2014): 70-83.

[19] Zofia Szarota. *Gerontologia społeczna i oświatowa. Zarys problematyki*. (Krakow: Wydawnictwo Naukowe AP, 2004): 58-61.

age and successful ageing, namely, a constructive attitude towards 'growing old.'

Projects involving physical activation

The physical-activity habit helps maintain physical fitness, independence, and good health, as well as prolonging active life. An increased physical activity of seniors such as strolls, marches, pedestrian tourist excursions, and cycling trips improve physical fitness, and prevent or support the treatment of many diseases. There are classes for elderly persons organized by sports and recreation centres, including fitness classes, stretching, yoga, aqua aerobic and the promotion of Nordic walking. Seniors also have an opportunity to participate in dancing lessons organized especially for their age group. Meetings with dieticians, doctors, and specialists in various medical conditions are also organized.

An example of such an activity in Poland has been the national "Physical activity of the elderly" project[20] which provides for the organization of ventures that stimulate the activity of elderly people in the following forms: 1. 'recreational activity,' that is, the promotion of various forms of individual- or group-active recreation based on physical activity; and 2. 'preventive activity,' that is, an activity designed to prevent early- and pathological-ageing, an activity rooted in a healthy lifestyle, proper nutrition, and social activity. The main goals to be achieved that derive from systematic movement by the elderly individual are 'maintained fitness,' 'maintained self-reliance,' and 'maintained independence.' Also, the National Olympics of the Universities of the Third Age (U3As) and Seniors' Organizations "3rd Age for the Start" is an interesting project. In the National Olympics, elderly contestants participated in ten disciplines, including swimming, athletics, shooting, table-tennis, chess, cross-country cycling, a bridge tournament, and canoeing, each competition being divided along gender lines and into age groups, namely, 50 years old and over, 60 years old and over, 70 years old and over, and 80 years old and over.

Projects to promote mental activation

Projects to promote mental activation involve environmental activities aimed at the development of skills such as self-cognition, healthy egotism, positive

---

[20] See Ministry of Labour and Social Policy, Warsaw. *Government programme for senior citizens' social activity for 2014-2020.* [*Rządowy Program na rzecz Aktywności Społecznej Osób Starszych na lata 2014-2020*] Warsaw: Ministry of Labour and Social Policy; 2013. <www.mpips.gov.pl/seniorzyaktywne-starzenie/rzadowy-program-asos/>

thinking about the future, and the elimination of the fear of late-age that, as a result, helps the elderly individual to understand and accept late-age as a natural phase and continuation of life, to accept oneself, and to enjoy life. One simple example is *"Przemarsz Kapeluszowy"* (the "Hat March"), an innovative project organized on a regular basis that enjoys great favour amongst elderly people. The objective of the "Hat March" is to activate elderly people who are alone and disabled, and to offer them integration with other elderly persons and with members of the younger generation. It is also a parade that allows the elderly to show how the age of their social group need be neither a limitation nor an obstacle to the pursuit of their personal interests. The 'march' takes place once a year. A colourful procession of people equipped with colourful hats, balloons, and other accessories passes along the city streets and stops at the central point of the city where associated events are held. The satisfaction of the need to feel useful is attained by helping their children to care for their grandchildren, or by participating in social activities in the form of volunteer work carried out by many organizations, such as Caritas, PCK, Little Brothers of the Poor Association, and Dar Czasu i Serca (Gift of Time and Heart). Feeling attractive improves the elderly persons' feeling of confidence; hence the organization of meetings with beauticians, make-up artists, fashion designers, and masseurs.

Furthermore, overcoming personal resistance regarding the use of new technologies can help an elderly individual to live without stress and frustration. E-activation of the elderly can be observed in the last few years in the form of courses that result in increasing numbers of elderly persons present on discussion forums, contacting others by e-mail or Skype, reading news on portals addressed to seniors or electronic newspapers, opening personal accounts on community portals, and skilfully using cellular phones. When it comes to social participation, activity of the elderly in Poland is generally less intense than it is among younger people. This is the reason why the main goal of social policy on active citizenship relating to the elderly is to increase the commitment of seniors to the social life of local communities and an intensification of their role in resolving social issues. Seniors' councils play the integrating and coordinating role in the actions promoting social policy in the local community. The goal of this initiative is to intensify the cooperation of communal seniors' councils with local government.

Projects of activation related to intellectual operation
Elderly persons have lectures, seminars, and faculty classes organized by the Universities of the Third Age (U3As), together with various language, computer, Internet, electronic banking, and memory and concentration courses at their disposal, to improve their skills as part of project for the activation of people aged 50 years old and over. Intellectual development is also stimulated thanks to book- or film-discussion clubs organized by local cultural centres and libraries, amateur theatre groups, theme meetings, fitness for the mind classes, encouragement to solve crosswords, and puzzles.

Social-life projects
Interpersonal skills and the ability to live in a group are important for the modelling of a positive attitude to late-age. Teamwork, joint projects, and volunteering help to promote that attitude. Elderly persons frequently feel lonely after retirement. There is the loss of the social role as a worker, the weakening of contacts with previous co-workers until they cease completely, and the effect of an 'empty nest' in family relations. Organized inter-generational projects become helpful in this area, for example, "A Senior in Action" of the "ę" Society of Creative Initiatives. Other good examples are the Lublin School of Super grandma and Super grandpa (supervised by Dr Zofia Zaorska), along with intergenerational meetings, cultural workshops, classes in Senior Activation Centres, Seniors' Clubs, and Universities of the Third Age (U3A) that promote the building of new interpersonal relations and participation in ecclesiastic group meetings for people of deep faith. Many cities care for elderly citizens and offer special prices for theatre and cinema tickets on selected days of the month, and special offers of cafés promoting the meetings of seniors, such actions taking place under names like "Seniors' Days," "Discounts for the Senior," "Senior-friendly theatre," "Seniors' Cinema," "Café for the Senior," and "Coffee for the Senior." Information about activities taking place in the city is available from the websites of city halls, institutions organizing discounts, and frequently from websites of social welfare centres. Seniors staying at home and not reluctant to use computer technologies have opportunities to meet others on the Internet. Various discussion forums organized by elderly persons for elderly persons are available, for example, Senior Café Club.[21]

---

[21] <www.klub.senior.pl/><www.50plus50.pl/forum_dla_seniorow><forum.senior.pl>
<www.bycseniorem.pl>

Economic functionality projects

Elderly persons can use the Senior's Card which offers many discounts when purchasing railway and air tickets. Also, travel agencies organize holidays for seniors at a promotional price, and cheaper tickets to the cinema, the theatre, reduced charges for courses, and even cheaper shopping in selected hypermarkets and pharmacies are all available to the elderly customer.

Pension benefits are the only source of sustenance for most seniors. Few elderly persons work to supplement their pension. For this reason, training courses on an appropriate management of the home budget are organized. To improve the possibility of replenishing the home budget, the Polish Agency for Enterprise Development (PARP)[22] organized the "Active Pensioner" project preparing elderly persons for the management of their own businesses. Various institutions organize handicraft workshops as a part of the professional activation programme, for example, wickerwork, crocheting, knitting, embroidery, modelling objects out of clay, salt dough or gypsum, and paper crafts. Electronic banking courses can be encountered more and more frequently, a service which promotes savings related to the lack of charges for account maintenance and transfers. A 'social cooperative' is a legal format that makes it possible to use business activities to carry out social objectives, especially the professional and social integration of people in a difficult life situation. A 'social cooperative' is a work-cooperative based on its members' personal work experience. Members of the cooperative are mostly people in danger of social exclusion.

Conclusion

Activities taken up by seniors in various areas of their lives perform the following functions:

1. prophylactic, that is, preventing and postponing physical and mental ailments, and counteracting loneliness;

2. therapeutic, that is, recovering the health of culturally- and educationally-active people, reinstating mental balance by directing their attention away from sorrow, suffering, and pain;

3. compensatory, that is, compensating for the deficiencies in other areas of life;

---

[22] Polish Agency for Enterprise Development (PARP)

4. informational, that is, making it possible to gain knowledge of current events;

5. integrative, that is, strengthening relations of seniors with their peers and with members of younger generations;

6. socialization, that is, improving interpersonal skills;

7. educational, that is, improving mental skills, aesthetic preferences, social and moral attitudes;

8. recreational and entertainment, that is, eliminating tiredness and weariness for the benefit of the continued active lifestyle; and

9. the prestigious function, that is, giving personal satisfaction to an individual, and, to the authority, demonstrating improvement and recognition for those people who take up a cultural activity from the social perspective.

Works Cited

Atchley, Robert C. *The social forces in later life: An introduction to social gerontology.* Belmont, CA: Wadsworth, 1972.

Błędowski, Piotr, *et al. Raport na temat osób starszych w Polsce.* Warsaw: Institute of Labour and Social Studies, 2012.

Central Statistical Office, Warsaw. *Sytuacja demograficzna osób starszych i konsekwencje starzenia się ludności Polski w świetle prognozy na lata 2014-2050.* Warsaw: Central Statistical Office: 2014.

—. *Ludność w wieku 60 lat i więcej. Struktura demograficzna i zdrowie.* Warsaw: Central Statistical Office, 2016.
    <stat.gov.pl/download/gfx/.../pl/.../18/.../ludnosc_w_starszym_wieku.pdf>
    <stat.gov.pl/obszary-tematyczne/ludnosc/ludnosc/ludnosc-w-wieku-60-struktura-demograficzna-i-zdrowie,24,1.html>

Cumming, Elaine, and William Earl Henry. *Growing old: The process of disengagement.* New York: Basic Books, 1961.

Czerniawska, Olga. *Drogi i bezdroża andragogiki.* Lodz: Wydawnictwo Wyższej Szkoły Humanistyczno-Ekonomicznej w Łodzi, 2000.

Halicki, Jerzy. *Obrazy starości rysowane przeżyciami seniorów.* Bialystok: Trans Humana, 2003.

Ministry of Labour and Social Policy, Warsaw. *Government programme for senior citizens' social activity for 2014-2020.* [*Rządowy Program na rzecz Aktywności Społecznej Osób Starszych na lata 2014-2020*] Warsaw: Ministry of Labour and Social Policy; 2013. <www.mpips.gov.pl/seniorzyaktywne-starzenie/rzadowy-program-asos/>

Szarota, Zofia., and Remigiusz J. Kijak. *Starość. Między diagnozą a działaniem.* Warsaw: CRZL, 2013.

Szarota, Zofia. *Gerontologia społeczna i oświatowa. Zarys problematyki.* Krakow: Wydawnictwo Naukowe AP, 2004.

Ziomek-Michalak, Katarzyna. "Uczenie się przez całe życie na przykładzie uniwersytetu trzeciego wieku." Wiktor Żłobicki, and Beata Maj. Eds. *Nierówność szans edukacyjnych – przyczyny, skutki, koncepcje zmian.* Krakow: Oficyna Wydawnicza Impuls, 2012.

—. "Wykorzystanie potencjału środowiska lokalnego do pracy na rzecz seniorów." Marta Mikołajczyk. Ed. *Praca socjalna i pomoc społeczna.* Warsaw: Wydawnictwo Akademii Pedagogiki Specjalnej, 2014.

Webpages

<stat.gov.pl/download/gfx/.../pl/.../18/.../ludnosc_w_starszym_wieku.pdf>

<senior.gov.pl/source/raport_osoby%20starsze.pdf>

<www.mpips.gov.pl/seniorzyaktywne-starzenie/zalozenia-dlugofalowej-polityki-senioralnej-w-polsce-na-lata-20142020/>

<www.mpips.gov.pl/seniorzyaktywne-starzenie/rzadowy-program-asos>

<www.50plus50.pl/forum_dla_seniorow>

<forum.senior.pl>

<www.bycseniorem.pl>

Long-term Senior Policy in Poland for the years 2014-2020
<das.mpips.gov.pl/source/Long-term%20Senior%20Policy.pdf>

Polish Agency for Enterprise Development (PARP)
<<u>en.parp.gov.pl/</u>>

Notes on contributors

Editors

ELENA URDANETA has a PhD in Pharmacy from the University of Navarra. After defending her PhD thesis on Nutrition Physiology, she lectured in Physiology and Physiopathology. She also undertook a post-doctoral stay at UCLA (Los Angeles, USA) in the Department of Physiology, under the supervision of Dr E.M. Wright.

Elena Urdaneta later worked as Senior Lecturer in the Department of Natural Environmental Sciences at the State University of Navarra (UPNA). She has been endorsed as Full Professor of Health Sciences by the Spanish National Quality Evaluation and Accreditation Agency (ANECA). From 2009 until 2012, she was Director of Research and Development (R&D) for the Ingema Foundation, and later for the Basque Culinary Centre.

In April 2017, after having managed a variety of complex international and interdisciplinary projects over the years, Elene Urdaneta joined the Euskampus project <euskampus.eus/es> as Director of Cooperative Innovation.

Elena Urdaenta holds that motivation and cooperation are key factors in the search for answers to complex challenges such as those our society is currently facing. She has taken great pleasure in being able to grow and learn from other people – researchers, professionals, and students – and from their questions and doubts that have always led to even deeper enquiry and investigation.

BRIAN WORSFOLD is Emeritus Professor of English in the Department of English and Linguistics at the University of Lleida (Catalunya, Spain). A graduate of Rhodes University (Grahamstown, South Africa), he holds a PhD from the University of Barcelona. His doctoral thesis focused on novels in English by Black South African writers. Since obtaining his doctorate, he has published articles on various aspects of literatures from Africa in English, especially from Southern Africa, and is author of *South Africa Backdrop: An historical introduction of South African literary and cultural studies* (1999). Since 1999, he has undertaken research on ageing as represented in literatures in English, and has published widely on the subject, especially as presented in fiction in English from Africa. He has been the General Editor of the Dedal-Lit collection, published at the University of Lleida, and is editor of *Women Ageing Through Literature and Experience* (2005), *The Art of Ageing: Textualising the Phases of Life* (2005), and *Acculturating Age: Approaches to Cultural Gerontology* (2011). He is co-editor, with Núria Casado-Gual and Emma Domínguez-Rué, of *Literary Creativity and the Older Woman Writer* (Berne: Peter Lang, 2016). As member of the research group Grup Dedal-Lit, he has co-ordinated the group's participation as a partner institution in the European Network in Aging Studies (ENAS) and in the European Project "Social Innovation in Active and Healthy Ageing for sustainable economic growth" (SIforAGE).

Authors

JAN ALEXANDERSSON (PhD) is a senior researcher at the Intelligent User Interfaces laboratory at the German Research Institute of Artificial Intelligence (DFKI GmbH). He received his MSc from the University of Linköping in 1993. He has been a member of the scientific advisory board of the ACL Special Interest Group of Dialogue (SIGDial) and has been working since 1993 at DFKI on topics such as spoken-language translation (Project VerbMobi), multimodal human-computer interaction (Project SmartKom), Corpus and Summarization (Project AMI/AMIDA), and more recently, assistive and accessible technology for the elderly and persons with disabilities (projects i2home, and VITAL).

ELEONORA BARONE (PhD Architecture, sp. Urban Planning) is a Social Entrepreneur and considers herself lucky to have worked in very different contexts, from universities to private firms through public administration and NGOs, and so be able to interact in multicultural environments, developing transversal competences. She loves the collective intelligence, and she thinks we have great opportunities ahead, thanks to what both the economic and financial crisis and demographic changes are offering us. Of course, we are in the "gray revolution," and this is good news for everyone. Currently, as Founder and Director of "memory in motion between Young and Old" (mYmO, Spain), she works to value senior talent and foster intergenerational dialogue, developing 'a society for all ages.'

BAIBA BELA (Dr.sc.soc. in Sociology, University of Latvia, 2004) is Senior Researcher at the Advanced Political and Social Research Institute, and Associate Professor in Social Anthropology and Sociology, at the University of Latvia. Her research and publications focus on oral history and identity, and recently on sustainable development, social security, and 'active ageing.' She is the author of more than forty articles, and she has co-authored and edited several publications, among them the *Latvia. Human Development Report. Sustainable Nation* (2014).

GEMA BELCHÍ-ROMERO graduated in social education from the University of Murcia in 2013. She holds a Master's Degree in educational intervention in social contexts, specializing in the quality-of-life of adults and the elderly, from the National University of Distance Education (UNED), Spain. She is currently conducting doctoral studies in education, policy-research, practice and evaluation in training, and socio-educational contexts. She is the representative of the 'active ageing' area of the professional College of Social Educators of the Region of Murcia. She is a member of the Research Group on "Education, quality-of-life, and development."

DANIEL BIEBER (PhD Economics, University of Dortmund, Germany) works as General Manager and Academic Director of the Institute for Social Research and Social Economics (iso-Institut e.V.) in Saarbrücken. He also lectures at the Karls-Ruprecht University of Heidelberg. Daniel Bieber studied Social and Economic Sciences in Frankfurt/Main. His research focuses on the following subject areas: non-technical success factors of technical innovation; innovative services; socio-scientific market research; future technologies and their social requirements and effects; the Internet of things and its implications; cooperation in the face of demographic change; the evolution of further professional training; business consultancy; and political consulting and evaluation. He was awarded an Honorary Professorship at the Karls-Ruprecht University in Heidelberg in 2006.

DARIO BRACCO is a graduate in Sociology. He is also a journalist. He has been an entrepreneur in the medical field. For twenty-five years, he has focused his activities on the study of and research into ageing. He has been president of CeRRCo (www.centrocornaglia.org), a not-for-profit Research and Relationship Centre, based in Turin (Italy), since 1982. Currently, he holds courses and lectures on the quality of services and clinical governance.

JOCHEN BRITZ is a Researcher at the German Research Centre for Artificial Intelligence (DFKI). He graduated in Computer and Communications Technology (CuK) at the University of Saarland in 2013. Since 2012, he has been working in the research team on Intelligent User Interfaces. In the AAL domain, he is involved in the national, government-funded project SUCH, and in the projects 'mobisaar' and "AdAPT," both partly funded by the German Federal Ministry of Education and Research (BMBF).

PEI-WEN CHU is a PhD candidate at the Graduate School of Education at the University of Bristol in England. She expects to be awarded her PhD in the summer of 2018. Her PhD study explores the relationship between older people in retirement and their use of digital technologies in contexts in everyday life. Her research interests focus on exploring the use of digital technology in retired older adults within a rapidly-ageing society in Taiwan, and the impact of digital technologies usage on social inclusion and exclusion. She is also interested in using digital technologies as tools to enhance teaching and learning in primary schools, and in undergraduates' use of social media for enhancing social interactions. Pei-Wen is a qualified primary school teacher in Taiwan, and acquired several years teaching experience before starting the master's degree course. She holds a Master's Degree in Education, Technology and Society from the University of Bristol. Between 2009 and 2010, Pei-Wen was involved in the research project "Science, Technology, and Cultural Sustainability," which is about an online collaboration science programme based in Taiwan for rural, indigenous students aged between 7 and 13 years old.

ANDRÉS ESCARBAJAL-DE HARO (PhD Philosophy and Educational Sciences, University of Murcia) has a degree in Philosophy, Psychology, and Education Sciences from the University of Murcia, Spain. He is University Specialist in Gerontagogy: Socio-educative Intervention with the Elderly, and Intercultural Education. He is the Principal Researcher of the Research Group E050-05 – "Education, Quality-of-Life, and Development," at the University of Murcia.

Andrés Escarbajal-de Haro has participated as a researcher in seventeen projects and another five Educational Innovation meetings. He has published thirty-five scientific articles; four books, among which *Non-formal Education and Community Development*, and *Seniors, Education and Emancipation* (2004); and he has collaborated in fifteen collections, among them *Socio-educational Alternatives for Older People* (2009), and *Old Age, Women, and Education. A Qualitative Approach to Social Educational Work* (2014). He is co-editor of *Active Ageing, Intergenerational Programmes, and Social Education* (2017). In addition, he has contributed forty chapters, and has presented numerous papers at national and international conferences.

Andrés Escarbajal-de Haro is currently Professor of Social Pedagogy in the Department of Theory and History of Education at the University of Murcia.

CRISTINA GARRIGÓS (PhD – Philology: English Literature, University of Seville) is Full Professor of English and American Literature at the National University of Distance Education (UNED) in Spain. She has published books and articles on authors such as John Barth, Kathy Acker, Don DeLillo, Gloria Anzaldúa, Giannina Braschi, Ruth Ozeki, and Rabih Alameddine, among others. Her main research interests are postmodernist theory and gender studies.

Cristina Garrigós was Secretary of the Spanish Association for American Studies (SAAS) from 2003 until 2011. She has taught at several universities in Spain (Autonomous University of Madrid, University of León), and in the United States of America (UNC Chapel Hill, University of Mississippi, University of Texas A&M International). She has been a visiting lecturer in Poland, Italy, and Germany. Currently, she is working on memory loss from an interdisciplinary perspective and writing a book on Alzheimer's in contemporary fiction from the United States of America.

MARÍA DEL ROCÍO GONZÁLEZ-TORRES was born in Córdoba, Spain. She has a degree in English Studies from the University of Córdoba, and she received her Master's Degree in Multilingual and Intercultural Communication at the University of Málaga, where she is currently doing her PhD on *Material Memory in Contemporary Fiction about Ageing*. Her thesis deals with the personal bonding that elderly people establish with their material possessions. Furthermore, her research focuses on female British novelists in their attempt to give voice to women coming of age within the setting of their material and personal mementos. She is also interested in memory studies, environmental psychology, and spatial studies.

María del Rocío González-Torres has been working for the General Foundation at the University of Málaga for the last four years, teaching "Gender Issues in North America and the Hispanic World: Cross Cultural Perspectives," "Art and Architecture," "Intercultural Management," and "Cross-Cultural Psychology."

UGO MARCHISIO (MD sp. Internal Medicine and Respiratory Diseases) has been Head of the Emergency Medicine ward and the whole Medical Department at the Maria Vittoria Hospital in Turin (Italy) from 2000 to 2016.

Now he is a freelance consultant in respiratory diseases, and medical coordinator for the private clinic LARC.

He is a member of CeRRCo <www.centrocornaglia.org>, a not-for-profit Research and Relationship Centre, based in Turin, and is deeply committed to the empowerment and advocacy of elderly persons, especially in the medical field. He holds courses and lectures on elderly people's health, health management, and international medicine.

SILVIA MARTÍNEZ DE MIGUEL-LÓPEZ (PhD Education, sp. Education for the Elderly, 2001) has a degree in Pedagogy from the University of Murcia (1997). She is University Gerontagogy Specialist: Educational Intervention with Older People. She is currently Professor in the Department of Theory and History of Education, Faculty of Education, and she lectures in the area of social education. She is a member of the Faculty Research Group E050-05 – "Education, Quality-of-Life, and Development," and Coordinator of the Degree in Social Education, at the University of Murcia.

Among Silvia Martínez de Miguel-López's latest published research are: "The perception of the quality-of-life in older women and active aging through social and educational activities in social centres" (2015), published in the journal *Revista de Investigación Educativa* (*RIE*); and "Mild cognitive impairment in elderly users of municipal centers of the Region of Murcia" in the journal *Annals of Psychology* (2016). She has collaborated in recently-published books, such as *Old Age, Women, and Education. A Qualitative Approach to Social Educational Work* (2014), and *Active Ageing, Intergenerational Programmes, and Social Education* (2017). She is a participant in and director of several research projects, among which the ESium Project, awarded the European Social Innovation Research Prize 2014 (SIforAGE).

GLÒRIA MATEU-VIVES (PhD Personality, Evaluation, and Psychological Treatment, 2003) was a nursery-school teacher from 1975 to 1980, and a primary school teacher from 1980 until 1987. She worked as an Educational psychologist and as a Clinical psychologist from 1987 to 1995. Since 1995, she has been working as a Clinical psychotherapist for both individuals and groups, and she has been a Clinical associate at Tavistock Clinic. In 1999, she was a visiting fellow at the Anna Freud Centre. In 2010, she began working as a psychoanalytic group psychotherapist with elderly people at the Primary Care Services.

Glòria Mateu-Vives is the author of several publications that deal with educational and clinical settings relating to persons from early-age until late-age. Since 2017, she has been a Mentalization-Based Treatment Practitioner at the Anna Freud Centre, and she is currently working in both private and public Mental Health Services.

PEDRO MORENO-ABELLÁN (PhD Education Sciences, sp. Intergenerational Programmes and Elderly, 2015) has a degree in Education (2001) and Pedagogy (2007) from the University of Murcia. He has a Master's Degree in Educational Professions, Quality-of-Life, and Social Well-being (2007-2009). His thesis for a Diploma of Advanced Studies in Education Sciences (2011) is based on research into "Intergenerational relationships between grandparents and grandchildren." His most recent research looks into "The role of the grandparent from the socio-educational perspective," the findings of which were published in the proceedings of the "Conference of Active Ageing and Solidarity between Generations" (2013). He is editor of the book, *Active Ageing, Intergenerational Programmes, and Social Education* (2017).

Pedro Moreno-Abellán participates in the ESium research projects with a lecture on "The Importance of the Intergenerational Programmes." This project was awarded the European Social Innovation Research Prize 2014 (SIforAGE). Currently, he lectures in the Department of Theory and History of Education, Faculty of Education, on the History of Education, Social Education, and Elderly People. Pedro Moreno-Abellán, is a member of the Faculty Research Group E050-05 – "Education, Quality-of-Life, and Development," at the University of Murcia.

EMINE ÖZMETE (PhD University of Ankara, Turkey, 2002) is a Professor at the University of Ankara, Turkey, in the Department of Social Work. She is the Head of the Centre on Aging Studies: Implementation and Research, at the University of Ankara. She is conducting studies on quality-of-life, well-being, social capital, life-skill education, financial behaviour, financial planning, resource management in the family, and ageing studies.

Emine Özmete received her MSc in Family and Consumer Sciences from the University of Ankara in 1997, on quality-of-life and values. As a Scholar, she visited the Department of Family Studies and Human Development at Iowa State University, and the Department of Gerontology at the University of Southampton.

Emine Özmete is a respected member of the International Federation on Aging and the International Federation on Social Work. She has carried out several projects, such as "Elderly Poverty Project: Analysis of Economic, Social and Cultural Needs (2012)," "Assessment of Intergenerational Solidarity in Turkey (2015-2016)," "Healthy Aging and Encountered

Problems Project (2015)," "Turkey Active and Healthy Aging Research," and "Elder Abuse Research (2015)," supported by the National Scientific Council, the Development Agency, and the Ministry of Health. She is an Advisory Member of the Ministry of Family and Social Politics.

DAVID RAMPTON (DPhil English and American Studies, University of Sussex, England, 1983) is Professor of English at the University of Ottawa (Canada). He served as Chair of the Department of English from 2002 to 2007. A specialist in American and Comparative Literature, his publications include *Vladimir Nabokov: A Critical Study of the Novels* (1984), *Vladimir Nabokov* (1992), *William Faulkner: A Literary Life* (2008), and *Vladimir Nabokov: A Literary Life* (2012). He has edited a number of anthologies, including *Prose Models* (3rd edition 1997), and *Short Fiction* (2nd edition 2005), *The Government Inspector and Other Works* (2014), and *Notes From Underground and Other Stories* (2015).

LIGA RASNACA (PhD) is Senior Researcher at the Advanced Political and Social Research Institute, Associate Professor in Social policy and Social Work organization, and Director of the master's programme of Professional Social Work at the University of Latvia. Her scientific interests are social welfare, social justice, and regional inequality, and she has paid special attention to analyses of vulnerable groups in society (ex-offenders, older persons, the homeless). She is the author of more than thirty scientific articles. She has co-authored and edited several publications about particularities of the labour market and housing problems in post-communist society. She is one of the authors of *Contemporary Challenges of Ageing Policy in the Central and Eastern European Countries* (2017). She has participated in The SIforAGE Project as a member of the Latvian team.

MAURICE REKRUT is Researcher at the German Research Centre for Artificial Intelligence (DFKI). He graduated in Biomedical Engineering at the University of Applied Sciences Saarland (HTW Saarland) with focus on Neural Engineering, and he received his MSc in 2013. Since then, he has been working at DFKI in the research team on Intelligent User Interfaces. In the AAL Domain, he is involved in the national government-funded Project SUCH, and in the projects 'Mobia' and 'mobisaar.'

JUAN ANTONIO SALMERÓN-AROCA (PhD Education, sp. Education for the Elderly, 2012) has a degree in Psychology from the University of Murcia, Spain. He holds a Master's Degree in Education and Integration of people with disabilities, social problems, and the elderly, from the University of Rome.

Juan Antonio Salmerón-Aroca has published several works in the field of the elderly and education, among them, in the journal *Rie*, "The perception of the quality-of-life in older women and active aging through social and educational activities in social centres" (2015); in the journal *Education*, "The Social Educator in centres for the elderly. Social and educational responses to a new generation of older" (2016); and in the journal *Reifop*, "The socio-educational approach in working with older people. The view of the professionals." (2016).

Juan Antonio Salmerón-Aroca is currently Associate Professor at the Faculty of Education in the Department of Theory and History of Education at the University of Murcia. He lectures in the area of Social Education. He is a member of the Faculty research group "Education, Quality-of-Life, and Development" (E050-05), of the University of Murcia, the research group that was awarded the European Social Innovation Research Prize 2014 (SIforAGE).

ANTONIA MARÍA SÁNCHEZ-LÁZARO (PhD in Education, University of Murcia, 2006) has a degree in Pedagogy from the University of Murcia, Spain, and is University Specialist in Gerontagogy, a position which led to her being awarded a training-stay at the University of Quebec in Montreal, Canada.

Antonia María Sánchez-Lázaro is a Lecturer in the Department of Theory and History of Education of the Faculty of Education at the University of Murcia. She lectures in the area of Social Education and is a member of the Faculty research group "Education, Quality-of-Life, and Development" (E050-05), at the University of Murcia. She has contributed chapters to several books, among them, "Proposed Methodology of Health Education for Cultural Diversity. A Working Tool: Method Apprêt" (*Procedia – Social and Behavioral Sciences*. 132, 15th May 2014. 330-335), the chapter "Promoción de la salud. Balance y perspectivas" in Juan Agustín Morón-Marchena. (Coord.) *Investigar e intervenir en Educación para la Salud*. (Madrid: Narcea, 2015), the chapter "Identidad-Diferencia," in Juan Sáez Carreras and Manuel Esteban Albert (Coords.) *Dialéctica de los Conceptos en Educación*. (Valencia: Nau Llibres, 2015), and "Envejecimiento saludable, envejecimiento activo y solidario intergeneracional" in Silvia Martínez de Miguel-López, Pedro Moreno-Abellán, and Andrés Escarbajal-de Haro. Eds. *Envejecimiento activo, programas intergeneracionales y educación social.* (Madrid: Dykinson, 2017).

KATHLEEN SCHWARZ received her MA in Social Science and Labour Science from the University of Bremen in 2009. Since 2010, she has worked for the Institute for Social Research and Social Economics (iso-Institut e.V.) in Saarbrücken. One of her main topics is applied research about handling technologies in man-machine-interaction, especially intending to contribute to an innovative alliance between technology development and corresponding development of new innovative services. Currently, projects are working on the quantitative and qualitative analysis of needs and demands for senior citizens and people with reduced mobility, especially referring to service-technology-combination in their everyday life. To do that, specific user-centred methods are used, to adapt the developed technologies to the needs of the target group.

ANNA STEPCENKO (PhD in Philosophy) is Researcher and Project manager at the Advanced Social and Political Research Institute of the University of Latvia. At the University of Latvia, she lectured in History of Philosophy, Theories of Classical Sociology, Social Gerontology, Sociology of Violence, and Management of Voluntary Work for students of both the Sociology and Social Work study programmes. Her research and publications focus on the sociology of Georg Simmel, social gerontology and ageing, and civil society and voluntary work. She has edited publications on Georg Simmel, and quality-of-life in gerontological institutions, and she has published many articles on ageing issues and voluntary work. From 2016 until 2019, she is researcher and manager of the project "Social Empowerment in Rural Areas" (SEMPRE) of the EU Interreg Baltic Sea Region programme at the University of Latvia.

JOHANNES TRÖGER is Researcher at DFKI in the department of Intelligent User Interfaces. He is part of the competence centre for Ambient-Assisted Living, led by Dr Jan Alexandersson. Within the EIT project Fit2Perform, his work focuses on user-acceptance and participatory design methodology, and within the 'MOBIA'/'mobisaar' projects <www.mobia-saar.de>, he works in multidisciplinary teams on accessible user interfaces and user experience. His research expertise lies in the field of adaptable user interfaces and designing with and for vulnerable users. During his studies for an MSc in Educational Technology and a BSc in Psychology, he gained comprehensive expertise in designing user interfaces based on user-centred approaches and the use of qualitative and quantitative research methods.

P.J. WHITE (PhD Product Design, sp. Product Design for Older Adults) is a research director, supervisor, and lecturer at designCORE research centre at the Institute of Technology Carlow (Ireland). As a Product Designer, he has extensive experience innovating for small to multi-national businesses. He was recently co-chair of 'Faultlines,' the 1st Irish Design Research Conference, hosted in Carlow, and he has been lead-editor of the research review *Iterations*. P.J. holds a PhD in Product Design, specifically in the areas of Design Ethnography and Product Design for older adults. His academic interests include Social Design, Design and Gerontology, designing interdisciplinary research, Design Anthropology, and Human Centric Design as a means of understanding human behaviours and cultures.

KATARZYNA ZIOMEK-MICHALAK (Ph.D.) is an assistant lecturer at the Institute of Social Prophylactics and Social Work at The Maria Grzegorzewska Pedagogical University in Warsaw (Poland). She works on the following scientific interests: activities in education, andragogy and gerontology, and the ageing process and old age. She has carried out research projects in the gerontologic and has also developed and implemented education and animation projects for elderly people. She has published several articles on the subject, and a book entitled *Personal Resources versus health expectations of seniors in Poland* (Warsaw, 2016).